Before and After 9/11

BEFORE AND AFTER 9/11

A Philosophical Examination of Globalization, Terror, and History

by

Tom Rockmore

continuum

2011

The Continuum International Publishing Group
80 Maiden Lane, New York, NY 10038
The Tower Building, 11 York Road, London SE1 7NX

www.continuumbooks.com

Library of Congress Cataloging-in-Publication Data
Rockmore, Tom, 1942–
Before and after 9/11 : a philosophical examination of globalization, terror, and history / by Tom Rockmore.
p. cm.
Includes bibliographical references and index.
ISBN-13: 978-1-4411-4891-9 (hardcover : alk. paper)
ISBN-10: 1-4411-4891-4 (hardcover : alk. paper)
ISBN-13: 978-1-4411-1892-9 (paperback : alk. paper)
ISBN-10: 1-4411-1892-6 (paperback : alk. paper) 1. September 11 Terrorist Attacks, 2001. 2. Terrorism. 3. Globalization. 4. Islam and world politics. 5. Islam–21st century. I. Title.

HV6432.7.R63 2011
363.3250973–dc22

2010037293

ISBN: 978-1-4411-4891-9 (HB)
978-1-4411-1892-9 (PB)

Typeset by Newgen Imaging Systems Pvt Ltd, Chennai, India
Printed and bound in the United States of America

Contents

Foreword

This study is intended as a philosophical contribution to understanding the terrorist attack on the United States on September 11, 2001, known as "9/11." This multidimensional series of events invites analyses from many perspectives, including philosophy. If philosophers have so far mainly been silent about 9/11,[1] perhaps it is because their normative conception of the discipline suggests it is independent of, but relevant to time and place, whose changes do not affect it, and for which (under one interpretation) it can supply, as has been suggested, the last word.[2] My own view is that philosophy is not independent of its surroundings, which affect it, but to which it is unfortunately only incidentally relevant.

A main thrust in modern Western philosophy is toward the formulation of positions that supposedly cannot be revised.[3] The aim here is different in that I have in mind no more than the formulation of a general analysis with which one can agree or disagree, in whole or in part, and which does not pretend to end the debate, but rather at most only to begin it, by calling for further discussion.

One often advises rulers, statesmen, and peoples to learn from the experiences of history. But what experience and history teach is that peoples and governments have never yet learned from history, let alone acted according to its lessons. Every age has conditions of its own and is an individual situation; decisions must and can be made only within, and in accordance with, the age itself. In the turmoil of world affairs no universal principle, no memory of similar conditions in the past can help us. . . .

G.W.F. Hegel[4]

Far from ushering in a new era of global governance, globalization is producing a rebirth of empire.

Paul Gray[5]

The only way to conceive of what happened on September 11 is to locate it in the context of the antagonisms of global capitalism.

Slavoj Zizek[6]

Empire is emerging today as the center that supports the globalization of productive networks and casts its widely inclusive net to try to envelop all power relations within its world order—and yet at the same time it deploys a powerful police function against the new barbarians and the rebellious slaves who threaten its order.

Michael Hardt and Antonio Negri[7]

We're an empire now, and when we act, we create our own reality. And while you're studying that reality—judiciously, as you will—we'll act again, creating other new realities, which you can study too, and that's how things will sort out. We're history's actors, and you, all of you, will be left to just study what we do.

An unnamed advisor to George W. Bush[8]

Surely it is possible for a Muslim fundamentalist quite reasonably to see President Bush's aim of making the whole world safe for democratic capitalism as a no less mortal threat to his traditional way of life, or his traditional sacred values, as we saw the threats from Stalin and Hitler, or even from the Kaiser and Napoleon, as a mortal threat to our ways of life or sacred values. Once that effort of imagination is made, Muslim terrorism becomes understandable not so much as a rational act to turn back the irresistible forces of modern capitalism, but rather as a form of madness which has many historical precedents—particularly in the cause of national self-determination—many of which posterity applauds.

Peregrine Worsthorne[9]

Every single empire, in its official discourse, has said that it is not like all the others, that its circumstances are special, that it has a mission to enlighten, civilize, bring order and democracy, and that it uses force only as a last resort.

Edward Said[10]

Notes

1. See, for exceptions, Giovanna Borradori, *Philosophy In a Time of Terror: Dialogues with Jürgen Habermas and Jacques Derrida*, Chicago: University of Chicago Press, 2003; Sam Harris, *The End of Faith: Religion, Terror and the Future of Reason*, New York: W. W. Norton, 2004; and *The Philosophical Challenges of September 11*, edited by Tom Rockmore, Joseph Margolis and Armen Marsoobian, Oxford: Blackwell, 2005; Jennifer Ang Mei Sze, *Sartre and the Moral Limits of War and Terrorism*, London: Routledge, 2010; and Allen Buchanan, *Human Rights, Legitimacy, and the Use of Force*, Oxford UP, 2010; Michael Gross, *Moral Dilemmas of Modern War*, New York: Cambridge University Press, 2009; Stephen Nathanson, *Terrorism and the Ethics of War*, New York: Cambridge University Press, 2010.
2. For this normative view of philosophy, see Thomas Nagel, *The View From Nowhere*, New York: Oxford, 1986.
3. Kant, for instance, states that to change anything in his theory of pure reason would introduce contradictions into human reason itself. See preface to second edition, in Immanuel Kant, *Critique of Pure Reason*, translated by Paul Guyer and Allen W. Wood, New York: Cambridge University Press, 1998, B xxxviii, p. 120.

4. G.W.F. Hegel, *Reason in History*, translated, with an introduction, by Robert S. Hartman, Indianapolis: LLA, 1953, p. 8.
5. Paul Gray, *Al Qaeda and What It Means To Be Modern*, New York: New Press, 2003, p. 97.
6. Slavoj Zizek, *Welcome To the Desert of the Real*, London: Verso, 2002, p. 49.
7. Michael Hardt and Antonio Negri, *Empire*, Cambridge, MA: Harvard University Press, 2000, p. 20.
8. George Packer, *The Assassin's Gate: America in Iraq*, New York: Farrar, Straus and Giroux, 2005, pp. 390–91.
9. Letter to the editor, in *The Guardian*, July 12, 2005, p. 23.
10. Cited in Kevin Phillips, *American Theocracy: The Peril and Politics of Radical Religion, Oil, and Borrowed Money in the 21st Century*, New York: Viking, 2006.

Introduction

This is a book about 9/11, understood in the wider sense as the series of events leading up to and away from that day. Steve Coll ends his detailed, important account of the secret history of the CIA, Afghanistan, and bin Laden from the time of the Soviet invasion until 9/11 by conceding it is easier to describe the past than the present.[1] The hypothesis guiding this work is that we can only understand the aftermath, or what comes later, in terms of antecedent events, hence the events before and after 9/11 as a single, ongoing, complex historical process, with roots in the sometimes distant past and with consequences that are likely to be felt for generations, perhaps even centuries, to come.

The problem of "understanding" historical events is complex. It seems obvious that, at a minimum, to "diagnose" historical phenomena we must not only be able to document, to collect and assemble "facts" about, but also to interpret, them—for instance by placing them within an ongoing historical narrative, which in turn presupposes they can be ("rationally") grasped. This book will argue that the main theories so far advanced about 9/11 fail to provide a satisfactory account. At the same time, this book proposes an alternative theory.

It is often assumed, especially by political figures in the United States and among its political allies, that the main contours of 9/11 were sufficiently clear to justify swift and decisive retaliation intended to reassure Americans and their allies, to "heal" the nation, to punish the "evildoers," and to "win" the war on terror. It is tempting, even reassuring, to buy into this simplistic view, which suggests that no matter what the problem is or, on reflection and later study might turn out to be, the US could reliably hope to "solve" it through an important military blow producing in its wake "shock and awe" at American military might. It is, then, not surprising that many around the world, especially Americans, "bought into" this or similar interpretations of 9/11. Swift and decisive action was undertaken in a series of military engagements, including the Afghanistan War, and then later in the war in Iraq, accompanied by the global war on terror, followed by the Israeli invasion of Lebanon, and perhaps by other conflicts still to come. Yet there seems no reason to believe that in this way the US has, by any reasonable interpretation, come closer to "protecting" the nation. Indeed, if "terrorism," however understood, is the problem, it would seem that the actions and strategies of the government headed by President George W. Bush, and perhaps even those of his successor, Barack Obama, have only increased the number of terrorists, hence arguably heightened the danger. This study will consider 9/11 in the wider sense, in which there is important disagreement about the "facts" as well as their interpretation.

All observers agree that on September 11, 2001, foreign terrorists launched a series of attacks in the US by commandeering four planes, of which two were deliberately crashed into the Twin Towers of the World Trade Center in Manhattan, killing almost 3,000 people; a third crashed into the Pentagon in Washington, D.C., and a fourth fell to earth in western Pennsylvania. Yet there is disagreement about other aspects, such as the number of highjackers. Were there 19 or 20 highjackers? If there were 20, who was the twentieth highjacker? This lack of knowledge is not unprecedented. Uncertainty is pervasive in catastrophic national events. For example, there is still no general agreement about whether, as the Warren Commission reported, Lee Harvey Oswald was the only assassin of President John F. Kennedy in 1963.[2]

It is common, by analogy with natural science, to understand or interpret historical events through their causes. Still, there is as yet nothing approaching agreement about the cause or causes of 9/11. It is still not reliably known why this series of attacks took place or what can be reliably be said to have "caused" them? Can they be explained in reference to religious or cultural (civilizational) differences? Or through other factors, such as the supposed "irrationality" of the enemies of the United States? Who (or what) is the main enemy? It makes good strategic sense, from the point of view of winning the battle of world opinion, for Osama bin Laden to claim truthfully (or perhaps not) to have been the main organizer of 9/11 to attract a segment of the Islamic community to his cause. It makes equal strategic sense for the United States to create an identifiable enemy by attributing this capacity to him, whether or not these were events he or his colleagues organized. Yet it remains unclear whether a "mad" Saudi was able, from a cave in Afghanistan, to coordinate that major attack on the United States on September 11, 2001.[3]

It is sometimes suggested that 9/11 constitutes a clean break with the past. In that case, it would be *sui generis*, and could not be understood. If there were a genuine break with the ongoing historical process, then events after it could not be explained or grasped in relation to it. The events of 9/11 would then have the status of an uncaused, or a self-caused series of events, as God is sometimes said to be *causa sui*. Adhering to this or similar beliefs is tacit acknowledgment there is no way to comprehend God, because God lies beyond scientific explanation or even human understanding. Yet to assert there is a radical break between 9/11 and preceding events is to concede that we do understand them. If, on the contrary, 9/11 does not break with, but perpetuates the effects of preceding events while amplifying tendencies already underway, then under certain conditions we can understand it.

What would a convincing account of 9/11 look like?[4] Only a small fraction of the already numerous and rapidly increasing number of works on 9/11 concerns the causes, understood as the proximal and more distant sources, or origins—the many antecedents, leading up to 9/11—and probably still fewer studies are concerned with analyzing the events leading away from it.

Discussion of the antecedents of 9/11 tends to coalesce around three conceptual models: the political view associated with President George W. Bush that our enemies are evil; the cultural (or civilizational) model worked out by Samuel Huntington; and the religious model that is identified with Bernard Lewis.

Chapter 1, entitled "Bush's Political Interpretation of Terrorism," studies the political view that the enemies of America are simply evil, which was frequently asserted by President Bush. Throughout his administrations this was one of the slogans justifying American military intervention around the world, especially in Iraq. This chapter examines the relationship of Bush's view to the history of the United States, to Bush's own religious commitment, and to political "neoconservatism". One of the main themes of this chapter is that Bush's approach, hence the neoconservatism it manifests, is less innovative than is often believed. It prolongs tendencies already strongly present in the history of the American republic, including an expansionist tendency both within and outside the continental United States, and closely linked to religion.

Chapter 2, entitled "Huntington's Political–Scientific Analysis of the Clash of Civilizations, (or Cultures)," examines Huntington's view, formulated in the early 1990s, that the wars of the future will be due to differences of culture (or civilization), which he later applied to understanding 9/11. I relate Huntington's thesis to so-called identity politics as well as to Fukuyama's thesis of the end of history. I criticize Huntington for omitting consideration of the economic dimension of international conflict.

Chapter 3, "Lewis's Historical Account of Religious Difference," considers Lewis' approach to 9/11. His religious approach takes the form of an ad hoc theory, invented for this purpose, according to which, 9/11 resulted from a clash between two different religions: Islam, which is essentially ill-adapted to the modern world, and Christianity, which is supposedly up to date. According to Lewis, the Islamic world tried but failed to adjust to the modern world, by which he apparently means acceptance of a largely Western model.

With respect to historical events, 9/11 poses a cognitive problem, more precisely as concerns a series of events situated in the course of an ongoing historical process. To understand these events requires us to comprehend not only what occurred but also why the actors did what they did. This suggests that, at a minimum, a grasp of 9/11 requires a general approach to historical phenomena, and a specific understanding of 9/11 in terms of its historical antecedents, with which it is seamlessly linked, and which are manifest in the events of that day and are further ingredient in events leading away from it.

Chapter 4, entitled "Models of Historical Knowledge," examines the epistemological conditions of grasping a historical process by reviewing various models. The chapter begins with an account of Hempel's covering law model, which is still widely popular at present. Next the chapter considers other strategies for an epistemology of history. If history is the record of human actions through time, and if human actions are intentional, then human history can be understood in terms of the intentions motivating finite human beings. Building on intentional conceptions of activity in Aristotle and Hegel, I recommend a form of epistemological constructivism as a promising approach to cognizing historical phenomena.

I propose a model of historical knowledge in which human beings are the actors of human history. I believe we must understand human history, and a fortiori 9/11, as a function of human activity in particular times and places. Human activity is teleological, hence directed toward realizing goals. History, which is the record of this activity, is always "rational," even in its darkest moments.

Chapter 5, "Economics, Globalization, and History," calls attention to the economic component of human activity, particularly as concerns 9/11. I focus on the economic component of international relations. All too often attention is drawn to a series of things Americans and the US government do without giving attention to their economic component.[5]

Bush, Huntington, and Lewis suggest that history is now being made in the clash between the Islamic world and the West in which Islam is the "aggressor" and in which the US is the main "victim." All three depict human activity in basically noneconomic terms. In their views, a noneconomic model takes the place of the economic dimension of social reality, thereby masking a crucial explanatory factor of social phenomena. A. Smith, Hegel, Marx, M. Weber and others suggest modern times can best be understood against its economic background. Incessant capitalist expansion, or economic globalization, is increasingly the main theme of the modern world. Globalization engenders a basic opposition between Western countries committed to economic expansion and the fundamentalist form of Islam present throughout the Islamic world.

In part, my argument consists in rejecting approaches to 9/11 that turn away from, or otherwise minimize, their economic dimension. The economic component is a crucial explanatory factor for understanding the modern world, including the antecedent events and further consequences of 9/11. There is a clear link between economic globalization and 9/11. It is not an accident that 9/11 occurred after the end of the cold war, in a period when the US was increasingly asserting itself in the international arena as the world's only remaining superpower.

I believe that capitalism, hence economics, provides a crucial dimension of the conceptual framework for understanding modern social life, specifically including modern history. This claim is widely contested by proponents of cultural, religious, and other explanatory models. Huntington intends his cultural approach as a post-capitalist explanatory model. He believes that as a result of the historical evolution of the modern world, for purposes of historical understanding, cultural factors take the place of such other factors as economics. The religious model presents a pre-modern effort to analyze history as, in one familiar formulation, the record of God's march through the world. Yet we live now in an increasingly secular age. From this perspective, to deny the importance of an economic explanation of human history is to turn attention from a real to a merely apparent analysis of events like 9/11.

My interpretation of 9/11 is based on three hypotheses. First, the events of 9/11 need to be understood in relation to earlier and later events. Second, these events need to be grasped within an increasingly economic context. This suggests that, at a minimum, to understand 9/11 requires us to comprehend the way economic and other factors influence human actions in the modern world. It would be as mistaken to reduce history, including 9/11, to economic history, as it would be to consider it in isolation from economic factors. Third, the interaction between economic globalization and conservative Islam results in, and can be understood as, an objective contradiction, the social consequences of which continue to play out on social, economic, political, religious, military, and other levels in the aftermath of 9/11.

Chapter 6, "Globalization and Terrorism: Modernity or Jihad," applies my model to understanding the terrorist campaign, which still emanates from elements in the Islamic world more than a decade after 9/11. Capitalism, which is mainly but not exclusively Western, is doubly incompatible with most traditional forms of Islam, but not with Islam as such. Malaysia exemplifies countries in which Islam is the official religion, but which is largely and very successfully capitalist. Capitalism tends to replace all existing indigenous social systems. Its relentless expansion threatens the very existence of Islam in any meaningful form. We see this, for instance, with respect to *jihad*, which goes back to early Islamic times and has more recently been transformed into a fundamentalist instrument directed both against Islamic moderates and the capitalist West, above all the US, the most powerful capitalist nation.

In chapter 7, entitled "Economic Globalism and Empire," I apply my model to the West, especially the US. The Western view of the Western world is largely a variation of Adam Smith's famous concept of the invisible hand, his term for what is now often called enlightened self-interest. According to this perspective, capitalism is on the whole good for capitalists as well as for everyone else. It follows that in exporting capitalism—or its variant form popular during the presidency of George W. Bush, which can be described as "capitalism + democracy"—to the far corners of the earth, the capitalists, though not necessarily everyone else, believe the rudiments of the good life are being extended to everyone.

This undemonstrated, and indemonstrable, assumption was a main source of the three wars that occurred in the wake of 9/11. In the war in Afghanistan, the US and its allies were reacting against al Qaeda and the Taliban. Another is the war in Iraq, in which the US managed to convince itself, its allies, and the American public that the security of the US was threatened by nonexistent weapons of mass destruction. It changed little that these weapons were never shown to exist, which means the war was entered into on a false premise. Finally, there is what is routinely called the global war on terror, the goals of which were never specified, and which presumably cannot be won. The result is to create what looks like a permanent state of siege as capitalism barricades itself, increasingly armed to the teeth, against its real and imagined enemies.

Economic globalism and Islamic terror are dialectical opposites, whose opposition to each other is working itself out in a social contradiction. The incessant expansion of capitalism is not without its price or limits. Its continued expansion is not limitless but limited, since it finally runs up against barriers to further expansion, barriers that do not precede it, but which are generated by itself. One such barrier, whose consequences are now being experienced in the aftermath of 9/11, is the tendency of capitalism to mobilize opposition to itself in certain sectors of the Islamic world. Capitalism, in which, if Max Weber is to be believed, religion plays an enabling role, is opposed by the fundamentalist form of Islam in which economics is not liberated from, but still in thrall to, religious criteria. In asserting itself against Islam, or at least against a certain form of Islam, as perceived by conservative Muslims, the capitalist West mobilizes against itself a significant part of the non-Western Islamic world in creating its "other," so to speak, as a limit to its further development. What is at stake is not the reaction of a few fringe elements that are not part of "genuine" Islam, however defined, nor mere differences of culture or religion, but a kind of social Darwinian struggle for survival between a way of life based on ceaseless economic change, and a very different way of life based on ceaseless, ahistorical repetition of itself without change.

The political problem we now face is as old as the modern world. As capitalism was emerging in England in the middle of the eighteenth century, Rousseau maintained that what he deemed our natural freedom either had been a form of self-induced slavery, or was being transformed into that slavery. Capitalism is good and bad: good in making available financial resources and material comforts that reduce poverty and enable a better life for many, but not all, individuals; but also bad in that such results often come at a terrible price. What we face now is a crisis engendered by capitalism, which is neither merely incidental, nor fortuitous, but central to the modern world, which turns on incessant capitalist expansion. The problem is a crisis of capitalism—a crisis of an arguably new kind. This crisis is not merely economic, nor as Marx insists due to a failure to find new markets, resulting in oversupply, but rather the result of capitalism's inability to limit itself.

Notes

1. "In such a tempestuous present, an examination of the past seems a relative luxury. It is now far easier for a researcher to explain how and why September 11 happened than it is to explain the aftermath." Steve Coll, *Ghost Wars: The Secret History of the CIA, Afghanistan and bin Laden, from the Soviet Invasion to September 10, 2001*, New York: Penguin, 2004, p. 588.
2. The literature is enormous. See, e.g., Richard Popkin, *The Second Oswald*, New York: Avon Books, 1996.
3. See Noam Chomsky, *9–11*, New York: Seven Stories Press, 2002.
4. This is different from the question of why the various US responses to the attack on the country can be regarded as a dismal failure. For discussion of books on this theme, see Mark Leonard, "Drinking the Kool-Aid: An Anatomy of the Iraq Debacle," in *The Chronicle of Higher Education*, volume 52, issue 19, page B 6, January 13, 2006.
5. Johnson, who is keenly aware of the way the US treats others, is a case in point. He writes: "The answer was not some people hate us because of our democracy, wealth, lifestyle, or values but because of things our government did to various peoples around the world." Chalmers Johnson, *Nemesis: The Last Days of the American Republic*, New York: Metropolitan-Henry Holt and Company, 2006, p. 2.

CHAPTER ONE

Bush's Religious Interpretation of Terrorism

Since it occurred, 9/11 has been the object of intensive discussion from many points of view. Many suggestions have been offered.[1] These analyses tend to coalesce around three main lines of interpretation, which can be identified with the names of George W. Bush, Samuel Huntington, and Bernard Lewis.

This is the first of three chapters devoted to examining these three lines of interpretation as part of the process of arriving at an analysis of this series of events. Throughout I will consider the various actors in the context of a single overriding conceptual framework, intended not to judge one participant in the conflict by the standards of another, since this is not a work in moral (or ethical) theory, but rather an endeavor to understand the main (causal) factors governing the ongoing interaction of these actors. In other words: it is not my intention to pass (moral) judgment on the actors in the interlocking series of problems that led up to, and are now leading away from, 9/11. My sole aim is to understand the process.

In what follows, I will consider in cursory fashion the view of 9/11 and terrorism that I attribute to Bush, and the views of Huntington and Lewis in more detail. In each case, I will be concerned with evaluating these approaches on their own inherent merits, hence not with respect to another, presupposed view. When I refer to Bush I have in mind not only opinions he may or may not privately hold and publicly represent, but also the convictions held by those who worked together with him in forging, amending, and defending the religiously based policies that characterized his administrations. In discussing religion, I will have in mind the series of Christian beliefs motivating his actions, as distinguished from their theological justification.[2]

The views of 9/11 I will be attributing to Bush, Huntington, and Lewis obviously differ. Bush, who is not an academic, always approached 9/11 as a politician. The politician is almost by definition someone who needs to act, often to act quickly in a relatively short interval, which can preclude careful consideration of what is known about a particular situation as well as alternative policy recommendations, and so on. On the contrary, Huntington and Lewis, who were academics, and who came to 9/11 from their respective fields of political science and Middle Eastern history, were more interested in arriving at a theoretical explanation of these events.

All three views overlap in a number of ways, including sharing a recognizably Western bias. There is a common tendency to assess the conflict from a dualistic,

Western perspective based on prior adoption of Western standards, as well as a further tendency to reject even the semblance of adopting Islamic standards of evaluation. This bias results in three limitations, rendering them unsuitable for an overall interpretation of the ongoing events. First, this bias creates a spurious link between the problem of understanding the ongoing struggle between Islam and the West by tending to evaluate it in familiar Western moral terms. Yet, since neither the non-Muslim West nor the Muslim world has a monopoly on morality, the impression that moral right is uniquely situated on one side but absent on the other is misleading. Second, since a moral judgment cannot be formulated before the problem has been successfully characterized, it is premature to render a moral judgment prior to identifying the problem. Third, identification of any kind with one of the parties to the conflict prevents the formulation of a general theory encompassing all the parties within the wider framework of a single analysis.

Terrorism and 9/11

Since 9/11 involved a series of terrorist acts, it will be useful to clarify the meaning of "terrorism." There is profound ambiguity about "terrorism." It is well said that one person's terrorist is another person's freedom fighter. Terrorism takes many different forms, running from assassination—widely practiced by many, perhaps all the major industrialized countries as well as many third and fourth world nations—to instilling a sense of deep, paralyzing fear, or terror.

Western definitions tend to associate terrorism with physical force, especially assassination. Terrorism consists in the use of violence and intimidation in the pursuit of political aims. "Terrorism," from the word "terror," seems to have originated in the aptly named period of terror (*la terreur*, 1793–94) during the French Revolution. The term refers to a series of measures taken during the emergency situation, or state of exception, decreed by the revolutionary government from the time of the fall of the Girondins to the fall of Robespierre.

Terrorism is notoriously difficult to define. Virginia Held offers two somewhat different definitions of "terrorism" as "political violence that usually spreads fear beyond those attacked" and "perhaps more than anything else . . . resembles small-scale war"[3]; and as political violence employed with "the intention either to spread fear or to harm non-combatants."[4] Both definitions appear to run war and terrorism together in implying that an act of war, proper, which is aimed at a *legitimate* military target, counts as terrorism. For, as Trotsky points out in his defense of the "red terror," "war . . . is founded upon intimidation. . . [It] destroys only an insignificant part of the conquered army, intimidating the remainder and breaking their will."[5]

Understood as physical violence, terrorism has a long history, going back to ancient times.[6] A well known early instance is the Athenian intimidation, and finally mass murder, of the Melians during the Peloponnesian Wars. Much later, terrorism became firmly associated with assassination. The term "assassin" apparently derives from the Hashshashin, also known as the Hashishin, or Hashashiyyin, a group of Ismali Muslims from the Nizari subsect, whose members are believed to have been active in the eighth to the fourteenth centuries, and who specialized in assassinating members of the Abbasid elite.

Terrorism is a constant of modern life. Such incidents include the St. Bartholomew's Day massacre of thousands of French Protestants in 1572, atrocities committed by Spanish troops in the Netherlands, and, in perhaps the single most notorious incident, the Gunpowder Plot in which Guy Fawkes, who thought that Catholicism was being persecuted in England, attempted to blow up Parliament on November 5, 1605.

Terrorism has long been a part of Russian life. Russian nihilists attempted to assassinate Tsar Alexander II in 1866. Stalin infamously orchestrated a reign of terror in Russia, including show trials, mass starvation, a series of prisons and concentration camps based on forced labor chronicled by Solzhenitsyn, and so on. The most recent instance of Russian terrorism is the ongoing war against the Tchechens in Tchechnya, which has resulted in thousands of deaths.

Terrorism plays an important role in American history. The Ku Klux Klan arose after the Civil War to counter Reconstruction by enforcing white supremacy. Until relatively recently, it was a significant source of terrorism directed by whites against black people. In 1868, there were some 336 cases of murder or attempted murder of blacks by the KKK in Georgia alone. In 1886, during a strike at the McCormick Reaper plant in Chicago, a bomb exploded during the so-called Haymarket Riots, killing six policemen and wounding some 60 others. Eight people were indicted and four were later hanged for this incident. In 1892, during the Homestead Strike at the Carnegie plant in Homestead, Pennsylvania, near Pittsburgh, the managing director of the plant, Henry Clay Frick, brought in the Pinkertons. In the resulting battle, 12 people—three detectives and nine workers—lost their lives.

Terrorism has long been a part of American presidential politics. Roughly every tenth president in American history has been assassinated. President Abraham Lincoln was shot and killed in 1865 by John Wilkes Booth, in turn later shot during his escape. President James Garfield was assassinated in 1881 by Charles Guiteau. In 1901, President William McKinley was killed by Leon Czolgosz, later electrocuted for his crime. President John F. Kennedy was assassinated in 1963 by Lee Harvey Oswald, subsequently killed by Jack Ruby, a nightclub owner, a shooting seen on live television.

The infamous Japanese attack on Pearl Harbor in 1941, perhaps the only single event to occur in the United States comparable to 9/11 in terms of loss of life, is too well known to require description here. Yet unlike 9/11, since the attack on Pearl Harbor did not take place in the continental US, its effect was perhaps felt less acutely. In 1954, four Puerto Rican nationalists opened fire from the Ladies' Gallery in the US House of Representatives, wounding five representatives. Recent incidents cited as contributing to the present American focus on terrorism include the World Trade Center bombing in 1993, the 1998 US embassy bombings, suicide bombings in Israel, and the Lockerbie, Scotland, bombing in 1998. Major international terrorist incidents after 9/11 include the Bali nightclub bombing, the Madrid train bombing, and the London underground bombings.

Some observers take terrorism, understood as physical violence or intimidation in the pursuit of political aims, to be new, even the salient fact of our times. It is sometimes asserted that the supposed pervasiveness of terrorism justifies emergency measures, even something like a permanent state of emergency that has increasingly become the norm in the United States.[7] Terrorism is not new in the US. What is new is the palpable uncertainty raised about the ability of the world's only remaining superpower to defend itself. In the general political euphoria following the collapse and breakup of the Soviet Union in the 1980s, many incorrectly believed the US would henceforth be able to dictate its policies, wishes, and desires to the rest of the world. An attack on some of its most visible symbols has shown that, despite its unprecedented economic and military strength, the US, like other modern industrialized countries, is probably unable despite the midst stringent measures devised by the Department of Homeland Security as well as other government agencies to protect itself against the permanent possibility of terrorism.

Bush's Political Approach to 9/11

We can be relatively brief in discussing the views of George W. Bush as illustrated during his two administrations. As the political leader of the US, in his role as president of the United States (often regarded as the most powerful person in the world), and as supposedly the main architect of an ongoing series of responses to the initial attacks, Bush played a major role in determining US foreign policy in this period of crisis. One can acknowledge the obvious influence of his views on the world stage, while denying that those views need to be taken seriously as an interpretation of the causes of 9/11.

Bush's approach to 9/11 is political (and religious) but not intellectual in even an extended, attenuated sense of the term. As President of the United States, Bush's job was not to formulate intellectual theories, but to exert political guidance for the country as a whole, specifically in rallying American citizens after a large-scale attack on important symbols of the nation and in organizing the reaction against terrorism. In the immediate wake of 9/11, he was responsible for taking a long series of defensive measures against terrorism, such as creating the Office of Homeland Security, improving security for air travel in the US, and for rallying North Atlantic Treaty Organization (NATO) members, as well as other countries, to the defense of American interests.

Yet he was also responsible, at least in principle, for articulating an American analysis, thus for guiding the American response to 9/11. Capable intellectuals have sometimes occupied high office in the US—Woodrow Wilson was an important historian and political scientist before becoming president—but Bush was not one of them. His views are conceptually undeveloped, on examination even incoherent—as could be anticipated, since he is a politician, neither an academic nor a scholar.

This is not necessarily a defect, at least not for someone in his line of work, since his aim was not to convince the American public through reasoned argument, which is not relevant to the office of the president of the US, but, whenever possible, convince them through political rhetoric. Yet, it can be a defect if he (or perhaps more precisely those around him, since his own precise role in formulating policies he represents is not known) is intellectually incapable of articulating a credible American vision of these events or at least of identifying and espousing such a vision created by someone in his administration.

Presidents are neither foreign policy analysts, political theorists, nor philosophers. They are obviously often under considerable pressure (especially in cases of grave national emergency like 9/11) to react as quickly as possible to events as they occur. Though they have an array of advisors, they themselves have little time to work out anything so grand as general principles of political action. Under the pressure of events, politicians tend to adhere to slogans, to make vague and contradictory statements providing their reaction to ongoing events, perhaps to fall back on campaign statements, to continue to curry favor with the electorate—for instance in claiming that the other party is "soft" on defense—and whenever necessary to deflect rather than answer embarrassing questions.

Bush never showed deep knowledge of, or curiosity about, the world outside the United States, about which he knew little when he became president. He never formally worked out a theory of political beliefs. This was hardly surprising, since nothing in Bush's background indicated his capacity to do so, not even interest in such an exercise. Yet, since actions are motivated by intentions, his core beliefs can be inferred from his actions.

It will be useful to distinguish between the public actions, including typical statements about Muslim terrorists, and the beliefs we can suppose are behind those statements. Like other politicians, Bush's references to Muslim terrorists, which routinely accused them of perpetrating a heinous attack on the US on 9/11, and his comments on related themes, were mainly formulated in vague generalities and simplistic dualisms, which changed according to the situation or occasion. In the immediate aftermath of the attacks, he naturally sought, in his role as national leader, to reassure the country. In brief remarks at Barksdale Air Force Base on the same day, he said freedom had been attacked by "a faceless coward." His statement indirectly depicted the US as a (brave) source of freedom, and any opponent as opposed to freedom. This kind of dualistic, unnuanced thinking, which excludes any other possibilities, appeared frequently in his speeches, in which those who disagreed with him were routinely described as evil and countries are assigned, as in the State of the Union Address on January 1, 2001, to the so-called "axis of evil." In this supposed opposition between good and evil, Americans were represented as "good" people who are victims of "bad" people, of those who are "evil," in what sounded like a morality play. As an example of a vague generality, consider the statement in a speech on September 20, 2001, in which Bush linked Muslim terrorists to fascism, Nazism, and totalitarianism in that they are willing to sacrifice their lives for a cause, temporarily forgetting that he was asking members of the armed forces to make a similar sacrifice. Indeed, several years later as the number of Americans killed in Iraq ballooned well beyond 3,000 soldiers, hence beyond the estimate of Americans who died on 9/11, Bush was still requiring the same sacrifice from Americans, a willingness to sacrifice their lives for a cause, a sacrifice he earlier had rejected in the case of Muslim militants.

There is no reliable way to distinguish between the exoteric and esoteric components of the views driving Bush's politics. Nothing is gained or lost by assuming he was sincere or insincere in his public declarations or actions. Nothing is gained or lost by assuming he was or was not the author of, or at least an important contributor to, the policies of his own administration. It seems at least plausible that whether or not he contributed in important ways to the policies his administrations espoused, they could not have been adopted if they ran counter to his own basic intuitions. The only way we will ever be able to judge more precisely is when, over time, the historical record is filled in. It is clear that many important details are not on the public record. An instance among many is the existence of secret CIA prisons in which captives thought to be important for connections to 9/11 were held, off the public record, but which has now been revealed. Yet, enough is known to make it possible to understand at least in outline the main components of the political analysis driving the administration's response to 9/11, and, on the assumption that Bush at least largely agrees with this analysis, the main views to which Bush is himself committed.

Bush and Religion

Arguably the two main factors determining Bush's reaction to 9/11 are his commitments to organized religion (in his case a particular form of Protestantism), and to political neoconservatism. The former derives loosely from his general life experience, and the latter depends on his relationship to a particular brand of American politics stemming from Ronald Reagan.

Religion, which has always been important in America, functions differently in American politics, in Bush's life, and in his politics. The religious dimension of American life,[8] especially American politics, including among the temporary residents at the White House,[9] is well known and has often been discussed. The US is regularly described as one of the most religious countries the world has ever seen, but what that means is not easy to understand. Though there is in principle a separation of church and state in the US, it is safe to say that, however understood, this boundary is regularly breached. It has long been considered crucial that candidates for public office manifest a public attachment to religion, for instance by attending religious services, by consulting religious leaders, by talking on occasion in public about their religious beliefs, by invoking divine guidance in crucial situations, and in other ways. There is, further, a well-established tendency to appeal to religion, religious symbols, religious figures, and what is sometimes characterized as a specifically American relationship to religion to justify actions taken on behalf of the country.

Since there is more continuity than change in the function of religion in American political life, it is useful to point to its continuous presence since the early seventeenth-century colonial era. Religion serves a complex function in American political life, above all in justifying American claims to be a special people picked out by God. This conviction helps justify specific political practices, moral outrage in difficult times, and even the claim to represent God in one's political life.

The religious dimension of the Puritan migration to the New World was clear from the very beginning. Perhaps the most famous reference occurs in a sermon, "A Model of Christian Charity," delivered in 1630 by the Calvinist John Winthrop, the first governor of Massachusetts Bay Colony, on the *Arabella*, the ship bringing him to the New World. In the sermon he asserted that the Puritan colonists emigrating to the New World had a special pact with God to create a holy community. The reference to the "city on the hill" alludes to Matthew 5, 13–16 in which Jesus compares a believer to a city on a hill. Winthrop makes two points in his sermon, both of which seem to have been widely believed by the Puritans: Americans are in effect God's chosen people, and the rich must look after the poor. The first point, which was and still is very influential, continues to echo through American history. It is regularly invoked even now, albeit in implicit fashion, in the idea that the US is engaged in bringing democracy to the world through a series of wars. This suggests a responsibility of individuals to God, who in return is likely to reward them. The second point was quickly forgotten. This latter point indicates a responsibility of individuals to each other, or the more fortunate to the less fortunate, of the rich to the poor, which runs against the supposition underlying liberal capitalism—that is, that the system itself will take care of everyone. In this regard, the latest incident in a long line of such incidents is the passage by Congress in early 2010 of legislation concerning supposedly universal medical coverage in which both major parties implausibly claimed to be the sole legitimate representative of the American people.

The view that Americans are chosen by God suggests they are in some recognizable sense exceptional, different from other people, hence capable of, allowed or permitted, and indeed expected, to do exceptional things. There is a strongly held American view that, on religious grounds, all the other countries depend on the US. In 1912, then presidential candidate Woodrow Wilson, said: "I believe that God planted in us visions of liberty . . . that we are chosen and prominently chosen to show the way to the nations of the world how they shall walk in the paths of liberty."[10] One can interpret Wilson to be saying that by virtue of who Americans are, America was designated by God to lead the way for the free world. The view that Americans are God's chosen people continues to attract attention. Ronald Reagan returned to Winthrop's sermon in a speech in 1974. According to Reagan—who noted that for Pope Pius XII God has entrusted the destiny of human beings to the United States—God has not withdrawn his support from America since the time of Winthrop. Reagan specifically claimed that America is "the last best hope of mankind."[11]

The idea that America is God's chosen people is apparent in a series of views many Americans hold about themselves, and which are periodically invoked to justify various political practices, including "manifest destiny," and what is widely known as "American exceptionalism." These beliefs, which overlap, point to the widespread American conviction that exceptional people, who are not bound by ordinary moral considerations, can do exceptional things by virtue of their special relationship to God. The only difference I can detect between these views—roughly, special rules for special people—and Nietzsche's concept of the "superman," is that Americans invoke God while Nietzsche is content to base his argument on a self-proclaimed superiority.

The belief that Americans and America differ from any other people and country on religious or other grounds is a frequent refrain. Some observers regard this belief as explaining an expansionist tendency that goes all the way back to the founding of the American republic.[12] This tendency, which seems always to have existed in America, later came to be known as manifest destiny. This doctrine, which covers a variety of ideas, was prominently invoked by Jackson Democrats in the 1840s to justify westward expansion across the North American continent toward the Pacific Ocean in the process of acquiring much of the American West. This concept was invoked to justify the right of Americans to spread their vision of self-government and freedom throughout the continent. At the time, manifest destiny justified expansion across the continent to the West in response to a high birth rate, economic depressions in 1818 and 1839, and the search for cheap land. Under the heading of the so-called war on terrorism, manifest destiny currently underwrites what is described as an effort to spread democracy throughout the world. In the nineteenth century, manifest destiny naturally excluded peoples believed to be incapable of realizing American democracy, such as American Indians and those of non-European origin, specifically including slaves imported from Africa and East Asians. John L. O'Sullivan, who coined the term in 1845, believed the US had the right to claim the whole of Oregon, since the higher moral law expressed in the concept of manifest destiny superseded all other laws. This specific idea was later revived by Republicans in the 1890s to justify American expansion, not within, but rather outside North America.[13] During the Bush administrations, what were believed to be the legitimate interests of the only remaining superpower are understood as permitting, indeed even requiring, the extension of democracy as Americans understand it around the world.

American exceptionalism, which is closely related to manifest destiny, differs, if at all, only in the emphasis on the supposed virtue of the American people and their institutions because of their supposedly special relationship to God. The term, coined by Alexis de Tocqueville in 1831, is usually understood to refer to the view that Americans and America differ from other countries and peoples because of their origins, beliefs, historical development, and distinctive institutions. American exceptionalism is often understood to indicate that America and Americans have a special place in the world, for instance as the beacon of hope that the message on the

Statue of Liberty proclaims. Some regard this concept as pointing to the moral superiority of Americans, which in turn dispenses them from following recognized international standards, adhering to international treaties, or observing the proprieties of international behavior.

Bush's political usage of religion was ambiguous, difficult to specify, not easy to clarify. It was determined by at least four main factors: the traditional role of religion in American politics, which he prolonged in his own political practice; his own personal religious beliefs; the rising religious tide dominated by evangelical Protestantism in the US in the wake of 9/11; and the beliefs of his own inner circle of advisers.

Bush's specific religious commitment seems to have arisen through a series of personal "mishaps," including what is described as a drinking problem, which led him to evangelical, or born-again Christianity through the intervention of Reverend Billy Graham, a family friend. As part of his rededication to religion, and perhaps also because much of his popular support (more during his first term than his second) derived from evangelical Christians, Bush publicly displayed interest in this type of Christianity in various ways, for instance in opposing abortion, in blocking funds allocated for United Nations programs to control population growth, in appointing fundamentalist Christian John Ashcroft, as attorney general, in vetoing a proposed law legalizing federal support for stem cell research, and in other ways.

The administration of George W. Bush skillfully exploited the religious nationalism featured by Protestant evangelicals, while seeking to appeal to Catholics (abortion, gay marriage) and Jews (support of Israel) on selected issues, and arguably to all of the above whenever possible. The exploitation of religion for political purposes was part of the political strategy sketched out for electoral ends by Karl Rove, Bush's chief political strategist, and was something he also seemed to believe in. There was a messianic aspect in Bush's relationship to religion. More than once he has indicated that he believed he was picked out by God to lead the nation in this time of trouble.

In Bush's speeches and remarks about 9/11, religion and religious references often hovered in the background, as it were, in a way suggesting that a religious conflict is the root of the problem. His comments on 9/11 depicted the United States as an exceptional nation populated by an exceptional people in a way consistent with the American view of history as described by a long series of American presidents, notably Reagan, as well as the version currently popular among representatives of the Christian religious right. One innovation consisted in drawing attention to a specific link between the familiar dualistic, self-congratulatory, religious view of the United States as enjoying God's backing, and 9/11. From Bush's references to 9/11, we detect a view of the adversaries the United States and its coalition as being composed of fringe Muslims, who are grouped around Al Qaeda, which is led by Osama Bin Laden, and are out of the mainstream. They are fighting to destroy the American way of life of the country, which now as in the past is God's favored nation.

This innovation was not a change of direction, but rather a reinforcement of the traditional American link between religion and politics. The other innovation that also reinforced this link marked, however, an important change. Rather than calling attention to the country or the American people, Bush presented himself as having a special relationship to God, for whom he functioned in effect as a prophet. Consider, for instance, the following statement in which Bush, a so-called born again Christian, drew attention to his conception of politics as based in his personal relationship to God: "Going into this period, I was praying for strength to do the Lord's will. . . . I'm surely not going to justify the war based upon God. Understand that. Nevertheless, in my case, I pray to be as good a messenger of his will as possible."[14]

One can take Bush to be saying two things: first, he was telling everyone who would listen that his approach to politics is based on his religious conviction. Here, one might note an apparent contradiction between this claim, the Christian view of the infinite worth of every individual, and the readiness of the US to engage in military action in which innocents are obviously being killed. Second, Bush is also suggesting that through his political action he in fact directly represented—in fact has been chosen by God as a divine messenger to proclaim—the divine will. This has led some observers to suggest that Bush created a faith-based presidency, in which, since he believed he is God's messenger, there is never any doubt on any issue.[15]

Many texts could be cited to illustrate George W. Bush's religious analysis of 9/11 with a political purpose. On September 11, 2001, the day of the attack, the president spoke to the nation in calling attention to the need to fight evil, referring to Psalm 23, and in asking that Americans unite for justice, peace, and freedom.[16] In a speech to a joint session of Congress nine days later, Bush went into more detail in identifying the terrorists as a fringe group of Muslim extremists, who intended to kill all Americans, an intent which, he claimed, perverted the peaceful nature of Islam. He further affirmed that the terrorists were led by bin Laden, harbored by the Taliban, concerned with overthrowing existing governments in many Muslim countries, desired to drive Israel out of the Middle East, and were opposed to the American way of life. In taking a dualistic stance, he said that you are either with us or against us. Bush insisted the terrorists are against pluralism, freedom, progress, and tolerance while reaffirming faith in the American economy.[17] Nearly four years later, on June 28, 2005, in a speech delivered to soldiers at Fort Bragg, Bush again linked the war on terrorism to the war in Iraq. The aim of terrorism is, he claimed, to remake the Middle East through wanton killing. But, he insisted, America will not retreat in the defense of freedom, which requires resisting evil wherever it may be. The American mission in Iraq, he continued, is to build a free nation; and he asserted that the liberation of Afghanistan and the liberation of Iraq are great turning points in the fight for freedom.

Political Neoconservatism

Bush's political agenda was determined as much by political neoconservatism as by religion. Neoconservatism, which in the Obama administration is now in retreat, was central to the two Bush administrations. Neoconservatism is a recent American form of political conservatism. Political conservatism is often understood as a defense of the status quo, broadly construed. According to Richard Rorty, conservatives look to the past, and progressives or social liberals look to the future.[18] It is usually believed that conservatism in Anglo-American circles goes back to Edmund Burke, who was a member of parliament, a philosopher, and a political theorist. He is now chiefly remembered for supporting the struggle of the American colonies against King George III, and for opposing the French Revolution. Conservatism in American politics brings together a strange group of bedfellows including fiscal conservatives, free market or economic liberals, social or religious conservatives, supporters of a strong American military, enemies of internationalism, proponents of states' rights, advocates of a flat tax who believe everyone should pay the same percentage of income tax on earned income, and even those (right wing libertarians) opposed to any income tax. American political conservatism really took off during the Reagan years, which were dominated by strenuous commitments to so-called supply-side economics and to opposition to international Communism.

Since there is no consensus about conservatism, it remains unclear whether George H. W. Bush and George W. Bush are "true" conservatives. The latter, who has often emphasized his link to the conservative movement, campaigned in 2000 as a "compassionate" conservative. But he, perhaps inconsistently, also expanded the Medicare program, increased federal spending and federal deficits, and began a series of enormously costly wars, all things many conservatives might have shunned.

There are many differences, some obvious, some less so, between political conservatives and political liberals. Conservatives are often ideologically rigid, wedded to tradition, more resistant to change than social liberals. The latter tend to be more flexible, not to take tradition seriously, or as seriously, as their fellow conservatives, and to desire change. Despite his consistently conservative rhetoric, president George W. Bush was comparatively and consistently more pragmatic, more interested in working with his supporters than in following a single ideological line. Yet, on social issues and foreign policy he was often very close to what came to be known as neoconservatism. Speaking generally, neoconservatives resist social change, upholding social tradition in supporting their concept of traditional morality and social mores. An example among many is the staunch resistance displayed by Bush to changes in sexual policy, both at home and abroad. This took the form of resisting, whenever possible, the utilization of "artificial" methods of birth control, both in the US as well as in programs administered by UNESCO or other branches of the UN. Unlike political isolationists, who turn away from international involvement, neoconservatives tend to support an activist foreign policy.

Neoconservative support for activism in foreign policy belongs to the lengthy American activist tradition, a tradition that has often resulted in American intervention in the affairs of other countries. I will return to this point below. I prefer to concentrate here on the relationship of neoconservative foreign policy to other foreign policy options.

According to Francis Fukuyama, a disaffected former neoconservative turned critic, there are four contemporary approaches to American foreign policy. They include realists in the tradition of former secretary of state Henry Kissinger, who play power politics; liberal internationalists who hope to transcend power politics in favor of a stable international order, including American nationalists, or isolationists, and neoconservatives.[19] Fukuyama, who traces the neoconservative movement to the 1940s, depicts neoconservatives as committed to four ideas, up to the end of the cold war: concern with democracy, human rights and internal politics of different states; a belief that American power can be used for moral purposes; skepticism about the ability of international law and institutions to solve security problems; and a view that social engineering often leads to unexpected and unwanted consequences.[20]

Fukuyama's description of neoconservatism reflects a kind of idealism about it that seems to be missing in some of its more recent incarnations. The concern with democracy, human rights, and internal policies of various states is still part of the rhetoric, hence germane to neoconservative theory, but often absent or at least slighted in practice. "Democracy" in the form of democratic elections was rejected when it led to the electoral victory of Hamas in Palestine, a democratic electoral victory which both the US and Israel regarded as unfriendly. There was no sign of concern about living conditions in the Gaza Strip when the US cut off its assistance to the beleaguered population. And the US turned a blind eye to events in Uzbekistan, one of its allies in Central Asia, when demonstrators, who were calling for democracy, which the US claims to favor everywhere in the world, were murdered by the police. Pervez Musharraf, a military dictator and for a time the president of Pakistan, a staunch US ally in Southeast Asia, assumed power as the result of a coup in 1999, though that never seemed to bother the US.

The conservative belief that US power is always, or nearly always, used for moral purposes is also questionable. It is more likely mainly used to further the current view of the US agenda at a given moment in time, whatever that may be. It is sometimes said that the US went into Iraq to help the Iraqis suffering under Saddam Hussein, but no one seems to take this claim seriously. On the contrary, there is obvious skepticism about the role of international law and institutions in solving security problems. A clear example is that the Bush administration appointed as its ambassador to the UN, William Bolton, a career diplomat in several Republican administrations, hence in principle qualified for this post, but someone who was opposed to the UN's very existence.

The conviction that social engineering often leads to unexpected and unwanted consequences, which traditionally has made conservatives timid in engaging abroad, was entirely disregarded by the Bush administration. Even before he became president, George W. Bush was committed to so-called regime change in Iraq as part of an ambitious project developed by Bush's future vice president, Richard Cheney, as early as 1992—that is, immediately in the wake of the Gulf war.

These American policies were interwoven with those of other countries. Regime change is linked to bringing about a fresh start by changing the dynamics of an existing situation. The idea of somehow making a fresh start was also interesting to one of America's traditional allies: Israel. A public report, prepared for the hawkish Netanyahu government in 1996, recommended what it called a new strategy, based on a clean break with past efforts. This turned out to include hot pursuit of Palestinians, preemptive warfare, and abandoning the peace process the US in principle officially supported through "land for peace" in favor of "peace through strength."[21] These measures in the Israeli context anticipated similar but more drastic measures that were later taken in the American context prior to, and after, 9/11.

At the request of Dick Cheney, who was secretary of defense in the administration of President George H. W. Bush, I. Lewis Libby[22] and Paul Wolfowitz[23] wrote a secret report, which was later leaked to the press, entitled 1992 Draft Defense Policy Guidance. Widely regarded as an early formulation of the neoconservative post–cold war agenda, this document outlined several objectives. The first objective was to prevent the reemergence of a new rival of the US, if necessary through force. It further called for unilateral military action in parts of the world considered important to US interests, specifically including preemptive action against potential threats. This latter policy later became law through the revision of the National Security Strategy in 2002. I come back to this point below.

Several years later, Cheney's program for the US in the post–cold war era led to the Project for the New American Century (PNAC). The PNAC, cofounded by Cheney, is a Washington think tank, established in 1997 and chaired by William Kristol, political commentator and founding editor of *The New Standard*. Present and former associates include such prominent members of the two George W. Bush administrations as Donald Rumsfeld, Paul Wolfowitz, Richard Perle, Richard Armitage, Dick Cheney, I. Lewis Libby, William J. Bennett, Zalmay Khalilzad, Jeb Bush, the president's brother, and Ellen Bork, the wife of Robert Bork. The PNAC has clearly hegemonic intentions. It is associated with plans to create American dominance of land, space, and cyberspace, as well as to establish American dominance in world affairs. The basic plan was laid out in a document entitled "Rebuilding America's Defenses: Strategies, Forces and Resources For a New Century," which the PNAC published in 2000. Even before the presidential election, in this document the PNAC called for military dominance in the Persian Gulf, including overthrowing Saddam Hussein, with the aim of consolidating American power in the region as well as throughout the world, and even in outer space. With that in mind, it is not difficult to infer that the policies worked out for American hegemony, even before George W. Bush was "appointed" as president by decision of the Supreme Court, were applied as soon as the opportunity arose as a result of the massive 9/11 terrorist attack on the US. In fact, years later they were still being applied.

In a short "Statement of Principles" published on June 3, 1997, the PNAC expressed the intention to rally support for America's global leadership in offering a vision to follow up on the US's alleged victory in the cold war, crediting the supposed insights of the Reagan administration. The statement preached the familiar, reassuring doctrine of peace through strength. The overall premise seemed to be that strong

American leadership, including shaping circumstances to fit American interests, is the practical prerequisite to keeping the peace. According to the statement, this requires a strong military to meet all challenges; a foreign policy that promotes American principles abroad; and national leadership that accepts the United States's (self-assigned) global responsibilities. Such a policy must be based on four principles: a significant increase in defense spending; strengthening ties to democratic allies and challenging regimes hostile to our interests and values; promotion of political and economic freedom abroad, and responsibility for what is described as the unique American role in securing a world friendly to our security, prosperity and principles. In short, in the wake of the cold war, when for some the main external threat had disappeared or at least sharply declined, the neoconservatives in the PNAC drew the opposite inference. The statement proposed not to decrease but rather sharply to increase military spending. It further proposed confronting any country that differs from the US, even to seek out quarrels. It further insisted that American views of politics and economics, hence freedom to continue the policies of advanced industrial capitalism, must prevail throughout the world. Finally it argued that, since the US is unique, it has the right, when countries differ from American views, to transform the world in its own image.

This short statement was followed up in September 2000 by a longer document entitled "Rebuilding America's Defenses: Strategy, Forces and Resources for a New Century: A Report of the Project for the New American Century." This document notes that a bilateral world featuring opposition between the US and the Soviet Union in a cold war has been replaced by a mono-polar world with a single superpower. It seeks to understand the real situation of bringing about a so-called *pax Americana*, a peace to be monitored and assured through targeting four military objectives. These are: defending the US; fighting and winning several wars simultaneously; forward placement of troops to prevent difficulties from arising, in practice stationing troops around the world in a large number of military bases; and modernizing the armed forces.

The goal of national defense is a given, which the remaining three objectives are intended to realize. In this case, practice followed theory as outlined by the neoconservatives. In direct line with the objectives outlined in the document, when George W. Bush took office in his first term as president an important modernization program of national defense capabilities was begun. The Bush administration also took steps to station troops permanently in Southeast Asia and East Asia.

The document published in 2000 by the PNAC ends with a statement, intended to call attention to a fateful alternative, even a turn in the road of world history from the neoconservative viewpoint, an alternative described as "the choice whether or not to maintain American military preeminence, to secure American geopolitical leadership, and to preserve the American peace."[24] It is at least plausible that the main thrust of this view also "drove" the Bush administration's foreign policy. So, 9/11 presented an opportunity, which the administration seized with both hands, so to speak. This led to building up and modernizing the military, to reviving various weapons programs, to taking a defensive, but also an offensive, stance with respect to US interests, and not least to embarking on a series of military "adventures," which arguably have still not come to an end. In that vein, the war in Afghanistan served two purposes: first, as noted, it met the need to respond rapidly and decisively. Second, it enabled the US to establish a foothold in the region, which it has steadily expanded through establishing a series of bases in surrounding countries.

The idea that neoconservatives should abandon caution about social engineering in actively utilizing US military power for political purposes rapidly became, and remained, one of the driving principles of Bush's foreign policy. Neoconservatives detect a clear antecedent of this policy in an interpretation of the view of Woodrow Wilson. According to Fukuyama, who was earlier very close to the neoconservatives, this is a form of "hard Wilsonianism," which, in rejecting Jean Kirkpatrick's plea for normalcy after the end of the cold war, called for benevolent hegemony.[25] The reference to Wilson requires some interpretation. Wilson, who favored international law, famously called for institutions to bolster policy. This is something that neoconservatives, who reject even the concept of international law and revel in their view of American power, tend to reject. In the neoconservative restatement, the result is a kind of Wilsonianism minus international institutions, without, for instance, the League of Nations, originally promoted by Wilson, or its contemporary equivalent the United Nations. What contemporary neoconservatives have in mind can be described as a go-it-alone policy based on military superiority, dedication to US alliances, and missile defense.

This view is articulated by a number of figures, earlier by Fukuyama before he became a critic of the Iraq War he never supported, and later and more consistently by Robert Kagan, one of the cofounders of the PNAC. In the wake of 9/11, Kagan presented what some observers regarded as a plea for unilateralism, on the grounds that the US no longer needs alliances, which are for the weak.[26] According to Kagan, the US has always defended a liberal progressive society, which has long been adopted by the world as its ideal, though not always with regard to such Westphalian "niceties" as respect for national sovereignty and noninterference. In Kagan's view, and despite the pious image of the temple on the hill, the tendency toward empire to the detriment of others—initially throughout the North American continent and then later abroad—is one of the central thrusts of American history.[27] Kagan is certainly correct about the failure to respect the claims of other nations when it suits the US not to do so. Yet he is wrong in suggesting that the American model is universally accepted. The opposition between the US and the European Union precisely turns on whether to adopt a social form of capitalism or a less economically restrictive American political liberalism.

For Kagan, only the US now possesses the power to defend liberal democracy.[28] Though Kagan is right that the US is enormously strong, the strongest nation the world has ever seen, the jury is still out about whether the US can effectively defend liberal democracy, and for two reasons. On the one hand, it is doubtful anyone who has recently been at an airport in the United States has been impressed with the practical utility of the very costly show of security as an effective deterrent to any but the most amateur potential terrorist. On the other hand, human rights are an integral part of liberal democracy, however defined. But it is becoming increasingly likely that the series of measures abridging civil rights that have been put in place since 9/11 will transform the political liberalism Kagan favors into political illiberalism, which has only the name in common with liberal democracy.

The far-flung intellectual sources of neoconservatism take into account American history, which records many instances of intervention in the internal affairs of other nations. These include the Roosevelt Corollary to the Monroe Doctrine, introduced by Theodore Roosevelt, which launched a period of what has been described as "big stick" diplomacy; Woodrow Wilson, who insisted on the role of America in spreading freedom and democracy; and the political philosopher Leo Strauss, who has influenced a number of members of Bush's inner circle.[29] Strauss held what today would be called a postmodern political view. There is some disagreement about what Strauss personally thought. It has recently been argued that he was a liberal democrat skeptical about claims for political certainty as well as the political uses of political theory.[30] This skepticism does not seem to have been passed on to his conservative followers.

Strauss is more often understood to believe that the modern world is on the wrong track, that modernity reaches its high point in the United States, and that the most pressing task is to rescue the United States from such modernity. "Good" politicians need to reassert absolute moral values that unite society in order to overcome moral relativism that liberalism has created. Strauss's belief that government needs to promote morality by deceiving its citizens, who need to be led, recalls Dostoyevsky's grand inquisitor. Strauss's political approach, which features deliberate deception, is regarded as highly appealing by some politicians. Mark Taylor, who bases himself on Drury, identifies four main ideas in Strauss: an aversion to modern liberal democracy in favor of a return to the original conception of democracy; the embrace of deception by governing elites; the affirmation of an aggressive nationalism; and an explicit embrace of hierarchical religion.[31] Taylor points to a long list of Straussian neoconservatives associated with the Bush government. Paul Wolfowitz, for instance, wrote his doctorate under Strauss's direction.[32] According to Taylor, almost all of those who signed the 2000 document of the Project for the New American Century, as well as most of the 41 signers of an earlier 1998 letter urging President Bill Clinton to remove Saddam Hussein from power, are neoconservative Straussians.

Christian Neoconservatism, 9/11 and Terrorism

Bush's dual commitment to evangelical Christianity and American neoconservatism created an important synergy that, in refuting traditional conservative isolationist tendencies, arguably impelled him to act boldly in the international arena. His attachment to Christianity offers a strong moral justification for political action in a least three ways. First, it presents a simplistic approach to practical problems that, from the religious perspective, is routinely depicted in dualistic terms and lacking nuance as finally only a choice between two possibilities: good and evil, freedom and "unfreedom," democracy and dictatorship. Bernard Lewis, the historian of the Middle East, and one of the academic intellectuals closest to Bush foreign policy, puts the case for a dualistic analysis with clarity: "The war against terror and the quest for freedom are inextricably linked, and neither can succeed without the other."[33] The result is a stance toward the world remarkably similar to that advanced at the beginning of National Socialism by the Nazi legal theoretician Carl Schmitt. Schmitt argued that we must look away from conceptual and other differences in assembling our forces, since in the final analysis there are only two camps face-to-face, among whom we must choose: friends and foes.[34] A similar approach reemerged in the religiously tinted rhetoric of Bush, who similarly divides the world into terrorists and those who comfort them, on the one hand, and those willing to join with America to combat them, on the other.

Second, religious conviction makes it easy to attach a moral stigma to 9/11, which links seamlessly to the American exceptionalist view that America is a land uniquely favored by God. This idea plays out in various ways. One is the view that if something has happened to the US, it is because Americans collectively and individually somehow have fallen below the proper level required by religious faith. Just as earlier some clergy suggested that HIV AIDS is a punishment sent by God, others claimed 9/11 occurred because of American sins. In a television program two days after the 9/11 attacks, Rev. Jerry Falwell made it clear that he believed God allowed it to happen because Americans were supporting gays, abortion, and feminism. In response, Rev. Pat Robertson publicly agreed with him in insisting the agenda he was criticizing was in fact adopted in the US by the courts and the highest level of government.[35]

Third, the commitment to Christianity supports the idea that if and when the US acts to strike down those opposing us, it will be morally justified by its special relationship to God. Bush, as noted above, carried this religious justification of political action further still in suggesting that in a time of travail he had been personally selected to perform this mission. His claim was that in acting against those who attacked the US he was not only acting on behalf of a nation favored by God but also acting as God's own emissary.

Bush's presidency was predicated on a commitment to two causes, Christianity and political neoconservatism, which he joined together in an adamantine link driving a foreign as well as a domestic agenda. His commitment to evangelical Christianity provided a justification for the underlying morality of any action that America, God's favored nation, might undertake against its enemies. His evangelical religious commitment was linked to the war in Iraq that, he believed, will bring about the spread of Jesus Christ's teachings in Iraq and throughout the Middle East.[36]

His form of commitment to neoconservatism called for such action as might be deemed necessary to forestall any possible threat to American hegemony after the end of the cold war. The cynical conservative conviction that since moral rules do not hold in foreign policy anything is possible gives way to the neoconservative view of the world, which in turn leads to the view that Americans must act, since not to do so would be a moral failure. In the opinion of American neoconservatives, at the end of the cold war the world was not friendlier and safer, but was an even more dangerous place, where danger lurked in ways that called for decisive action at the slightest hint of a threat—if necessary even preemptive war. This view was not dampened but rather heightened by 9/11, which justified the worst fears of neoconservatives while simultaneously creating the possibility for them to act aggressively in initiating a series of wars that, in more normal situations, would probably not have been possible.

Notes

1. One of the wilder views is that idea that the source of 9/11 lies in the so-called cultural left, including the filmmaker Michael Moore, the linguist Noam Chomsky, mainstream politicians like Hillary Rodham Clinton, Robert Byrd, and Jimmy Carter, and journalists such as Garry Wills and Seymour Hersh. See Dinesh D'Souza, *The Enemy at Home: The Cultural Left and Its Responsibility for 9/11*, New York: Random House, 2006.
2. See, for the distinction between religion and theology, Herbert Schnädelbach, *Religion in der modernen Welt*, Frankfurt A.M: Fischer, 2009.
3. Virginia Held, *How Terrorism Is Wrong: Morality and Political Violence*, New York: Oxford University Press, 2008, p. 21.
4. Held, *How Terrorism Is Wrong: Morality and Political Violence*, p. 76.
5. Leon Trotsky, *Terrorism and Communism*, Ann Arbor: The University of Michigan Press, 1961, p. 58.
6. For an overview, see Milton Meltzer, *The Terrorists*, New York: Harper and Row, 1983.
7. For recent discussion of the concept of a state of emergency, see Giorgio Agamben, *Etat d'exception. Homo sacer*, trans. By Joël Gayraud, Paris: Editions du Seuil, 2003.
8. For an updated version of an older, comprehensive study, Sydney Ahlstrom, *A Religious History of the American People*, 2nd ed., foreword and concluding chapter by David D. Hall, New Haven: Yale University Press, 2004.
9. See Sébastien Fath, *Dieu bénisse l'Amérique. La religion de la maison–blanche*, Paris: Editions du Seuil, 2004.
10. Cited in T. J. Knock, *To End All Wars*. Princeton: Princeton University Press, 1992, p. 11.
11. "City Upon a Hill," The president at the first annual CPAC conference, January 25, 1974.
12. In the wake of the enormous debacle in Iraq, neo-conservatives are scrambling to depict their views, which led to this war, as simply mainstream. Kagan has recently argued that the US has never been isolationist but has always been

prone to expansionist policies. See Robert Kagan, *Dangerous Nation*, New York: Knopf, 2006.

13. Kagan specifically compares the Spanish-American War and the decision to invade Iraq. See chapter 12: "Morality and Hegemony," in Kagan, *Dangerous Nation*, pp. 357–416.
14. Bob Woodward, *Plan of Attack*, cited in Ron Suskind, "Faith, Certainty and the Presidency of George W. Bush," *New York Times Magazine*, October 17, 2004.
15. See Ron Suskind, "Faith, Certainty and the Presidency of George W. Bush," in *New York Times Magazine*, October 17, 2004.
16. Office of the Press Secretary, September 11, 2001.
17. Office of the Press Secretary, September 20, 2001.
18. See Richard Rorty, *Achieving Our Country: Leftist Thought in Twentieth Century America*. Cambridge: Harvard University Press, 1998.
19. See Francis Fukuyama, *America At the Crossroads: Democracy, Power and the Neoconservative Legacy*, New Haven: Yale University Press, 2006, p. 7.
20. See Fukuyama, *America At the Crossroads*, pp. 4–5, 48–49.
21. See "A Clean Break: A New Strategy for Securing the Realm." This is a report prepared by The Institute for Advanced Strategic and Political Studies' "Study Group on a New Israeli Strategy Toward 2000." The lead author of the report was Richard Perle, a close associate of Defense Secretary Donald Rumsfeld. Perle was later forced, because of a conflict of interest, to resign from his position as chair of the Pentagon's Defense Policy Board in March 2003.
22. Libby was later convicted of federal charges of obstruction of justice and perjury. His prison time was later commuted by Bush, who did not pardon him.
23. As US deputy director of defense under Donald Rumsfeld, Wolfowitz was a main architect of the Iraq War. He was later appointed president of the World Bank from which he was forced to resign in questionable circumstances.
24. "Rebuilding America's Defenses: Strategy, Forces and Resources For a New Century: A Report of the Project for the New American Century," p. 76.
25. See Fukuyama, *America At the Crossroads: Democracy, Power and the Neoconservative Legacy*, p. 41.
26. See Packer, *Assassin's Gate*, pp. 52–53.
27. For Kagan's view of this tendency, see Robert Kagan, *Dangerous Nation*, New York: Random House, 2006.
28. See Robert Kagan, *Of Paradise and Power: America and Europe in the New World Order*, New York: Vintage, 2003.
29. This relationship has been studied in detail by Drury. See Shadia Drury, *Terror and Civilization: Christianity, Politics, and the Western Psyche*, St. Martins, 2004; see also Drury, *Leo Strauss and the American Right*, New York: St. Martin's Press, 1997.
30. See Steven B. Smith, *Reading Leo Strauss: Politics, Philosophy, Judaism*, Chicago: University of Chicago Press, 2006.

31. See Mark Taylor, "Liberation, Neocons and the Christian Right: Options for Pro-Active Christian Witness in Post-9/11," in *Constellation*, Fall 2003.
32. Paul Wolfowitz (Reagan's ambassador to Indonesia, then deputy secretary of defense, and later president of the World Bank) [61], Abram Shulsky (director of Rumsfeld's and Wolfowitz's Office of Special Plans), Seth Cropsey (Caspar Weinberger's former speechwriter), John T. Agresto (former chair, National Endowment for the Humanities Deputy), Carnes Lord (served on the National Security Council), Gary L. McDowell (served as adviser to Attorney General Edwin Meese III), Alan Keyes (Assistant Secretary of State for International Organization Affairs), Gary Schmitt (head of President Ronald Reagan's National Advisory Board of Foreign Intelligence, now executive chairman of the Project for a New American Century), William Bennett (former secretary of education, drug czar, and author on values), William Kristol (former chief of staff for Vice President Dan Quayle, now chairman of the New American Century Project), and many more.
33. Bernard Lewis, *The Crisis of Islam: Holy War and Unholy Terror*, New York: Random House, 2003, p. 169.
34. See Carl Schmitt, *The Concept of the Political*, translated by George Schwab, Chicago: University of Chicago Press, 1996.
35. See "You Helped This Happen"; Jerry Falwell and Pat Robertson react to the September 11 terrorist attacks on American soil. Partial transcript of comments from the Thursday, September 13, 2001 edition of the "700 Club."
36. See "Evangelical Missionaries Rush To Win Iraq as Middle East Mission Base" quoted in *Christian Today*, March 22, 2004, accessed on www.christiantoday.com.

CHAPTER TWO

Huntington's Political–Scientific Analysis of the Clash of Civilizations (or Cultures)

There is an obvious difference between politicians, who act but do not "know," and intellectuals who may "know" but only rarely act. In discussing George W. Bush, we focused on someone who, during his two mandates as president of the United States, was undeniably a major actor on the world stage. Though he was not in any sense an intellectual, he was called upon in his role as the American president to act before an understanding of the situation was worked out. He was someone who was arguably not well equipped to provide anything approaching an academic analysis of the problems to which he was called upon to react. In turning now to Huntington and Lewis, I will be considering academic intellectuals. Both belong to those whose views receive a hearing in the intellectual academy but, though Lewis is an exception to this practice, since his views were listened to by George W. Bush's administration, are routinely ignored by those in a position to act. Bush offers what is basically a populist political defense of the Western point of view as the aggrieved party, the victim of Islamic terrorism. From this perspective, the US was justified by its supposed privileged relationship to God as well as by neoconservative political analysis in acting vigorously against an enemy it does not pretend to understand. A more thoughtful defense of the Western point of view was independently worked out in more academic fashion by Huntington and Lewis, two leading members of the American academic community.

Fukuyama, Kojève, Hegel and the *End of History*

Huntington's theory arose in the heady days of the early 1990s after the break up of the Soviet Union and after the claimed capitalist "defeat" of international Communism. To understand Huntington's position, it useful to see it as a possible answer to ideas that were attracting attention at the time, especially the view of Francis Fukuyama. It was a moment when Fukuyama, inspired by Ronald Reagan's conservatism, was confidently proclaiming the end of history. Fukuyama, earlier a leading neoconservative (who has in the meantime turned against neoconservatism), in turn builds on Hegel, as famously misinterpreted by the French Marxist philosopher Alexandre Kojève.

When Hegel died in 1831, his followers quickly split up into what were known as right-wing Hegelians, all situated in the universities, and left wing Hegelians, also called young Hegelians, who, with the exception of Eduard Gans, on the law faculty in Berlin, were situated outside the universities. The right-wing Hegelians attributed a conception of religion as central to Hegel's position, which they celebrated. The left-wing Hegelians accepted this attribution, which is arguable in criticizing Hegel's support of organized religion.[1]

The left-wing Hegelians, who included Karl Marx, were more influential than the right-wing Hegelians. We owe to the left-wing Hegelians the suggestion, most clearly formulated by Friedrich Engels, that Hegel brings philosophy to a peak and to an end.[2] Kojève, who was impressed by this claim, which he further develops as an even more extreme doctrine, misreads Hegel as claiming that not only philosophy, but even history has ended. According to Kojève, history ends when man disappears through the disappearance of "Action," with a capital letter, as well wars and bloody revolutions.[3]

In this regard, Kojève makes two points: first, we have already arrived at the end of history, hence we are now in an era of political stability that has replaced change; and, second, its price is the loss of the human nature of the human being. The first suggestion, made in the late 1930s as Europe was preparing for the Second World War, is clearly false. The second suggestion about a loss of character in times of peace is difficult to grasp. In his book,[4] which builds on an article,[5] Fukuyama takes over the first point but drops the second one. For Fukuyama, the United States, hence the so-called American way of life, represents the end of history with all the advantages and few or none of the drawbacks on which Kojève, who is critical of the American way of life, insists.

Fukuyama, like Kagan and other conservatives, claims to detect a consensus concerning the "legitimacy of liberal democracy," which "conquered rival ideologies like hereditary monarchy, fascism, and most recently communism."[6] This book, the work of a young man, not surprisingly contains some extreme views. Fukuyama describes liberal democracy as perhaps the "end point of mankind's ideological evolution," "the final form of human government," hence "the end of history." Though earlier forms of government suffered from "grave defects and irrationalities that led to their collapse," liberal democracy suffers from nothing more than the "incomplete implementation of the twin principles of liberty and equality."[7]

Fukuyama asks whether in the present historical moment "it makes sense for us once again to speak of a coherent and directional History of mankind that will eventually lead the greater part of humanity to liberal democracy?"[8] He answers affirmatively since liberal democracy is the only "coherent political aspiration" and "liberal principles in economics—the 'free market'—have spread, and have succeeded in producing unprecedented levels of material prosperity."[9]

Marxism used to argue that history culminates in Communism. In much the same way, Fukuyama now argues that history culminates in American liberal democracy. In part 1 of his book, he insists we need to return to this theme.

In part 2, he maintains that modern natural science, "the only important social activity that is cumulative and directional[10]," moves history toward capitalism. In part 3, going beyond the economic level, he returns to Hegel's view of recognition, which he applies in part 4 to interpret disparate social phenomena and, as Huntington will later do, to anticipate some main lines of future international struggles. Part 5, which addresses the intrinsic stability of liberal democracy, examines two main criticisms: the left-wing view (e.g., Marx) that in liberal democracy universal recognition is necessarily incomplete, and the right-wing view (e.g., Nietzsche) that the commitment to equality reduces everyone to a common denominator.

Fukuyama's approach is based on the assumption that liberal democracy has now carried the day. He concedes a difference between the theory and practice of liberal democracy, which he understands as the ability to participate in the electoral process. Yet this criterion seems mainly to be honored in the breach. In many "democratic" countries, such as the US, it is difficult to be a candidate for high office without important financial resources. And there are "democracies," such as Switzerland, where not everyone can vote.

Fukuyama, who concedes that liberal democracy does not always work in practice, believes the free market is the most efficient form of economy and the most efficient mechanism yet devised for accumulating capital. Yet, accumulation of capital is not necessarily useful for society as a whole, even if it is obviously useful for some people, for instance the owners of the means of production. The full development of human beings as individuals is arguably unlikely to be realized within the free market that is oriented toward a different goal than the accumulation of capital. Other observers, such as Daniel Bell, deny that liberal democracy is appropriate in all times and places, for instance in East Asia at present.[11]

Fukuyama, who thinks there is no alternative to the free market, assumes a free market enterprise system is best, if not for everyone, at least for the majority. It is sometimes useful for everyone that some people act only for their own advantage. Yet it seems unlikely that general social utility, what J.S. Mill calls the greater good of the greater number of people, is more likely to be served by ignoring their interests. His book was written before the great recession that began in late 2008. It would be interesting to see how he could defend his claim that the free market system is best for the majority in view of the great recession to which it led and from which only the privileged few profited.

Fukuyama's position is contradictory. He favors a free market economy, as free as possible, as being best suited, against all possible rivals, to liberal democracy. Yet he also favors mutual recognition over an analysis of the human being as *homo economicus*. Fukuyama, who thinks that the best way we can help others is to forget about them and go about our business, seems to believe that enlightened self-interest coupled with benign neglect is about the best thing I can do for my fellow human beings. But there is no reason to believe, and Fukuyama offers none, that economics leads, will lead, or conceivably might lead to mutual recognition.

Huntington's Cultural Thesis: Multiculturalism, Identity Politics, and the Nation-State

Huntington refutes Fukuyama through an approach to 9/11 based on identity politics and a conception of the nation-state. The second half of the twentieth century saw the emergence of a number of political movements focused on claims of injustices done to particular social groups that have been historically mistreated. These include women, denied equal treatment in many significant ways, Blacks, denied civil rights, gays and lesbians, and the American Indians, each of whom can be understood as possessing a collective identity. Huntington, who applies a version of the identity thesis to world politics, thinks future international conflicts will be caused by differences between cultures or civilizations. In great detail, he elaborates this view, anticipated in the 1950s by Lester Pearson,[12] later the prime minister of Canada. If identity politics belongs to multiculturalism, and if multiculturalism is postmodern, then Huntington's view can be called a postmodern theory of international relations. His thesis—it was initially stated in an article in the early 1990s,[13] then developed in a book,[14] and later applied to 9/11[15]—is intended as a general hypothesis about the cause, hence the explanation, of future conflicts.

When he initially worked out his theory, Huntington was not concerned with a particular series of historical events, but rather with fundamental sources of conflict in the present historical moment. His position revises the view of the modern nation-state as a primary cause of historical events. It is usual to understand international conflict as due to, hence as "caused" by, nation-states, such as when Germany attacked the Soviet Union early in the Second World War. Huntington argues that the nation-state is still, and will continue to remain, important. But it has now been superseded as an explanatory concept for future conflicts that he thinks, unlike Fukuyama, will continue to occur.

According to Huntington, we are in a new phase of world politics. Views of "the end of history, the return of traditional rivalries between nation states, and the decline of the nation state" miss a crucial point, which he formulates as the hypothesis that "the fundamental source of conflict in this new world will be neither primarily ideological nor primarily economic."[16] His basic claim is that, "The great divisions among humankind and the dominating source of conflict will be cultural. Nation states will remain the most powerful actors in world affairs, but the principal conflicts of global politics will occur between nations and groups of different civilizations. The clash of civilizations will be the battle lines of the future."[17] In other words, the causal role earlier played by nation-states will shift to civilizations, or what he also calls cultures.

Ideology and Conflict

Huntington's view is unclear and difficult to interpret. He seems to hold that, whether or not the nation-state will be weaker in the future than in the past, conflicts will be mainly explicable through cultural divisions, not through ideology or economics.

Ideology has had a checkered career since the end of the eighteenth century, when Destutt de Tracy coined the term to refer to the science of ideas and their origins. After Daniel Bell declared the end of ideology, it became popular to decry it. Yet, depending on how the term is understood, ideology is arguably as widespread and important now as it has ever been. The increasing prevalence of large, influential special-interest groups creates pressure to make decisions on ideological grounds—or prior commitment to a particular view—rather than on the merits of the question. For example, though it seems likely many will die through the failure to make needed medical advances, it makes perfect ideological sense to impede, or even prevent, stem cell research if to permit it would alienate those committed to the right to life for the unborn, and these alienated individuals might later vote against the party in power. The Nobel Prize for Physiology and Medicine was awarded in 2005 to two Australian scientists whose scientifically demonstrable claim that a bacterium caused stomach inflammation and ulcers was, for years, strongly opposed by the pharmaceutical industry.[18]

Ideology operates as a means rather than as an end. Though Hitler notoriously hated Jews, it would be farfetched to regard his anti-Semitism as a basic cause of the Second World War. His desire to kill Jews was at most a secondary theme, enlisted as a means to realizing his vision for Germany, but not the main end in view. The fact that his virulent dislike of Jews was not the central point, enabled many intellectuals, like Martin Heidegger and Carl Schmitt, who did not necessarily share his anti-Semitism, to become enthusiastic Nazis.

"Ideology" is sometimes taken to mean a system of ideas characteristic of a particular group, social class, or collection of individuals. Huntington's reference to ideology and economics suggests a distinction between them. There are both non-economic and economic forms of ideology. Marxists refer to false consciousness based on group (or what they call class) identification with specific economic interests. Instances of ideology in recent American history include the so-called domino theory invoked to justify the Vietnam War[19] and the supposed existence of weapons of mass destruction invoked to justify the Iraq War. No one pretends the domino theory "caused" the Vietnam War, nor that WMD caused the Iraq War, but in each case an ideological myth that was later discredited proved politically useful for entering into, and carrying out, the conflict.

Economics and Conflict Between Nations and/or Different Civilizations

It would be as mistaken to disregard economics in conflicts between nation-states and even "civilizations" as it would be to reduce any and all international conflicts to such factors. Huntington's suggestion that economics is now less important than before can be interpreted in two ways. Either it has somehow become less significant in international conflict than it once was, or other, more important factors have emerged in the meantime. Yet, there is no evidence that the role of economics in international conflicts has diminished, especially in the period with which he is specifically concerned, the more than half century since the end of the Second World War.

Huntington's argument that differences in culture have recently become primary causes of international conflict derives from an account of the historical evolution of the modern world in four stages, during which conflict in the West was finally replaced by cultural conflict between the West and other regions. The Peace of Westphalia (1648), ending the Thirty Years War and resulting in the creation of nation-states, led to a series of conflicts between princes. Beginning with the French Revolution, these conflicts brought nation-states into opposition instead of princes. In the wake of the First World War, the conflict of nation-states was replaced by a conflict of ideologies. The cold war featured an opposition between two superpowers, each of which defined its identity in ideological terms as the negation of the other. This Western phase of international politics ended with the cold war. After that time, international politics assumed a new form as an opposition between Western and non-Western civilizations and among non-Western civilizations. For Huntington, "With the end of the Cold War, international politics moves out of its Western phase, and its center-piece becomes the interaction between the West and non-Western civilizations and among non-Western civilizations."[20]

This account is obviously controversial. It is at least arguable that the conflict of ideologies during the cold war did not replace, but only gave a new form to, a continuing conflict between nation-states. The conflict between the Soviet Union and the United States that took up much of the last century was mainly fought through ideology, since it never quite broke into classical forms of warfare. One could further argue that each of these two superpowers is no longer a nation-state in the earlier sense of the term. For instance, each was allied with other countries that these superpowers were not only stronger than, but also largely independent of.

Huntington analyzes international politics through a single but unclear primary cause: the difference between cultures (or civilizations). Yet, there is no reason to believe that at any given time there is only a single primary cause for international conflict. There is, for instance, no satisfactory mono-causal analysis of the Iraq War. I come back to this point below. There is also no reason to think that cultural difference, which is as old as civilization, has now become more important than such other causes of international conflict, such as ideology and economics.

Ideology is probably never absent from politics, including American politics. It was visible in many facets of the administrations of George W. Bush. It has arguably changed in the Obama administration, but has not somehow suddenly vanished. And it is an integral part of both the Muslim and Western sides of the global war on terror. Many observers regard the war on terror as serving two unrelated aims: the legitimate response to the 9/11 attack on the United States, and the illegitimate use of that event to establish American hegemony over world affairs through the use of force rendered legitimate by 9/11.

The economic dimension of international conflict is strongly represented in current events. A relatively neutral example is the American refusal to sign the Kyoto Protocol, a treaty on global warming, on the grounds that to do so would be harmful to the US economy. A more controversial example is the US attitude toward Iran after 9/11, a country that is apparently making progress toward developing nuclear weapons, but which also possesses oil as well as very large reserves of natural gas. A factor in the decision to enter into war with Iraq seemed to be the view that its oil would defray the costs of the conflict. I also return to this point below.

Huntington groups countries in terms of culture and/or civilization to explain conflict. Cultures belong to civilizations, which do not belong to any other entity. "Civilization is a cultural entity," hence, is composed of different cultures, and defined by "common objective elements, such as language, history, religion, customs, institutions, and by the subjective self-identification of people."[21] All villages in Italy share in Italian culture, hence are Italian and not, say, German. European countries share the cultural traits of Europe, which distinguish them from Arab lands or China. But Arabs, Chinese, and Westerners constitute civilizations, which do not belong to any further cultural grouping.

Huntington, who recognizes no more than seven or eight examples—"Western, Confucian, Japanese, Islamic, Hindu, Slavic-Orthodox, Latin American and possibly African civilization"[22]—thinks future conflict will occur along fault lines between them. Those who define their identity in ethnic and religious terms are likely to join with those with whom they identify in rejecting others who differ from them. Faced with the declining importance of ideology, "governments and groups will increasingly attempt to mobilize support by appealing to common religion and civilization identity."[23] This will lead to conflicts on two levels: on the micro level over territory; and on the macro level over military and economic power, the control of international institutions, and the promotion of political and religious values, such as Western values of democracy and liberalism.

In retrospect, Huntington's remarks on the clash between Islam and Christianity seem prophetic. He notes that the conflict between the West and Islam, which has been under way for some thirteen hundred years, is unlikely to decline, and might become more virulent. He cites a number of Muslims, including Saddam Hussein, Ayatollah Ali Khamenei, and King Hussein of Jordan as being convinced the Gulf wars were not merely a clash involving the US, its allies, and Iraq, but a conflict of civilizations. He argues that, as a result of the current political, military, and economic dominance of the West, world politics will increasingly turn on the difference between what, following Kishore Mahbubani, he calls: the West and the rest.[24]

Further Elaboration and Application of Huntington's Cultural Thesis

Huntington's book, which appeared several years later, extends his argument that since "clashes of civilizations are the greatest threat to world peace . . . an international order based on civilizations is the surest safeguard against world war."[25] The term "remaking," which figures in the title of the book—*The Clash of Civilizations and the Remaking of World Order*—can be understood in two ways: as referring to the historical change of the world order or even—in a way closer to the neoconservative view of hegemonic empire—as inviting (us) to modify it. In that sense, it is in principle consistent with so-called regime change dear to the heart of George W. Bush's presidency.

The interest of Huntington's approach lies in its claim to offer an improved conceptual framework grasping international conflict. In the preface, Huntington describes his hypothesis as a "more meaningful and useful lens through which to view international developments than any alternative paradigm."[26] He identifies four conceptual frameworks that were advanced after the end of the cold war—the one world model (e.g., Fukuyama); the two worlds model; the realist theory of international relations, or 184 states more or less; and the sheer chaos model (e.g., Zbigniew Brzezinski and Daniel Patrick Moynihan), before suggesting a fifth possibility. The new paradigm is supposedly quantitatively and qualitatively superior to available alternatives for interpreting world politics; it sacrifices neither reality to parsimony nor parsimony to reality; it is easily grasped; and it is more compatible with other alternatives than they are with it.[27] According to Huntington, it is further compatible with a series of events that took place in 1993.[28]

Huntington believes the age of Muslim wars, an age in which Muslims fight each other and everyone else, has replaced the cold war. The attacks of 9/11 are a continuation of violence involving Muslims. The causes do not lie in Muslim doctrine, hence not in religion, but rather in politics. "These do not include the inherent nature of Islamic doctrine and beliefs, which (like those of Christianity) its adherents can use to justify peace or war as they wish. The causes of contemporary Muslim wars lie in politics, not seventh-century religious doctrines."[29] These include an increase in Islamic consciousness as a response to modernization and globalization, resentment toward the West, intra-Islamic divisions that promote violence between Muslims, and high birthrates among Muslims.

Huntington holds open the possibility of a decrease in Muslim violence through a change in American policy toward Israel, and improvements in living conditions in the Middle East. His suggestions contradict his general thesis about the clash of civilizations as being due to cultural difference. Huntington mistakenly separates politics and social conditions. On the one hand, he ascribes the source of violence, not to Islamic religion or culture, but to Muslim politics. And on the other, he attributes Muslim violence to poor social, economic, and political conditions in Islamic countries. Yet, politics and social conditions are obviously interrelated. Bad politics produce poor social conditions, as Robert Mugabe has demonstrated in Zimbabwe. Conversely, poor social and economic conditions produce politics leading to conflict with neighbors and other countries.

Huntington's message is twofold: stop political and other forms of aggression through unlimited support of Israel, which is perceived in Islamic countries as radically unfair; and improve living conditions in Islamic countries, which will become less threatening to others. In other words, the Muslim threat to the West can be explained, and largely reduced, by taking the needs of Muslim populations into account instead of attributing this threat to cultural differences. It follows that, by Huntington's own account, cultural differences play a role in Muslim violence, but are not its root cause.

In calling attention to ideology and economics as explanatory factors, Huntington's suggestion—that 9/11 manifests less a clash of civilizations (and/or cultures) than it does difficulties resulting from Islamic politics and living conditions in the Islamic world—contradicts his "official" hypothesis that international conflict is currently best explained through the theory of a class of civilizations. If the problem of 9/11 is due to, and can be ameliorated through, a change in Islamic politics and living conditions, then the clash of civilizations is no more than an effect following from other, deeper causes. Huntington's cultural model, which is intended as an alternative to other models of international relations, is not useful directly or even indirectly to the analysis of 9/11 or international conflict. Since differences in civilizations, which Huntington regards as primary, are themselves caused by other, deeper factors, it is incorrect to attribute the primary cause of international conflict to this factor.

Notes

1. For an account of the split of the Hegelian school, see Emil Fackenheim, *The Religious Dimension in Hegel's Thought*, Chicago: University of Chicago Press, 1967.
2. See Friedrich Engels, *Ludwig Feuerbach and the Outcome of Classical German Philosophy*, New York: International Publishers, 1941.
3. In a note appended to the second edition of his book, Kojève argues that the end of history was not in the future but already in the present. It was represented by the American way of life, in which people who no longer had anything to achieve had regressed to the level of mere animality. According to Kojève, life in the United States instantiates the Marxist goal of a classless society. Yet, later, after a trip to Japan, he changed his mind and argued that postwar Japanese civilization, in which human beings had already returned to an animal state, would end up by transforming the West into the Orient. See Alexandre Kojève, *Introduction à la lecture de Hegel*, Paris: Editions Gallimard, 1947, pp. 436–38.
4. See Francis Fukuyama, *The End of History and the Last Man*, New York: The Free Press, 1992. All passages from this book are indicated in the text with F, followed by the page number.
5. See Francis Fukuyama, "The End of History?," in *The National Interest* 16, Summer 1989, pp. 3–18.
6. Fukuyama, ibid., p. xi.
7. Fukuyama, ibid., p. xi.
8. Fukuyama, ibid., p. xii.

9. Fukuyama, ibid., p. xiii.
10. Fukuyama, ibid., p. xiv.
11. See Daniel A. Bell, *Beyond Liberal Democracy: Political Thinking for an East Asian Context*, Princeton University Press, 2006.
12. See Lester B. Pearson, *Democracy in World Politics*, Princeton: Princeton University Press, 1955, pp. 82–83.
13. See Samuel P. Huntington, "The Clash of Civilizations?," in *Foreign Affairs*, Summer 1993.
14. See Samuel P. Huntington, *The Clash of Civilizations and the Remaking of World Order*, New York: Simon and Schuster, 1997.
15. See Samuel P. Huntington, "The Age of Muslim Wars," in *Newsweek*, vol. 138, No. 25, December 17, 2001, pp. 42–47.
16. Huntington, "The Clash of Civilizations?," in *Foreign Affairs*, p. 22.
17. Huntington, "The Clash of Civilizations?," in *Foreign Affairs*, p. 22.
18. Scc Lawrence K. Altman, "Nobel Came After Years of Battling The System," in *The New York Times*, Tuesday, October 11, 2005, D5.
19. The domino theory was initially introduced by then President Eisenhower during a news conference on April 7, 1954, and was applied to Indochina. According to Eisenhower, if the Communists succeeded in Indochina, they would then proceed to take over other countries in the region, such as Burma, Thailand, and Indonesia. This would result in a strategic foothold from which to invade other countries, such as Japan, Taiwan, the Philippines, Australia, and New Zealand. This theory was specifically applied during the Vietnamese War by President Johnson to justify committing more than half a million troops to that conflict.
20. Huntington, "The Clash of Civilizations?," in *Foreign Affairs*, Summer 1993, v. 72, p. 22.
21. Huntington, "The Clash of Civilizations?," in *Foreign Affairs*, Summer 1993, v. 72, p. 23.
22. Huntington, "The Clash of Civilizations?," in *Foreign Affairs*, Summer 1993, v. 72, p. 23.
23. Huntington, "The Clash of Civilizations?," in *Foreign Affairs*, Summer 1993, v. 72, p. 26.
24. See Kishore Mahbubani, "The West and the Rest," *The National Interest*, Summer 1992, pp. 3–13.
25. Huntington, *The Clash of Civilizations and the Remaking of World Order*, p. 13.
26. Huntington, *The Clash of Civilizations and the Remaking of World Order*, p. 14.
27. Huntington, *The Clash of Civilizations and the Remaking of World Order*, pp. 36–37.
28. Huntington, *The Clash of Civilizations and the Remaking of World Order*, p. 38.
29. Huntington, "The Age of Muslim Wars," in *Newsweek*, Dec. 2001–Feb. 2002, p. 9.

CHAPTER THREE

Lewis's Historical Account of Religious Difference

It is but a short step from Huntington's "official" view that 9/11 is explicable through a clash of civilizations to the further view that it is explicable through a clash of religions. This claim is an ad hoc thesis, invented specifically for the purpose of explaining 9/11 after it occurred. According to this thesis, 9/11 can be understood as a clash between two religions: Islam, which is ill-suited to the modern world, and Christianity, which is very much up to date.

This suggestion is a variation on Max Weber's well-known thesis that religion, especially Christianity, is particularly important for the rise of capitalism. As concerns 9/11, Weber's thesis can be reformulated as the general claim that various forms of religion are useful for, or on the contrary harmful to, the prospects of the democratic way of life.

This thesis distantly reflects the close American link to religion. Public opinion polls suggest Americans are overwhelmingly committed to Christianity, though what that means varies considerably according to the group in question. Since religion is so closely linked to life in the United States, it is not surprising to see an analysis of 9/11 emerge that features the religious theme. The connection between religion and democracy in America is hardly news. It was famously analyzed by Alexis de Tocqueville after his trip to the US in the 1830s. Democracy takes many forms. American democracy, sometimes characterized through the canonical phrase as "government of the people by the people," is very different from the elimination of privileges and class order that took place in France through the abolition of the *ancien régime*.[1] What seems to be new is the suggestion that 9/11 can be understood through an alleged disparity between a specific religion and the modern world.

The religion-based analysis of 9/11 exists in both popular and scholarly versions. The non-scholarly, popular form is a dualistic analysis, mentioned above, one that places good and evil in opposition, our religion and theirs, or one fundamentalism with another. As specifically applied to 9/11, it suggests Christianity is deeply attuned to democracy (and freedom), which, on the contrary, fundamentalist Islam opposes.

One of the constant factors driving current American foreign policy is a widespread ignorance of history. Americans, including those who formulate this policy, are often uninformed about their own history, and even less informed about the history of other countries. A grasp of the history of the Middle East is obviously relevant to understanding 9/11.[2] Bernard Lewis, the well-known historian of the Middle East, maintains the Islamic world has failed to adjust the modern world (by which he means the West), leading to a clash of religions that is the overall explanation of 9/11. According to Lewis, "President Bush was careful to stress that this was not a war against Islam or Muslims, nor against any particular ethnic group or country, but a war against a criminal conspiracy, waged in defense of human decency."[3]

Religious Explanation of Historical Phenomena

Lewis explains current events through the role of the religious dimension of modern life. This is different from the well-known concern to provide a religious explanation for both sacred and secular phenomena. The religious approach to history is basic to the effort common to all three main Abrahamic religions (e.g. Judaism, Christianity, Islam) to explain the events of human history, and finally history itself, through God. In Christianity, for instance, reliance on God as the ultimate and, finally, only explanatory factor has never wavered.

An approach to human life as unfolding in divine history is common to all three main forms of the Abrahamic religion. Christianity shares with the other Abrahamic religions the view that history is neither inherently meaningless, nor limited to the meaning we give it. It rather has an intrinsic meaning deriving from God. This religious belief transforms what for some is the result of the interaction of economic forces, for others the collision of different civilizations, and for still others a clash of differing ideologies, into a moral contest between good and evil. If God is the final cause of everything, then all events, literally everything, including 9/11, must be explained in religious terms. And since from the religious angle of vision, religion is the source and guarantee of morality, all of history, including 9/11, is the theater of a great moral war between good and evil.

The specifically religious approach to human history sometimes results in religious approaches to cognitive endeavors. A secular thinker works within a given field, unrestricted by religious convictions. A religious thinker, as distinguished from a religious person, is not only a believer but one whose scholarly approach is based on that religious belief. Obvious examples include such fields as philosophy, history, and modern science.

The distinction between religious and secular approaches is significant in philosophy, which belongs to the cognitive disciplines. Secular philosophers think within one or another philosophical tendency, according to the rules obtaining within it. Religious thinkers think within the conceptual philosophical framework deriving from their adherence to a specifically religious worldview. Secular thinkers work within the conceptual limits currently in vogue in the profession, and which are constantly being renegotiated. They do not, in principle, accept the religious conviction that reason is subordinate to faith, or philosophy to theology. Secular thinkers accept this idea as the cornerstone of their approach to philosophy. These differences are so profound that in an important sense secular and specifically religious thinkers, though both ostensibly concerned with philosophy, are really not engaged in the same pursuit.

A similar difference between secular and specifically religious approaches also obtains for historians. Religious historians tend to regard history through the lens of theology. Ibn Khaldun, the great fourteenth-century Muslim historian, is generally believed to be among the very first to study the economic, social, and religious forces determining history. He started on a great history of the world *(Kitab al-'Ibar)* for which he completed its introduction, the *Muqaddimah*, in 1377. As a practicing Muslim, his approach to history was conditioned by his religious belief. He explains human phenomena in human terms. But he also accepts the metaphysical structure of traditional Islam, specifically including the existence of exceptional individuals, such as the Prophet Muhammad, who transmitted the divine message.[4]

Just as Ibn Khaldun, a Muslim, approaches history through Muslim religious belief, Christian philosophers and historians elaborate variations on the Christian view of history. Christian historians select and interpret facts in the light of their religious conviction, in effect in writing a Christian history. They treat the entire range of topics, including those of specific Christian interest, such as the history of the Church, in a way that generally respects, hence does not call into question, the Christian view.[5] Just as there is no single way of interpreting Christianity, there is no single authorized version of the Christian approach to history. Different Christian historians follow different versions of a common Christian reading of history, including Church history. The specifically Christian approach to history unfolds in a long series of works, including recent studies that examine this general Christian approach,[6] older writings devoted to this theme,[7] and broader studies of the relationship between faith and the academy.[8]

The difference between secular and religious approaches is a main factor in the understanding of modern science. Three of the more important instances are the reactions to Copernicus, Galileo, and Darwin. Copernicus was greeted with scorn by Luther, but with prudent silence by the Roman Catholic Church. In his 1539 *Table Talks*, several years before Copernicus died (1543), Luther rejected the work of the fool who denies the statement in Joshua[9] that God caused the Sun to stand still.[10] Shortly after Copernicus died, Luther's disciple Melanchthon renewed Luther's criticism in suggesting it is a revealed truth that the Sun stands still.[11] Calvin, who pointed out the biblical view that the Earth does not move, further asked: "Who will venture to place the authority of Copernicus above that of the Holy Spirit?"[12] Yet, the attitude of later Protestants toward science seems to be more positive than this incident would indicate.

Catholic persecution of Galileo for denying the Christian Bible-based view in supporting Copernicus is a seminal even in the relationship between religion and science in the West. Catholic reaction to Galileo in the seventeenth century belongs to the Counter-Reformation. It is more difficult to justify continuing official Catholic hostility to Galileo today, such as the inability to find grounds to reverse the ecclesiastical judgment rendered during his trial three centuries ago.

A widely different gamut of religious reaction divides those who follow sacred texts more or less literally, those for whom Darwinian evolution simply falsifies the

Bible, and everyone else. Darwinism, which some religious Christians regard as hostile to Christianity, is often held responsible for a decline in religious belief. If the human being is understood as a product of a nonspiritual, mechanical process, there seems to be no relevant role in nature for God.

Darwinism affects Protestantism, which is theologically "decentered," and Catholicism, which is theologically highly centralized, differently. Over the centuries Christian investment in religious forms of explanation leads to the refusal of secular forms of explanation. Centuries after the emergence of modern science in the seventeenth century, Darwinism is still regarded by many Western religious authorities with suspicion. Different religions react differently to modern science. The three main Protestant reactions to Darwinism include: turning one's back on organized religion; working out a compromise between Darwinian evolution and religion, between science and faith; and turning one's back on science.

In the United States after the Civil War, the reaction to Darwin divided Protestantism in a way that still persists. This division can be characterized in terms of the well-known Protestant historical approach to biblical criticism that arose in the nineteenth century. Liberal Protestantism, for instance, is generally friendly to science, which it regards as contributing to the realization of God's work.

Mainline Protestant denominations do not teach the inerrancy of the Bible, which is taught by evangelical Protestants.[13] Evangelicals generally avoid coming into direct conflict with science. But Protestant fundamentalists, who strongly oppose those forms of Protestantism that admit rationalism, so-called higher biblical criticism, and political liberalism, routinely and strongly reject it.

The refusal of Darwinian evolution and the subsequent rejection of modern science are consistent with the conservative Protestant rejection of modern higher biblical criticism in favor of a more literal approach to the Bible. This opposition led to the famous Scopes ("monkey") trial in Tennessee in 1925. The Butler Act (1925), which was passed by Tennessee General Assembly, forbade the teaching of evolutionary theory in any school supported by public funds. In the trial, the defendant, John Scopes, a Tennessee high school teacher, was found guilty of teaching evolution. A more recent instance was the concerted effort in Pennsylvania and Kansas, in response to fundamentalist Protestant rejections of natural science. to substitute the argument of "intelligent design" for Darwinian evolution in secondary school education.[14]

On even a charitable interpretation, it appears the Catholic Church "officially" rejects, or at least by inference partially rejects, Darwinian evolution on the basis of a variant of the argument from intelligent design.[15] In 1996 Pope John Paul II asserted the teaching of the Catholic Church is directly concerned with evolution, since revelation teaches that man is created in the image of God (Genesis 1, 27–29).[16] He insisted the Church rejects the evolutionary idea that life arises from nonlife. "Consequently, theories of evolution which, in accordance with the philosophies inspiring them, consider the spirit as emerging from the forces of living matter or as a mere *epiphenomenon* of this matter, are incompatible with the truth about man.

Nor are they able to ground the dignity of the person."[17] This statement arguably reflects a misreading of evolutionary theory. This theory does not tell us how life arises from nonlife but rather how, once it has arisen, it is transformed by the evolutionary process into the various animals of which we have fossil records, including human beings. John Paul II went on to maintain that human beings have a spiritual dimension that escapes science, and that theology "brings out its ultimate meaning according to the Creator's plans."[18] In other words, through faith and the teachings of the Church we know the purpose of human history. Perhaps. But these views are unrelated to evolutionary theory.

The reaction to John Paul II's claim about evolutionary theory was mixed. *Time Magazine* incorrectly inferred the Church was endorsing evolutionary theory.[19] The opposite is closer to the mark. Catholic rejection of Darwinian evolution was later reaffirmed by Christoph Cardinal Schönborn. He makes two points that John Paul II also makes. On the one hand, through the natural light of reason human beings can discern purpose and design in the world. This claim is tantamount to saying the design of the world proves the existence of God, hence to providing support for the official religious version of the argument from design. On the other hand, a theory of evolution based on natural selection, widely regarded as Darwin's central insight, is simply false. "Evolution in the sense of common ancestry might be true, but evolution in the neo-Darwinian sense—an unguided, unplanned process of random variation and natural selection—is not. Any system of thought that denies or seeks to explain away the overwhelming evidence for design in biology is ideology, not science."[20] When science encounters religion, and religion perceives a conflict between it and science, then at least for religion faith triumphs over scientific reason.

Lewis's Academic Version of the Religious Interpretation of 9/11

Bernard Lewis is an unusual man, a highly respected, well-published, academic historian of the Middle East with decidedly rightwing political views, someone who has been officially convicted in a court of law of denying the Armenian genocide.[21] His writings on the Middle East, on which he has long been a leading Western academic authority, are influential, but controversial. For Edward Said, Lewis presents a severely distorted view[22] of the history of the region. Lewis's views are taken seriously in academia and also, during the presidency of George W. Bush, in government circles as well.

In a seminal 1990 article on the sources of Muslim anger, Lewis argues that we are at present facing a conflict between Western and Muslim civilizations. He depicts Muslim anger as irrational, while warning against the danger of being provoked into a similarly irrational reaction against Islam.[23]

In retrospect, this article is important for three reasons. First, it formulates an early version of the thesis about the "clash of civilizations" later popularized by Huntington. Huntington generalizes Lewis's conviction that over the centuries the real threat to the West has been Islam,[24] which conviction he applies to the postwar environment. Second, this article provides an early statement of Lewis's conviction about the religious basis of the conflict between Islam and the West. Shortly after 9/11, Lewis restated and developed this conviction in several books. Third, the view Lewis adumbrated in the article, and which became known as the Lewis Doctrine, has been highly influential in American political circles.

The Lewis Doctrine, which has never been explicitly stated, is regarded in government circles in the United States and the United Kingdom as a substitute for the very well-known Kennan Doctrine. In 1946, George F. Kennan, a senior State Department official with a special interest in Soviet affairs, sent a famous long telegram to the State Department, and followed it up with an equally well-known article in which he advocated containment of the Soviet bloc within the boundaries established at Yalta. This recommendation was adopted as a key element that later gave rise to the cold war.[25]

The term "Lewis Doctrine" seems to have been invented by the *Wall Street Journal* shortly after the invasion of Iraq. The article discusses Lewis's conviction that, since most Muslim societies have simply failed to adapt to modernity, the best policy is to introduce democracy in the Middle East by force—Lewis specifically recommended an invasion of Iraq.[26] Lewis has held this view for a very long time. About a half century ago, he published a volume on modern Turkey in which he argued in favor of the introduction by Kemal Ataturk of Western democracy to Turkey.[27] Though prominent scholars disagree with Lewis,[28] he gained the ear of George W. Bush's administration, starting with Vice President Cheney[29] and both recommendations were adopted.

Lewis campaigned for his view in two op-ed pieces in *The Wall Street Journal*. In a discussion of American resolve, he maintained that giving in to bin Laden would only embolden more moderate Arabs.[30] In a subsequent article, he weighed in on the side of "regime change" in Iraq in arguing that action was better than inaction and that there was in fact no good alternative policy.[31]

Lewis elaborated his view in two works published around this time. In the first book, completed before 9/11, he analyzes the familiar theme, *What Went Wrong? The Clash Between Islam and Modernity in the Middle East*, in adding many details. In his afterword, he notes that President George W. Bush clearly indicated the war against terror is not a war against Islam, although some, such as Osama bin Laden, who proclaimed a *jihad* in the classic sense of a war against infidels, depict it as a struggle between Christendom and Islam. Lewis points to the problematic nature of centuries of Western dominance over the Islamic world, dominance that reached its peak in the twentieth century. He detects Islamic pluralism in the difference between traditional and nontraditional forms of Islam. For some, such as bin Laden, the end in view is to return to an earlier, purer form of Islam through removing Western influence and restoring Islamic authenticity. But for other Muslims, the cause is freedom, including freedom from corrupt Muslim tyrants. According to Lewis, either Muslim moderates will triumph, or the prospect for the West is grim.[32]

In the second study, completed between the invasions of Afghanistan and Iraq, Lewis applies to 9/11 his theory about the inability of Islamic countries other than Turkey to modernize. This work is based on an article that appeared in *The New Yorker* in 2001,[33] in which Lewis once again insists on the significance of the failure of Islam to modernize. This failure leads, in turn, to a rejection of modernity in favor of what Lewis calls a return to the sacred past. This supposed return is fueled by the poverty and tyranny of the Islamic world, conditions made increasingly visible by the mass media. Lewis agrees with the Ayatollah Khomeini that the temptation of US culture is the greatest threat to a strict vision of Islam. Lewis ends by predicting that, if bin Laden can impose his leadership, a long and bitter struggle lies ahead.

In the appendix, Lewis indicates that the American objectives in the Afghanistan war are to deter and defeat terrorism, and "to bring freedom, sometimes called democracy to the peoples of these countries and beyond."[34] He repeats his view that Middle Eastern tyranny derives from a failure to modernize, and cautions it will not be easy to bring democracy to the region. Pointing to Turkey, his example for many years, he suggests that, though the task is difficult, democracy can be created in the region. What he does not say, which is just as significant, is that the Turkish brand of democracy is so different from what is understood by that term in the West, that the European Union asked for major governmental policy changes before Turkish candidacy for membership could even be discussed. A main instance is the continuing repressive treatment of the important Kurdish minority, whose rights (even to the right to speak their language in public), have consistently been violated.[35] Another problem is the massacre of the Armenian minority early in the twentieth century, which Turkey has never acknowledged as a crime against the Armenian people. Left unclear in Lewis's theory is what "democracy" can reasonably mean in a part of the world that has never known a system of government approaching any of the many forms of democracy that have long existed in the West.[36]

Notes

1. For a recent discussion, see Alain Renaut, *Qu'est-ce qu'un people libre?: Libéralisme ou républicanisme*, Paris: Grasset, 2005.
2. Khalidi, a specialist in the history of the region, sensibly claims that the American debacle in Iraq is largely due to American politicians who decided on the invasion but were ignorant of the history of the Middle East. See Rashid Khalidi, *Resurrecting Empire: Western Footprints and America's Perilous Path in the Middle East.* Boston: Beacon, 2005.
3. Bernard Lewis, *What Went Wrong?*, New York: Harper Collins, 2002, p. 163.
4. See Ibn Khaldun, *The Muqaddimah*, translated by Franz Rosenthal, Princeton: Princeton University Press, 1980, 3 vols.
5. Yet the Christian view of Christian history is far from monolithic, since there are important exceptions. For instance, John Dominic Crossan, instead of treating the history of the Church as unproblematic, suggests that the influence of

Paul caused it to develop in a way that does not enhance, but rather diminishes, the message of Jesus. See, e.g., John Dominic Crossan, *The Birth of Christianity: Discovering What Happened in the Years Immediately After the Execution of Jesus*, New York: Harper Collins, 1998. For another view of Paul, see also Gary Wills, *What Paul Meant*, New York: Viking, 2006.

6. See, e. g., George M. Marsden, *The Outrageous Idea of Christian Scholarship*, New York: Oxford University press, 1997; Bruce Kuklick and D.G. Hart, eds., *Religious Advocacy and American History*, Grand Rapids, Michigan: Eerdmans Publishing Co., 1997; Ronald A. Wells, ed., *History and the Christian Historian*, Grand Rapids, Michigan: Eerdman's Publishing Co., 1998.
7. See, e.g., Herbert Butterfield, *Christianity and History*, London: G. Bell and Sons, 1949; H. Christopher Dawson, *The Dynamics of World History*, London: Sheed and Ward, 1957; idem., *The Crisis of Western Education*, New York: Sheed and Ward, 1961; Van Harvey, *The Historian and the Believer*, New York: Macmillan, 1967; Frank Roberts and George Marsden, eds., *A Christian View of History?*, Grand Rapids, Michigan: Eerdmans Publ. Co., 1976; C.T. McIntire, *God, History and Historians*, New York: Oxford University Press, 1977; C.T. McIntire and Ronald Wells, *History and Historical Understanding*, Grand Rapids, Michigan: Eerdmans Publ. Co., 1984.
8. See e. g., George M. Marsden and Bradley J. Longfield, eds., *The Secularization of the Academy*, New York: Oxford University Press, 1992; Mark R. Schwehn, *Exiles from Eden: Religion and the Academic Vocation in America*, New York: Oxford University Press, 1993; George M. Marsden, *The Soul of the American University: From Protestant Establishment to Established Nonbelief*, New York: Oxford University Press, 1994; Mark Noll, *The Scandal of the Evangelical Mind*, Grand Rapids: Eerdmans Publishing Co., 1994; and Warren A. Nord, *Religion and American Education: Rethinking a National Dilemma*, Chapel Hill: University of North Carolina Press, 1995.
9. "People gave ear to an upstart astrologer who strove to show that the earth revolves, not the heavens or the firmament, the sun and the moon. . . . This fool wishes to reverse the entire science of astronomy; but sacred scripture tells us that Joshua commanded the sun to stand still, and not the earth." Martin Luther, *Table Talks*, 1539, cited in Andrew D. White, *A History of the Warfare of Science with Theology in Christendom*, New York: Appleton, 1896, I, p. 126.
10. "And the sun stood still, and the moon stayed, until the people had avenged themselves upon their enemies. . . . So the sun stood still in the midst of heaven, and hasted not to go down about a whole day." Joshua 10:13; King James version.
11. "The eyes are witnesses that the heavens revolve in the space of twenty-four hours. But certain men, either from the love of novelty, or to make a display of ingenuity, have concluded that the earth moves; and they maintain that neither the eighth sphere nor the sun revolves. . . . Now, it is a want of honesty and decency to assert such notions publicly, and the example is pernicious. It is the part of a good mind to accept the truth as revealed by God and to acquiesce

in it." Melanchthon, *Initia Doctrinae Physicae* (1550) cited in White, *A History of the Warfare of Science with Theology in Christendom*, pp. 126–27.

12. See John Calvin, *Commentary on Genesis* (1554) cited in White, *A History of the Warfare of Science with Theology in Christendom*, p. 127.
13. Thus the "Chicago Statement on Biblical Inerrancy" (1978) articulates evangelical views on this issue in point 4 of its summary: "Being wholly and verbally God-given, Scripture is without error or fault in all its teaching, no less in what it states about God's acts in creation, about the events of world history, and about its own literary origins under God, than in its witness to God's saving grace in individual lives." Summary statement, point 4. See International Council on Biblical Inerrancy, Chicago, Illinois, 1978. Reproduced from *Explaining Hermeneutics: A Commentary on the Chicago Statement on Biblical Hermeneutics*, Oakland, California: International Council on Biblical Inerrancy, 1983.
14. For a detailed, recent discussion of the relation between Darwinism and creationism, see Philip Kitcher, *Living with Darwin: Evolution, Design and the Future of Faith*, New York: Oxford University Press, 2007.
15. This argument was developed by the Reverend William Paley (1743–1805). In his study of *Natural Theology* (1800), he gives the example of someone finding a watch in the street and inferring from its complex structure, with an obvious purpose, that it had a creator. Paley's argument was famously attacked in a posthumously published work entitled *Dialogues Concerning Natural Religion* by the Scottish philosopher, David Hume. Hume criticizes the analogy between the workings of a watch and God. See David Hume, *Dialogues Concerning Natural Religion*, New York and London: Hafner, 1966. In parts X and XI (pp. 61–81), he goes on to refute empirical theism in refuting the idea that from the mechanical workings of the universe one can infer God's moral attributes.
16. See "Truth Cannot Contradict Truth," Address of Pope John Paul II to the Pontifical Academy of Sciences (October 22, 1996), Excerpted from the October 30 issue of the English edition of *L'Osservatore Romano*.
17. "Truth Cannot Contradict Truth," point 5.
18. "Truth Cannot Contradict Truth," point 6.
19. See James Collins, "Vatican Thinking Evolves: The Pope Gives His Blessing to Natural Selection—Though Man's Soul Remains Beyond Science's Reach," in *Time Magazine*, November 4, 1996.
20. Christoph Schönborn, "Finding Design in Nature," in the *New York Times*, Op Ed page, July 7, 2005.
21. He was fined a symbolic total of one franc by a Paris court after expressing doubt, in an interview with *Le Monde*, that the 1915 Turkish massacre of Armenians qualified as an act of genocide.
22. Said sharply criticized the views of Lewis and V. S. Naipul. See Edward W. Said, *Orientalism*, New York: Vintage Books, 1979.
23. "It should now be clear that we are facing a mood and a movement far transcending the level of issues and policies and the governments that pursue them. This is no

less than a clash of civilizations—that perhaps irrational but surely historical reaction of an ancient rival against our Judeo-Christian heritage, our secular present, and the worldwide expansion of both. It is crucially important that we on our side should not be provoked into an equally historic but also equally irrational reaction against that rival." Bernard Lewis, "The Roots of Muslim Rage: Why So Many Muslims Deeply Resent the West and Why Their Bitterness Will Not Be So Easily Mollified," in *The Atlantic Monthly*, no. 266, September 1990, p. 60.

24. See, e.g., Huntington, *The Clash of Civilizations*, p. 210.
25. The article, which presents the gist of a famous telegram sent by Kennan in 1946, was published anonymously. X, "The Sources of Soviet Conduct," in *Foreign Affairs*, July 1947.
26. See Peter Waldman, "A historian's take on Islam steers U.S. in terrorism fight : Bernard Lewis's blueprint—sowing Arab democracy—is facing a test in Iraq," in *Wall Street Journal*, February 3, 2004.
27. See Bernard Lewis, *The Emergence of Modern Turkey*, Oxford: Oxford University Press, 1961.
28. See Richard Bulliett, *The Case for Islamo-Christian Civilization*, New York: Columbia University Press, 2006.
29. See Michael Hersh, "Misreading Islam," in *Washington Monthly*, November 12, 2004.
30. See Bernard Lewis, "A War of Resolve," in *The Wall Street Journal*, Friday April 26, 2002.
31. See Bernard Lewis, "Time For Toppling," in *The Wall Street Journal*, September 27, 2002.
32. See Bernard Lewis, Afterword in *What Went Wrong? The Clash Between Islam and Modernity in the Middle East*, New York: Harper Collins, 2002, pp. 163–65.
33. See Bernard Lewis, "The Revolt of Islam: When did the conflict with the West begin, and how could it end?," in *The New Yorker*, November 19, 2001.
34. Bernard Lewis, *The Crisis of Islam: Holy War and Unholy Terror*, New York: Random House, 2004, p. 165.
35. See Christopher de Bellaigue, "Left Out in Turkey," in *The New York Review of Books*, vol. LII, number 12, July 14, 2005, pp. 43–47.
36. For recent discussion of the meaning of "democracy," see David R. Hiley, *Doubt and the Demands of Democratic Citizenship*, New York: Cambridge University Press, 2006.

CHAPTER FOUR

Models of Historical Knowledge

The discussion so far has restated, analyzed, and criticized the current three main approaches to 9/11. It shows we do not presently possess anything resembling an acceptable or even a widely shared view of this series of events. It remains to formulate an alternative framework (or conceptual matrix), in short a general theory to comprehend, understand, or interpret—three terms I will be using interchangeably here—the events comprising 9/11.

Greek philosophy takes an ahistorical approach to knowledge as the grasp of what is as it is. This view, which is already clear in Parmenides, is reinforced by Aristotle's famous claim that poetry is, as he says, "more philosophic and of graver import than history."[1] The reason is that poetry deals with general statements, or universals, but historical events only take place once. From Aristotle until modern philosophy, history was mainly thought to be irrelevant to theories of knowledge.

History, which is lurking in the conceptual wings as it were, emerges with increasing force in a series of modern thinkers, who understand it in often very different ways. The philosophy of history is replete with religiously inspired attempts to find meaning and structure in history by relating it to some specific, divinely ordered plan. Theologians and religious thinkers have attempted to find meaning in historical events as expressions of divine will.[2] One reason for theological interest in this question is the problem of evil. Thus Leibniz's *Theodicy* (1709)[3] attempts to provide a logical interpretation of history that makes the tragedies of history compatible with the will of a benevolent God. In the twentieth century theologians such as Jacques Maritain[4] offered systematic efforts to provide Christian interpretations of history.

The theological approach to history gradually gave way in the modern period to efforts to understand historical phenomena in terms of the finite human being. Vico and Herder provide two of the more influential approaches. Giambattista Vico's *New Science* (1725)[5] interprets history through the idea of a universal human nature and a universal history. His interpretation of the history of civilization offers the view that there is an underlying uniformity in human nature, across historical settings, that permits explanation of historical actions and processes.

Kant's former student, Johann Gottfried Herder, whom Kant severely criticizes, takes a very different approach from Kant to human nature and human ideas and motivations. Herder argues for the historical contextuality of human nature in his work in a series of writings, including *This Too A Philosophy of History For the Formation of Humanity* (1774).[6] He advances a historicized understanding of human nature, advocating the idea that human nature is itself a historical product and that human beings act differently in different periods of historical development. These views, opposed by Kant, were later influential on Hegel and, through him, on Marx.

Since 9/11 is composed of historical events, the task of formulating a theory of 9/11 belongs to the domain of the epistemology of history. There is a difference between writing about historical events or history in general, and the epistemology of history. "Rules" of how to go about writing history are not permanent, but are constantly being "negotiated" between working historians who arrive, through public debate, at views that are shared for a time and then later revised about the appropriate ways to approach historical phenomena. At any given moment, working historians presuppose more or less widely shared views about the discipline in gathering information in a wide variety of ways, which they narrate and interpret. The "construction" of a historical narrative may, but need not, touch on epistemological questions.[7]

The writing of history centers on an effort to "know" the past. The claim to "know" history is more frequently made than justified. Hegel, who affirms knowledge of historical events, never clearly says, but merely suggests, how "knowing history" is possible. The numerous views of historical knowledge that arose after Hegel include, in no particular order, the Marxist idea that history should be understood against the background of the development of political economy; Ranke's claim to know history as it really happened, which claim Sartre applied in his study of Flaubert; the well known religious approach to the eschatological explanation of historical phenomena by such thinkers as Augustine, Ernst Troeltsch, and Karl Löwith; Croce's idea that there is no difference between philosophy and history; R. G. Collingwood's view that to understand history requires one to be able to reenact it on the level of mind; Heidegger's claim that we must understand history against the background of the history of being, and so on.

The epistemology of history is similar to other forms of epistemology in requiring a theory of knowledge about a particular epistemological region. Observers distinguish between explanations based i. A. For instance, on common sense, science, social science, and history.[8] A central question is whether the form of historical knowledge is typically the same as that of the natural sciences. I will answer this question negatively, turning from a natural-scientific to an action-theoretical approach to historical knowledge. I will stress an approach to history which asserts it is the result of human actions, which can be understood (*verstehen*) but which cannot be explained (*erklären*).

Hempel's *Positivist* Approach to History

In turning to the epistemology of history, it will be useful to start with Carl Hempel's theory, for several reasons. First, it is a widely influential effort to describe the epistemology of history. Second, even if it now seems dated, at the time it appeared, during the heyday of Vienna Circle positivism, it attracted much attention. Third, it illustrates the strong commitment to science, as a main—even, as the only important—source of knowledge. Under the heading of scientism, this approach is still often featured in the current debate.[9]

Hempel's approach is motivated by two assumptions. On the one hand, science and only science serves as a reliable source of knowledge, since other cognitive strategies are insufficiently rigorous. On the other hand, the main elements of the scientific approach can, under the proper circumstances, be successfully applied to history. The suspicion that any acceptable cognitive approach needs to rely on a recognizable form of the scientific method is familiar in recent debate. An extreme form of this view is *physicalism*, or the claim that, once more under appropriate conditions, all other sciences can be "reduced" to, hence replaced by, physics, which incarnates the only acceptable model of knowledge. This view was important among thinkers active in or influenced by Vienna Circle *positivism*. Karl Popper applied a version of this model to Marxism[10] and Adolf Grunbaum applied it to psychoanalysis.[11] Each argues along similar lines that neither Marxism nor psychoanalysis meets proper scientific criteria, which they identify with physicalism; hence, from this perspective, neither Marxism nor psychoanalysis is an acceptable source of knowledge. Carl Hempel developed a very similar approach for the epistemology of history.[12]

Popper and Grunbaum were both interested in disqualifying rival theories. Hempel is not interested in disqualifying other claims to knowledge. He is rather concerned with identifying the conditions under which we can understand history as a reliable cognitive source. For Hempel as for Kant, we need to determine the conditions of the possibility of various forms of cognition Yet, unlike Kant, Hempel, who is influenced by later positivism, believes science is not an *a priori* but rather an *a posteriori* discipline, hence inevitably dependent on experience in all its many forms.

Hempel's theory of history is counterintuitive. At least intuitively, there is a difference in kind between natural occurrences, such as the rotation of a planet on its axis while revolving in its orbit around the sun, and historical events, such as the Peloponnesian War. Hempel's basic insight is that history can be taken as a source of rigorous knowledge if, and only if, it can be considered as if it were a natural science, hence can be evaluated according to natural scientific epistemological standards.

At least since Aristotle, it has often been thought that the approach to knowledge depends on, hence needs to be adjusted to, the particular domain. According to this view, there is one approach for chemistry, and another for physics. A weaker version of this idea is Wilhelm Dilthey's familiar distinction between interpretation and explanation as cognitive approaches respectively appropriate for the soft, or social sciences, and for the hard, or natural sciences. René Descartes denies any correlation between particular cognitive domains and appropriate methods through his insistence on a single universal method, a method applicable without exception in all the many domains. Positivists, who favor at least in principle the reduction of all forms of knowledge to physics, are neo-Cartesians, who tend for this reason to deny there is more than one approach to knowledge in a rigorous sense of the term.

For Hempel, who is closer to Descartes than to Dilthey or even Aristotle, there is finally only a single form of scientific knowledge, hence only a single scientific approach that holds across the board in all scientific domains. Hempel develops this view in an original conception of scientific law known as the *covering-law* model. This model is based on a distinction between so-called deductive-nomological and inductive-statistical types of explanation. Both types depend on a similar structure, composed of initial conditions and law-like generalizations to explain one or more events. According to Hempel, scientific explanation consists in deducing a statement to explain a fact in terms of scientific laws.[13]

The insight behind this covering law model is that no cognitive claim is acceptable in any cognitive domain that is not the consequence of "unbroken" laws. For Hempel, who detects symmetry between explanation and prediction, the former concerns what has already occurred, whereas prediction, for instance scientific prediction, explains what will occur. On this model, the occurrence of an future event is deduced from *general laws* and statements of antecedent conditions. A general law—a universal statement capable of being confirmed or disconfirmed empirically—functions in the same way in history and in the natural sciences.[14] On Hempel's model, a general law is "explained" when it is "deduced" from more comprehensive laws.[15]

This approach more closely resembles an unredeemed promissory note than a description of anything historians actually do in writing about historical phenomena. It is problematic both as philosophy of science and as an approach to the epistemology of history. An approach to science, which is defined by adherence to general laws, is not obviously adequate. In proposing this way of defining science, Hempel casts his net too narrowly. Cognitive domains such as archeology and paleontology—routinely accepted as forms of science, and which do not feature general laws in any obvious sense—would fall outside Hempel's view of the wider scientific domain.

Hempel's normative vision of history fails in practice. He points to, but never identifies, any general historical laws. He neglects the actual practice of writing history in favor of an *a priori* deductive model of historical knowledge. Professional historians, who believe they are offering genuine explanations, do not conform to Hempel's model. Hempel could counter that we should reject current approaches by working historians, since there are better ways to write history. Yet, if there are in fact no general historical laws, then the covering-law model cannot hold, even as an ideal of what historians ought to be doing. To the further objections that he simply assimilates people to things and history to natural science, Hempel could reply that this is how objective cognition should be understood in all the cognitive disciplines. Yet what if "objectivity" had a different meaning in different cognitive disciplines?

In part, the defense of Hempel's effort to apply natural scientific standards to history turns on finding an appropriate form of the claim that historical laws are similar to scientific laws. Clayton Roberts looks for middle ground between simply insisting on theoretical necessity or, on the contrary, denying that a covering-law model applies to human history. The distinction between the world in which we live and act, which defies mathematical description, and the subatomic world of particle physics, which can be mathematically described in terms of physical processes, is familiar. Roberts draws attention to an analogous distinction between so-called macro-events, such as wars and revolutions, where the covering law model is admittedly invalid, and so-called micro-events, where it supposedly holds.[16] Yet this defense simply concedes the point to working historians, who deny the covering law model applies to writings about human history.

Murray Murphey defends Hempel's conception of historical law in a different way. He suggests that universal laws in natural science take the form of law-like generalizations in the historical domain. According to Murphey, history chiefly consists in generalizations true of members of a given society at a given time.[17] He claims historians are in fact concerned with discovering laws, hence are required to provide statements relevantly similar to Hempel's conception of a covering law.[18] Yet, this argument conflates law-like regularities, which being regular are law-like, but are not laws, with laws in Hempel's sense of the term.

Murphey cites a series of authorities, who believe natural science deals with general statements, but history, as Aristotle thinks, deals only with singular statements.[19] This point undercuts any effort to understand science as resting on universal laws that apply across the board without restrictions. Murphey, who contends that historical interpretations are not different from scientific theories,[20] concedes only that historians are working with generalizations that apply within a limited spatio-temporal frame and not in general.[21] In other words, if we understand the circumstances in which events occur, and if we understand the intentions motivating the historical actors, we may be able to understand these events as a product of these circumstances from which, however, they cannot be said to follow in any necessary way. Obviously historians, anthropologists, psychologists and others can, and on occasion successfully do, generalize about a particular society, as do, e.g., Perry Miller in *The New England Mind: The Seventeenth Century*,[22] and Edmund Morgan in *The Puritan Family*.[23] But generalizations about society are not the same as natural scientific laws, hence such generalizations are incompatible with, and cannot be compared to, these laws. Murphey is right that we can successfully understand events in terms of circumstances from which they cannot be deduced. He is further correct that we can successfully generalize about a particular society. But he is incorrect to believe that historical laws are the same as, or similar in a relevant way, to scientific laws.

Realism and the Epistemology of History

Hempel's straightforward adaptation of a version of the modern scientific method to the epistemology of history fails because of the obvious disanalogy between knowledge of nature, which concerns natural objects, and knowledge of history, which concerns historical events. This failure is not unexpected, but expected. It is implausible to think historical events can be known in the same way as natural objects.

Hempel, a Cartesian with respect to history, presupposes that a single scientific method is applicable to all kinds of epistemological objects. His failure suggests the utility of a revised form of the Aristotelian view that the type of knowledge in a given domain depends on the specific type of object. This implies that any theory of historical knowledge needs to adapt to the historical events it seeks to cognize.

In part, the problem of historical knowledge turns on the question of realism. All theories of knowledge make at least an implicit commitment to realism, but there are many different ways of understanding reality as the object of knowledge. Ordinary realism is implicit in the conviction of the individual—one without a special philosophical background—who believes that in ordinary circumstances we in fact know the way the world is. Metaphysical realism, sometimes also called Platonic realism, is the more sophisticated, philosophical reformulation of ordinary realism as a variant of the general claim that under proper conditions we can reliably know the mind-independent external world as it is beyond mere appearance. Empirical realism is a popular form of the weaker counterclaim that at best we can only reliably know what is given to us in conscious experience, but which is nothing as grand as the way the world is in itself. Scientific realism is frequently associated with metaphysical realism as well as with *scientism*, or the idea that science and only science succeeds in uncovering, or exposing, the structure of the mind-independent reality as it is. Marxist aesthetics prefers socialist realism, a particular artistic style, as a source of knowledge about the world in which we live.

For the epistemology of history it is useful to focus on metaphysical realism. This view of realism is incompatible with any form of the epistemology of history. Metaphysical realism is characterized by stability, absence of change—hence, sameness from moment to moment. History is composed of a changing sequence of events, which are not stable but unstable, hence constantly subject to change, and different from moment to moment. If the epistemology of history concerns knowledge of a series of events, then it is incompatible with metaphysical realism. In cognizing historical events, one cannot reliably claim to cognize the mind-independent reality, as it is beyond appearance, and hence one cannot reliably claim to cognize the metaphysical reality of historical events. At most, in the epistemology of history, knowledge turns on making out claims to know the ever-changing sequence of historical events, which, since they change, cannot be said to be in one way rather than another, hence cannot be said to be known as they are in themselves.

Epistemological Strategy and the Epistemology of History

A similar problem arises about appropriate epistemological strategy. For present purposes, the various strategies for knowledge can be grouped around three main approaches, which one can call *intuitionism*, *foundationalism*, and *representationalism*.

Intuitionism is the view that, at least some of the time, we can reliably claim to grasp the world as it is in finding a way to go beyond mere appearance to mind-independent reality. The conviction that there is a way the world is, and that under appropriate conditions it can be reliably intuited as it is, runs throughout the entire Western discussion, and remains popular at present. Plato is often understood to suggest that if there is knowledge then, on grounds of nature and nurture, in appropriate circumstances at least some individuals can directly "see," or intuit, reality as it is.

Intuitionism is closely related to what is known as *commonsensism*. At the beginning of the twentieth century, in refuting idealism, the English common sense philosopher G.E. Moore maintained there are certain truths about the world that ordinary people just naturally know, which they grasp intuitively, and which cannot reasonably be denied. Moore famously suggested, holding up his hands, that the claim, "Here is one hand and here is another," is undeniably the case. His point can formulated as a general statement: intuition is quite sufficient for us to be convinced that under normal conditions we do in fact know, not merely believe we know, self-evident truths.[24] Yet, since intuitive claims are intrinsically individual and private, they are not considered reliable in modern times, when, under the influence of modern science, there is widespread insistence that claims to know must be publicly, hence intersubjectively, verifiable.

Foundationalism, also called epistemological foundationalism, or Cartesian foundationalism, is a second important epistemological strategy, which goes all the way back to ancient Greek philosophy. Foundationalism, which takes its name from a famous reference to an unshakeable foundation, or Archimedean point, is strongly identified with Descartes in modern philosophy.[25] He lays out an approach to knowledge that requires an inference from one or more indubitable principles, principles that in theory cannot possibly be doubted under any circumstances whatsoever. According to Descartes, we can reliably claim to know the world as it is on the basis of an initial principle, one which is known to be true and from which all further claims to know can be rigorously deduced.

Representationalism is a modern epistemological strategy that abandons the Cartesian claim for apodictic inference in invoking the suggestion that, in at least some circumstances, ideas can reliably be said to represent mind-independent reality as it is, just the way a picture correctly represents what it supposedly pictures. This strategy is followed in different ways throughout what is termed the *new way of ideas*. This term, originally applied to designate Locke's view of the relationship of ideas in the mind *about* the world to things *in* the world, can be applied impartially to Continental rationalism and English empiricism. The rationalist Descartes argues from an idea in the mind to apodictic claims to know the way the mind-independent external world is. Conversely, John Locke and a number of other English empiricists, clearly excepting Thomas Reid, argue that simple ideas (or their equivalents) correctly, hence reliably, depict the way the mind-independent external world is, to which they match up one-to-one, so to speak. Representationalism influences Immanuel Kant, who in his famous letter to Marcus Herz written early in the critical period, describes the epistemological problem (21 February 1772) as requiring an analysis of the relationship of the representation to the object being represented.[26] The early Wittgenstein similarly claims that propositions are pictures of the world. There are many other representationalist thinkers. But it has never been shown how a reliable inference is possible from a representation of the world, such as an idea in the mind, to the mind-independent world outside the world. Or, to put the same point differently, it has never been shown how to claim reliably that we know the way the world is through representing it.

The changing nature of the historical object undermines strategies to know it as it is through intuition, epistemological foundationalism, or by representing it. If there is no single way the world is, then it cannot be grasped intuitively as it is. Further, it cannot be shown that an epistemological inference is possible, from a principle or set of principles, to the world as it is. Finally, we cannot claim to correctly represent what is as it is if it is constantly changing. At most we can claim to represent a sequence of historical events, though to do so we require an epistemology of history, in other words a theory of how to do so.

Constructivism and the Epistemology of History

This rapid review shows that at least some main approaches to realism and to epistemological strategy do not "fit" the problem of cognizing history, which requires an approach more closely linked to the changing nature of historical events. Among the main options, the most promising for a specifically historical approach to epistemology appears to be *epistemological constructivism.*

Constructivism originates in ancient times in Euclidean geometry, which relies on the construction of plane figures. This led, in the late nineteenth century, through the extension of mathematical constructivism from plane figures to mathematical objects in general, to what is called mathematical intuitionism. In more technical language, philosophical constructivism can be described as the view that knowledge is possible if, and only if, the cognitive object is "constructed" by the epistemological subject as a condition of knowledge.

The starting point for constructivism, in that sense a second-best theory, lies in giving up the idea that the problem of knowledge must be formulated as a "solution" to the problem of knowing something independent of the subject, for instance in one formulation the world as it really is in itself. If this demand is maintained, the result is epistemological skepticism. From the constructivist perspective, this is an insoluble enigma.

Constructivism works out the basic insight that knowledge is possible because of an "identity" between subject and object. In knowing, the subject does not know an independent object; it rather knows only itself. This idea points to a nonstandard, metaphysical identity between the individual, or the subject, or again the person who knows, and the object, which is known—an identity brought about through the activity of the subject. In place of metaphysical realism, or the claim to know the mind-independent world as it is, constructivism substitutes the claim to know what the subject constructs, makes, or produces. The constructivist claim to know asserts that knowledge is not knowledge of something other than oneself, but rather knowledge of oneself, or self-knowledge, a grasp of oneself in the form of otherness. One way to put it is to say that rather than basing knowledge on consciousness of an independent object, a constructivist bases knowledge on the subject being conscious of itself in the form of externality of a dependent object.

This idea is intuitively familiar in ordinary human experience, particularly in the aesthetic realm. An artist who creates a work of art of any kind whatsoever gives "concrete" form to creative talents, the results of which are in principle recognizable as the work of that individual. We identify, say, a painting by Rembrandt, since there is an identity in externality between the artist and the work, which is brought about through his painterly activity. Similarly, we can identify a poem by Baudelaire through acquaintance with his distinctive style. This claim can be put more generally. All forms of artistic creation presuppose a metaphysical identity in externality between the artist, who creates the *objet d'art* of whatever kind and in whatever medium, on the one hand, and the artistic object on the other.

This view, though stated in different terminology, is familiar in the modern debate. Kant was impressed by the Copernican revolution in astronomy, which he believed was a crucial turning point in the rise of modern science. He sought to create a Copernican revolution in philosophy. In his Copernican revolution, Kant advances a highly abstract form of a constructivist approach to knowledge, or the claim that a condition of knowledge is that the subject construct what it knows, which he was later unable to work out. In a justly famous passage, Kant, who is an *a priori* thinker, examines and rejects the possibility of knowledge through intuition of objects. He does so by suggesting that objects must conform to the structure of the human mind. Kant writes[27]:

> If intuition has to conform to the constitution of the objects, then I do not see how we can know anything of them *a priori*; but if the object (as an object of the senses) conforms to the constitution of our faculty of intuition, then I can very well represent this possibility to myself. Yet because I cannot stop with these intuitions, if they are to become cognitions, but must refer them as representations to something as their object and determine this object through them, I can assume either that the concepts through which I bring about these determinations also conform to the objects, and then I am once again in the same difficulty about how I could know anything about them *a priori*, or else I assume that the objects, or what is the same thing, the *experience* in which alone they can be cognized (as given objects) conforms to those concepts, in which case I immediately see an easier way out of the difficulty, since experience is itself a kind of cognition requiring the understanding, whose rule I have to presuppose in myself before any object is given to me, hence *a priori*, to which all objects of experience must therefore necessarily conform, and with which they must agree. As for objects insofar as they are thought merely through reason, and necessarily at that, but that (at least as reason thinks them) they cannot be given in experience at all—the

> attempt to think them (they must be capable of being thought) will provide a splendid touchstone of what we assume as the altered method of our way of thinking, namely that we can cognize of things *a priori* only what we ourselves have put into them.

In Kant's wake, it was widely acknowledged that constructivism (though not as Kant proposed it) was a promising approach to knowledge. Post-Kantian German idealism largely turns on reformulating Kantian *a priori* constructivism in *a posteriori* terms. With regard to Kant's distinction between the spirit and the letter, the later idealist reaction to Kant carries his Copernican insight beyond the critical philosophy in attempting to realize its spirit. The debate in this period can be read as a series of contributions by a series of different thinkers (e.g., J.G. Fichte, F.W.J. Schelling, Hegel, and Marx). Each participates in ways consistent with different readings of Kant and the problem of knowledge in the ongoing project running throughout German idealism, beginning with Kant, of rethinking Kantian constructivism.

There is an analogy between a "solution" to the problem of knowledge understood ahistorically as the relationship of a subject to an independent object, or as a relationship to a series of historical events. The lesson of Kant's Copernican revolution seems to be that we cannot reliably claim to know either relationship. We do not know mind-independent external objects as they are, since if they are independent there is no epistemological link to them. And we do not know historical events if they are not due to the activity of finite human beings. But we can at least potentially claim to know what we in some sense "construct," whether in the form of objects or events. This conclusion emerges from the complex debate on knowledge in Kant's wake.

This debate features three main moves, each of which violates the letter of Kant's position in the course of attempting to realize its spirit. These include rethinking the subject as one or more finite human beings, hence as a real human subject as opposed to an abstract epistemological principle; then there is a shift toward *historicism*, that is a grasp of knowledge as impermanent, as dependent on history, and as indexed to the historical flux; and finally there is a revised approach to historical phenomena as a human construction, more precisely as constructed, made, or produced by, hence knowable to finite human beings.

In the process of this debate, which was intended to realize Kant's Copernican revolution, Kant's *a priori* approach to knowledge was, as it were, simply turned inside out. Kant responds to Hume, who formulates a theory of human knowledge, hence falls into what Edmund Husserl later diagnoses as the problem of *psychologism*. Psychologism roughly consists in wrongly equating nonpsychological objects with psychological objects, or again logical processes with psychological processes. An important instance might be analyzing claims to know, which concern instances of true or false knowledge (e.g., $7 + 5 = 12$) as merely psychological claims. Kant, who anticipates this difficulty, responds to it by depicting the subject of knowledge as a mere epistemological function, which in turn creates the difficulty of how to relate the "logic" of knowledge with what human beings are capable of in practice. In Kant's wake, Fichte rethinks the subject as one or more finite human beings in shifting toward historicism. Fichte's innovation is extremely promising. One way to put the point is in terms of what is often called *contextualism*. Human beings are always already in a social context, which cannot be ignored in any analysis of knowledge. Claims for human knowledge depend on the form of the social context in which they arise, hence are in some way—a way that remains to be decided—"indexed" to, or dependent on that context. It follows that cognitive claims are not merely in time but also of time, that is, in some sense dependent on, hence relative to, the historical moment.

Historical Epistemology and the Epistemology of History

As concerns knowledge of history, the key move in post-Kantian idealism is the transformation of Kant's ahistorical epistemology into historical epistemology. For history to be knowable, historical events must themselves be knowable. One of the reasons an epistemology of history was slow in developing is that early views of history tended to depict it as beyond the human grasp, hence as beyond human cognition. Historical events, which only occur once, cannot be known if, as Aristotle thinks, we can know universals only. They can also not be known if, as Augustine believes, history is the product of an unknown and unknowable God. Yet, they can in principle be known if they can be treated as a human "construction" or as the result of human actions in real historical space. In other words, knowledge of history becomes possible in rethinking knowledge itself as intrinsically historical. In this way, knowledge becomes historical and history becomes an object of knowledge.

Attention to the epistemological importance of history develops gradually in modern times. Descartes, an ahistorical thinker, still refers to history as a mere fable.[28] The link between history and knowledge is prefigured in Vico's anti-Cartesian thesis that human beings make human history, hence, can know it. This thesis, later "lost" until around the time of Marx, emerges independently in German idealism in the process of making a qualified return to Vico's position.

In the shift to a historical view of knowledge, three of the most significant figures are Fichte, Hegel, and Marx. Since this is not a study of the genesis of German idealism, there is no need to describe in any detail the complicated evolution of this period's philosophical debate. Suffice it to say that each reacts to his predecessors in the ongoing effort by different hands, to work out an acceptable conception of knowledge as historical. All three figures follow Fichte's lead in interpreting Kant's Copernican revolution in terms of what Hegel correctly, but obscurely, called the identity of identity and difference, unity and diversity, subject and object. In the process, what for Kant is a purely logical claim becomes a claim about human history.[29]

In reacting to Kant, Fichte makes a shift from the *a priori* to the *a posteriori*. He understands philosophy as providing theoretical solutions to practical problems that emerge out of human life. He comprehends the subject as being intrinsically active and never passive, and the cognitive object as constructed, hence knowable by human beings. Yet Fichte, who also studies history from a transcendental, logical viewpoint, never makes a transition to a view of knowledge as intrinsically historical.

Unlike Kant and Fichte, Hegel approaches the problem of knowledge as a problem of the construction—not of cognitive objects—but rather of conceptual frameworks adequate (or inadequate) to their cognition. Knowledge, according to Hegel, arises within a historical process leading to the formulation of a conceptual framework. In the *Phenomenology of Spirit*, Hegel provides a philosophical exposition of types (or levels) of knowing, ranging from cognition in general (*Erkennen*) to absolute knowing (*absolutes Wissen*), a designation for philosophy in his specific sense. In the introduction, Hegel argues for the construction of the required identity in a cognitive process. He presents a view of knowledge as unfolding through trial and error in a historical process in which one seeks to work out a concept (or concepts) that "fit(s)" the cognitive object. This view is *fallibilist*— from fallibilism, or the view that theories can be empirically refuted—in that it makes room for the possibility that the proposed claim is incorrect, hence that, in suitable empirical circumstances, it can be refuted. An important difference with respect to other epistemological fallibilists is that for Hegel it is not the case that the world is "stable" and unchanging, since when the theory changes its object also changes.[30]

Following Marxism, non-Marxists also think Marx is not a philosopher. Yet if constructivism is the criterion, Marx is a full-fledged member of the German idealist tradition. The idealist transformation of epistemology into historicism reaches a high point in Marx who, perhaps for the first time, clearly brings together the historical approach to knowledge and the epistemology of history through a theory of human being. Marx draws on the views of the main German idealists in formulating his own position. He shares with Fichte the fundamental thesis that human beings must be understood as basically active beings, that is, in terms of their activity. And he shares with Hegel the idea that all human phenomena are historical.

Marx's position combines social ontology and the epistemology of history through a theory of human beings as basically active. Marxian social ontology is the basis of his theory of capitalism. This theory extends and transforms Kant's constructivist conception of epistemological activity through a constructivist theory of the social world. Human beings construct (or produce) objects, themselves, the surrounding social world, the transition from capitalism to Communism, and finally human history. Marx also proposes a related constructivist theory of knowledge, which is basically different from the Marxist approach to knowledge.

Very much like Vico, Marx is committed to an anthropological approach to knowledge. In writing, "in all the universe man cannot find a well so deep that, leaning over it, he not does discover at the bottom his own face,"[31] Leszek Kolakowski suggests that for Marx we inevitably perceive and know from a human point of view. In *Capital*, Marx refers in passing to Vico's conviction that human history differs from nature in that we have made the former but not the latter.[32] He follows Vico's conviction that we know history but not nature because we make the former but not the latter. In other words, like Vico, he thinks human beings literally "make" history. He further thinks, again like Vico, that we can only know what we make, according to Marx by reconstructing what we make on the level of mind, in order to know it.

Intentionality and the Constructivist Approach to the Epistemology of History

The epistemology of history is akin to all other epistemological domains in that it requires a theory to explain knowledge of historical phenomena. My approach consists in a theory of history as the result of human actions, which can be understood (*verstehen*) but not explained (*erklären*).

I have been discussing German idealism, understood in a widened sense to include Marx, since we find here a very rich inquiry into the epistemology of history. German idealism contributes to the epistemology of history in two ways. Through the debate engendered by Kant's Copernican revolution, it "recovers" Vico's seminal insight linking knowledge and history in the historicist thesis that we can know history only because we "make" it. And it shows how to cognize, interpret or "know" history as the result of human activity. This is a view Hegel formulates as the claim that there is reason in history.[33] What this approach still lacks, and which is lacking in Vico as well, is a specific relationship between human actions and human history. That relationship can be grasped through human intentions, that is, by grasping human history in terms of the intentions and goals motivating human actions.

In practice, this means we can understand history if we regard historical events as caused by, and manifesting, the intentions of individual human agents. The same point can be put in other words. Murphey is correct that we can successfully understand events in terms of circumstances from which the events themselves cannot be deduced. In thinking about historical events, we do not attempt to deduce them but rather to marshal the various factors that can be considered as causing or bringing them about. Heidegger's turn to Nazism, which cannot in any sense be deduced, but which is also not a mere chance series of events, follows from his general political orientation as well as his specific philosophical orientation.[34]

In the West, an approach to human action in terms of human intentions goes all the way back to ancient Greek philosophy. Aristotle anticipates the modern theory of *intentionality* in his view of action as teleological. According to Aristotle, all action aims at the good, and if there is a choice, at the good for human beings.[35] The ascription of intentions to human beings is a way of calling attention to a distinction between people, who in normal circumstances act, and things, which at most do no more than move. This distinction is routinely overlooked by approaching people as if they were things, hence devoid of intentions, as if they did not act, but merely moved; or, on the contrary, in the less frequent approach to things, as if they acted, as if they were people. This basic insight is often overlooked. Hempel's approach to history as if it were a part of physics, hence could be described through a form of causality in use in modern science, fails to take into account human intentions in considering historical phenomena. In effect, the result is to reduce people to things. Conversely, in his fundamental ontology Heidegger mistakenly attributes action to things, which are obscurely said to "show" themselves.[36]

As concerns human agency, an intention can be parsed by saying that human actions are motivated (as well as constrained) by reasons, which accordingly act as causes in bringing human actions about. A short, incomplete list of such causes might include reasons, but also passions, as well as *akrasia* (or weakness of the will), psychological compulsions, economic constraint, appetite, and so on.[37] Some writers also include moral considerations, following from teaching, religious affiliation, and so on. But for the purposes of this discussion, I will bracket the relation of morality to human action.[38]

Socrates and then Aristotle each claim that human beings strive to realize what they consider to be the good. Socrates argues that no one willingly does other than the good or the good as it appears.[39] Aristotle examines the relationship between continence and incontinence. He agrees with Socrates that no one who fully understands the good consciously chooses to do evil. But he differs in noting that moral responsibility is possible if, and only if, one is able to do otherwise.[40]

There is a distinction between the analytic effort to distinguish action from motion;[41] the related debate on weakness of will, which is intended to carry forward and to react to the problem of *akrasia* analyzed by Socrates and Plato;[42] and the interest in action as an explanatory concept for understanding various facets of human life. The idea that human action is intrinsically rational, hence can be understood, occurs infrequently in the philosophical discussion. Nicholas Rescher, a philosopher of science, is an exception. He claims: "This presumption of rationality is not just a matter of generosity but one of self-interest too. It affords us an important labor-saving device by allowing us to explain people's actions by noting that they were, in the circumstances, rational."[43] David Hume presents a view of human behavior that is primarily driven by the peaceful pursuit of pleasure. His view is disputed by Adam Ferguson. Writing well before Friedrich Nietzsche, Ferguson holds that human behavior is driven not only by pleasure, but also primarily by a will to power, aggressiveness, a desire for conflict, and a susceptibility to corruption.[44]

Ferguson and other Scottish thinkers influenced Hegel.[45] Hegel's account of human action in terms of desire (*Begierde*) updates and develops the early Greek debate. His theory of action includes connected views of human self-realization in and through what one does,[46] as well as a theory of history as rational.[47] History, which manifests the rationality of human action, is not transparent, but is opaque by virtue of the difference between what one intends and what occurs. With this in mind, Hegel introduces the concept of the *cunning of reason*. It is in virtue of the cunning of reason that a particular person realizes a goal different from his intention.[48] In signing the Munich Agreement in 1938, British Prime Minister Neville Chamberlain intended to appease Hitler in order to bring about peace with honor, but the result differed from the intention. We now think Chamberlain naively misunderstood Hitler in undertaking a strategy unlikely to succeed, and which failed to prevent the Second World War, which he unintentionally facilitated.

Like physical theory, which cannot go beyond theories of nature to grasp the world as it is, the epistemology of history cannot surpass mere interpretation, or different ways of construing the historical process. It is always possible to produce another interpretation, always possible to understand historical events differently. The choice among competing interpretations of historical phenomena, which is not merely arbitrary, should consist in opting for a more powerful, or richer interpretation, hence in that sense a better one. An interpretation is said to be richer than others when it accounts for all the items its competitors do plus at least one item which belongs to its task but cannot be explained by competing explanations.

An obvious example lies in the difference between Einsteinian relativity theory and Newtonian mechanics. Mercury is the smallest planet in the solar system and the one closest to the Sun. By virtue of the gravitational effect of the other planets, it has an irregularity in its orbit technically known as the precession of the perihelion of Mercury. This irregularity, which is not explained by Newtonian mechanics, is explained by general relativity theory, and is an important reason to adopt it. With respect to its explanatory capacity, one can say that Einsteinian relativity theory is comparatively richer than Newtonian mechanics.

This same approach is useful to understanding the sequence of events leading up to and away from September 11, 2001. Interpretation of these events needs an understanding of them in terms of the intentions of the actors. An interpretation, which depicts them as irrational, or simply evil, is unacceptable for two reasons. Aristotle believes all actions aim at the good for human beings. Though human beings differ about what they think is good, if one always acts to realize the good, then no actions, even those resulting in great and wanton loss of life, are intrinsically evil. Further, the precondition in this and other cases to interpreting any and all events is to understand them as the attempted realization of the perceived interests of the human agents whose actions brought them about. From the perspective of explanatory richness, an interpretation that regards 9/11 as explicable merely as a clash between Islam and Christianity is less interesting than an interpretation that takes into account further factors, such as Western economic expansion in the Muslim space. By the same token, an interpretation that links, in a historical sequence, this ongoing series of events to those they follow in terms of the intentions of historical agents is preferable to efforts to grasp 9/11 in isolation—that is, apart from earlier and later events, as a rupture in the fabric of history as it were. It seems intuitively implausible to regard the Islamic attack on targets in the US on 9/11 as an isolated incident, more plausible to formulate an interpretation linking it to prior historical events, and more plausible still to "situate" it within the ongoing history over centuries of interaction between Islam and the West. An even stronger interpretation is one that is not merely retrospective, able to link a particular event to those preceding it, but also prospective, or able to interpret the relationship of an event to those that succeed it as the historical context continues to unfold. This does not mean predicting the future, as one might predict the Earth will continue, in the foreseeable future, to rotate on its axis while revolving around the Sun. Rather, it means that any interpretation should be able to understand in advance the main determinants of the political, economic, or other circumstances that are likely to evolve in ways that can be interpreted, but only incompletely anticipated.

To see how this approach works in practice, let us consider briefly the Israeli invasion of Lebanon in July 2006. This invasion can be understood as the immediate reaction to a specific event: the kidnapping of two Israeli soldiers. This incident preceded and—at least in that sense, depending on one's perspective—led to this war, just as the assassination of the Archduke Ferdinand preceded and led to the First World War. Yet, neither the kidnapping nor the assassination is more than an isolated incident. Each is at most a precipitating factor that is in no sense the deeper, or main, cause. The Israeli invasion of Lebanon, which simply cannot be understood through this single kidnapping incident, can easily be linked retrospectively to deep tensions in the wake of 9/11 between some forms of Islam and the mainly non-Islamic, largely capitalist West. The invasion can also be interpreted prospectively, since the Arab-Israeli dispute is overshadowed by the maneuvering between other countries in the Middle East, maneuvering that periodically gives rise to serious clashes, and in all probability will eventually continue to lead to a variety of other incidents. In this particular case, it makes interpretive sense to regard the war in southern Lebanon between Hezbollah and the Israeli army as a proxy conflict, pitting Iran and to a lesser extent Syria against the US (and its allies) as part of the further playing out of the consequences of 9/11 in the Middle East. An additional dimension is arguably the belief of President George W. Bush and Vice-President Cheney that Israeli security can be improved by eliminating Hezbollah.[49] As this example indicates, we understand these historical events, and indeed can arguably only understand them by interpreting them, not in respect to divine will or historical laws, but as being motivated by the intentional actions of human beings.

Notes

1. See Aristotle, *Poetics*, chapter 9 in *The Complete Works of Aristotle*, edited by Jonathan Barnes, Princeton: Princeton University Press, 1984, 2 vols., II, pp. 2322–23.
2. See, e.g., Karl Löwith, *Meaning in History*, Chicago: University of Chicago Press, 1949.
3. See Gottfried Wilhelm Leibniz, *Theodicy*, trans. by E.M. Huggard, with introduction by Austin Farrer, London: Routledge and Kegan Paul, 1952.
4. See Jacques Maritain, *On the Philosophy of History*, edited by Joseph W. Evans, New York: Scribners, 1957.
5. See *The New Science of Giambattista Vico*, trans. by Thomas Goddard Bergin and Max Harold Fisch, Ithaca: Cornell University Press, 1970.

6. See *This Too A Philosophy of History For the Formation of Humanity*, in *Johann Gottfried von Herder: Philosophical Writings*, trans. by Michael N. Forster, New York: Cambridge University Press, 2002, pp. 272–360.
7. See, for a recent discussion, Paul Veyne, *Comment on écrit l'histoire*, Paris: Editions du Seuil, 1978.
8. See Michael Stanford, *An Introduction to the Philosophy of History*, Oxford: Blackwell, 1998.
9. See Joseph Margolis, *The Unraveling of Scientism: American Philosophy at the End of the Twentieth Century*, Ithaca: Cornell University Press, 2003.
10. See Karl R. Popper, *The Poverty of Historicism* (2nd. ed.), London: Routledge, 1961.
11. See Adolf Grunbaum, *The Foundations of Psychoanalysis: A Philosophical Critique*, Berkeley: University of California Press, 1984.
12. Carl Hempel, "The Function of General Laws in History," in *The Journal of Philosophy*, vol. 39 (1942), reprinted in Herbert Feigl and Wilfrid Sellars, *Readings in Philosophical Analysis*, New York: Appleton-Century-Crofts, 1949, pp. 459–71.
13. See Carl Hempel and Paul Oppenheim, "Studies in the Logic of Explanation," in *Philosophy of Science* 15 (1948), pp. 135–75, reprinted in C. Hempel, *Aspects of Scientific Explanation and Other Essays in the Philosophy of Science*, New York: Free Press, 1965, pp. 245–90.
14. See Hempel, "The Function of General Laws in History," in Feigl and Sellars, p. 459.
15. Hempel later generalized the covering-law model to include statistical or probabilistic explanations. See Carl Hempel, *Aspects of Scientific Explanation and Other Essays in the Philosophy of Science*, New York: Free Press, 1965.
16. See Clayton Roberts, *The Logic of Historical Explanation*, University Park: Pennsylvania State University Press, 1996, p. viii.
17. See Murray G. Murphey, *Our Knowledge of the Historical Past*, Indianapolis: Hackett Publishing Company, 1980, p. 85.
18. See Murphey, *Our Knowledge of the Historical Past*, p. 91.
19. See Murphey, *Our Knowledge of the Historical Past*, p. 92.
20. See Murphey, *Our Knowledge of the Historical Past*, p. 131.
21. See Murphey, *Our Knowledge of the Historical Past*, p. 101.
22. See Perry Miller, *The New England Mind: The Seventeenth Century*, Cambridge, Harvard University Press, 1954.
23. See Edmund S. Morgan, *The Puritan Family: Essays on Religion and Domestic Relations in Seventeenth Century New England*, Boston: Trustees of the Public Library, 1944.
24. See G.E. Moore, *Principia Ethica, New York: Cambridge University Press*, § 86, pp. 143–44.
25. See Tom Rockmore, *On Foundationalism: A Strategy for Metaphysical Realism*, Lanham: Rowman and Littlefield, 2004.

26. See Immanuel Kant, Immanuel, *Philosophical Correspondence, 1759–99*, translated and edited by Arnulf Zweig,.Chicago: University of Chicago Press 1967, p. 71.
27. Kant, *Critique of Pure Reason*, B xvii–xvii, pp. 110–11.
28. There is a portrait of Descartes by J.-B. Weenix from around 1647 in which he is seated and holding an open book where one can read *mundus est fabula*. The original is found in the Rijksmuseum Het Catharijneconvent, in Utrecht, Holland.
29. See, for an early statement of the philosophy of identity (*Identitätsphilosophie*), G.W.F. Hegel, *The Difference Between Fichte's and Schelling's System of Philosophy*, translated by H.S. Harris and Walter Cerf, Albany: SUNY Press, 1977.
30. See G.W.F. Hegel, *Phenomenology of Spirit*, translated by A.V. Miller, New York: Oxford University Press, 1977, pp. 46–57.
31. "Karl Marx and the Classical Definition of Truth," in Leszek Kolakowski, *Toward a Marxist Humanism*, translated by Jane Zielonko Peel, New York: Grove Press, 1968, p. 66.
32. See Karl Marx, *Capital* I, edited by Frederick Engels, translated by Samuel Moore and Edward Aveling, New York: International Publishers, 1967, p. 372, fn. 3.
33. See G. W. F. Hegel, *Reason in History: A General Introduction to the Philosophy of History*, translated by Robert S. Hartman, Indianapolis: LLA, 1953.
34. For discussion, see Tom Rockmore, *On Heidegger's Nazism and Philosophy*, Berkeley: University of California Press, 1992.
35. See Aristotle, *Nicomachean Ethics* 1, i, 1094a1–3, in Aristotle, *The Complete Works of Aristotle*, II, p. 1729.
36. This is the basis of his theory of truth. See §44: "Dasein, disclosedness, and truth," in Heidegger, *Being and Time*, pp. 256–74.
37. See, e.g., "Paradoxes of Irrationality," in Donald Davidson, *Problems of Rationality*, Oxford: Clarendon Press, 2004, pp. 169–88.
38. This theme is central to Hume's view. In Book III, Part I, Section I of *A Treatise of Human Nature*, he is routinely understood to argue that moral distinctions are not founded on reason. For a recent effort to counter that interpretation, see Sophie Botros, *Hume, Reason and Morality: A Legacy of Contradiction*, London: Routledge, 2006.
39. See Plato, *Protagoras* 351b–59a.
40. See Aristotle, *Nicomachean Ethics*, VII, passim.
41. See, e.g., Georg von Wright, *Explanation and Understanding*, Ithaca: Cornell University Press, Ithaca, NY, 1971.
42. For a recent overview, see Julius Schälike, "Willenschwäche," in *Information Philosophie*, Dezember 2006, no. 5, pp. 1–29.
43. Nicholas Rescher, *Human Knowledge in Idealistic Perspective*, Princeton: Princeton University Press, 1992, p. 11.
44. See Adam Ferguson, *An Essay on the History of Civil Society (1767)*, edited by F. Oz-Salzberger, Cambridge: Cambridge University Press, 1995.

45. See Norbert Waszek, *The Scottish Enlightenment and Hegel's Account of "Civil Society,"* With a foreword by Duncan Forbes, in *International Archives of the History of Ideas*, vol. 120, Dordrecht/Boston/ London, Nijhoff-Kluwer, 1988, 1991.
46. Wood, who emphasizes Hegel's view of human self-realization in and through action, writes: "Its starting point is the conception of a certain self or identity to be exercised or actualized, to be embodied and expressed in action. The theory selects the actions to be performed and the ends to be pursued because they are the actions and ends of that kind of self." Allen Wood, *Hegel's Ethical Thought*, Cambridge: Cambridge University Press, 1990, pp. 31–32.
47. This is an epistemological approach to Hegel's view of history. For a nonepistemological approach, which emphasizes his relation to Fichte and Kant, see Jean Hyppolite, *Introduction à la philosophie de l'histoire de Hegel*, Paris: Editions du Seuil, 1983.
48. G.W.F. Hegel, *Reason in History: A General Introduction to the Philosophy of History*, translated, with an introduction, by Robert S. Hartman, Indianapolis: LLA, 1953, pp. 75, 89.
49. See Seymour M. Hersh, "Watching Lebanon: Washington's Interests in Israel's War," *The New Yorker*, August 21, 2006.

CHAPTER FIVE

Economics, Globalization, and History

I have been suggesting that to understand 9/11 it is useful to consider history as "constructed," that is as resulting from the intentional actions of normal and even abnormal human beings, of fools as well as madmen, which, since their actions are "rational," can always be understood.[1]

The problem of comprehending history lies in finding a plausible way, or ways, of comprehending the conditions under which individuals (and groups) act, the range of choices with which they are confronted, and the intentions motivating them in the choice of a particular series of actions. The enormous list of contexts, hence the constraints on human actions, and the choices actually available, though not infinite, are simply too numerous to be listed. Huntington and Lewis respectively identify differences of culture (or civilization) and religion as primary "causal" factors with respect to 9/11. The events of 9/11 constitute a highly unusual historical configuration denoting an important ongoing conflict, with roots in the history of the interaction between the Islamic Middle East and the mainly non-Islamic West, set against the background of incessant economic globalization. In more usual circumstances, many more such factors might be identified, specifically including those related to living, living better, and living well. A trivial example might be attending college in the belief that it is financially, culturally, or otherwise personally useful to do so before entering the labor market. A more important example with respect to understanding 9/11 from the Islamic perspective is the series of actions that can reasonably be required of an individual who wishes to live according to the precepts of an Abrahamic religion.

Factors impacting on human actions can be more or less important. In understanding historical events involving large numbers of individuals belonging to a given group, it is more useful to identify factors affecting many, most, or even all its members than factors affecting smaller numbers of people. Actions are both enabled as well as constrained by the contexts in which they occur. We can only partially grasp the context within which our actions take place. Actions are multiply determined by a variety of influences, the importance of which is often difficult to assess and may be unknown or even unknowable.

A college student might be influenced, hence constrained, to act in different ways, by the need to attend and to study for various classes; by interaction with roommates and others in the same dorm, college, or university; on occasion by whether or not that person identifies with a particular religion; by the availability of financial support from a particular educational institution; possible identification with a political party for which the student might volunteer, and so on. These and other factors contribute to the larger context impacting how an individual acts, might act, or conceivably could be expected to act, as well as the specific types of action that person might be expected to find attractive in normal and even abnormal circumstances.

Part of the problem in understanding historical events lies in knowing which factors are significant and, if there is a choice, which are likely to be regarded by a given individual as most significant, hence most important to act upon. Different observers understandably focus on different factors: historians on the weight of the past in determining the present; sociologists on patterns in contemporary society; theologians on the force of religious belief; psychologists on conscious and unconscious phenomena, and so on.

Well-known efforts to craft overall accounts of 9/11 on the basis of differences in civilization or religion are incomplete or erroneous. My hypothesis is that there is at least one other factor as important as, perhaps even more important than, those so far explored, a factor not usually regarded as basic or central with respect to grasping 9/11, and which has not so far been adequately explored. I have in mind the effect of free enterprise, liberal capitalism. which has often been absent, or mainly absent, from the debate over human history, including the debate over 9/11. As Merleau-Ponty observed, the question is not, to reduce history to economics, but rather to restore economics to its place as a major component in the rise and development of the modern world, hence as a major interpretive component of any effort to cognize the situation leading up to and away from 9/11.[2]

On Economics as an Explanatory Factor

The suspicion that economics plays a fundamental social role unites thinkers on the left such as Karl Marx, who are committed to socialism as the practical prerequisite of real human freedom in a social context; and thinkers on the right, such as Friedrich Hayek, who detect in socialism a basic danger to freedom.[3] Interest in economics as an important social factor is very old. Aristotle already suggests that ethics cannot be dissociated from the political and economic framework of the Greek city-state. Probably no one but the most blinkered observer doubts the relevance of economics to modern life. Yet, for a variety of reasons, little effort seems to have been given to assessing the role of economic factors for understanding 9/11, including the situation leading up to it, the events of that day, and subsequent developments.

Any claim that economics is a basic factor in understanding historical phenomena needs to confront several objections. These include the strong penetration of religion in contemporary American life, leading to an influential, eschatological view of history; the putative functioning of the American democratic system; and the consistently bad political press given to Marx and Marxism, which in turn "blocks" appreciation of the economic dimension of history. The eschatological view of history strongly ingrained in the history of the United States suggests there are factors at work in daily life that are unrelated to, or at least not dependent on, the actions of finite human beings. In its most extreme form, this leads to the conviction that everything is literally in the hands of God.

The US officially features the separation of church and state, religion and politics. The American republic was in part founded to guarantee religious freedom, including freedom from religious interference. Yet, politicians are fond of invoking religious themes for political benefit. President Ronald Reagan, who was enamored of casting America in the role of God's favorite country, was an adherent of "Armageddon theology." He was prone to suggesting that Armageddon was almost around the corner. Anyone persuaded of this view must hold that only a religious explanation can enable us to understand cataclysmic events like 9/11, and even more mundane occurrences such as Hurricane Katrina, which caused great damage in New Orleans in the fall of 2005. The "excuse" for an appeal to religious explanations resides in the conviction that the events of daily life (and *a fortiori* contemporary terrorism), cannot be understood merely in terms of human actions. The mere fact that none of this is verifiable is not relevant for someone committed to religious explanations. For as Hume pointed out in the middle of the eighteenth century, there is no prospect of verifying miracles by appealing to natural laws, which are by definition exceptions to miracles.[4]

A second factor is American democracy. According to some observers, the sudden decline and disappearance of the Soviet Union, rapidly followed by the disintegration of the Soviet bloc, represent a significant victory for what is often vaguely called the American way of life. This is variously construed as a triumph of democracy over totalitarianism, or capitalism over Communism. This vague claim is interpreted to mean that democracy as such is more desirable than other alternatives, that capitalism simply outperformed Communism, leading to the economic collapse of the Soviet Union, and that all or at least most economic problems have in the meantime been relegated to the past.

There seems to be no question that capitalism outperformed Communism in respect to usual economic criteria. Yet it does not follow that in Eastern Europe Communism "withered away" because capitalism was economically more successful. A cogent argument could be constructed that Communism was not a victim of capitalism but rather of the fact that at a certain point those whom Communist ideology was intended to convince simply ceased believing in it.[5]

The idea that economic difficulties have been relegated to the past is often suggested. It is expressed in a particularly blatant form by Fukuyama, who responds affirmatively to the question of whether "it makes sense for us once again to speak of a coherent and directional History of mankind that will eventually lead the greater part of humanity to liberal democracy?"[6] Fukuyama never pauses to inquire whether capitalism is economically problematic. Even Niall Ferguson, who is critical of the idea of a new American empire, does not detect a problem with capitalism. Rather, he objects to the possible economic overextension of capitalism that arguably is simply not in a position to pay for the empire that, in his opinion, its leaders (when George W. Bush was in office) sorely desired.[7] Chalmers Johnson, who agrees that American foreign policy is directed toward empire, believes this direction undermines American democracy in a way that will ultimately destroy it.[8] Others see, as intrinsic to capitalism, an expansionist tendency, which during Bush's tenure was expressed in hegemonic ambitions.[9] Still others, whom one might expect to be less interested in economics, are less sanguine about the prospects for capitalism. Pope Benedict XVI, in his encyclical "*Deus caritas est*" (2006), notes pointedly that the spread of industrialization in the nineteenth century brought to the forefront the relationship between capital and labor as the decisive issue. Benedict, who rejects Marxism, nevertheless partly agrees with it. He clearly says the nineteenth century concentration of power in the hands of the few to the detriment of the rights of the working classes justified rebellion.[10] Left unclear is why, if rebellion was justified in the nineteenth century, it is no longer justified.

Distrust of Marx and Marxism is more political than conceptual. Few of Marx's political opponents take the trouble to inform themselves about a position they reject on political grounds, and which, following the Marxist view of Marx, they all too frequently conflate with Marxism.[11] The mistaken assumption that Marx desired to bring about something even faintly resembling the form official Marxism assumed in the Soviet Union and its political satellites seriously impedes access to Marx's insights. Like all theories, his can be read (or misread) in myriad ways. It is arguable they were misread by Lenin and other Bolsheviks in the course of establishing a totalitarian state at the antipodes of Marx's own vision of the full social realization of human beings.[12]

Marx is arguably still the most interesting critic of capitalism. He helps us to discern the nature and limits of a free enterprise, market-oriented system of economy. In suggesting that economics lies at the foundation of the modern world, he provides a useful key to understanding historical phenomena, including the events of 9/11. To turn away from Marx on political grounds only blocks access to his insights about the economic component of such historical phenomena as 9/11.

Economics and History

Interest in economics, like interest in history, is very old. Yet, it is only in modern times, as interest in history grew, that attention was increasingly focused on the central role of economics in society and history.

As stated, ancient Greek philosophy was already concerned with economics. In formulating his theory of the ideal city-state, Plato treats economic issues as moral questions affecting the social life of individuals.[13] In the *Republic*, he indicates the guardians will not possess silver, gold, or private property;[14] and he insists on specialization as key to justice in the state, which he justifies on economic grounds.[15] In the unpublished *Laws*, he later remarks that virtue is incompatible with great wealth.[16]

Aristotle's treatment of economics is comparatively more rapid. He briefly discusses money in the context of economic reciprocity in the *Nicomachean Ethics*[17] and moneymaking at more length in the *Politics*.[18] In the latter text, he points out that money provides equality through commensurability. He identifies differences between moneymaking, or property-getting, both natural and unnatural, which concerns making money, and household management, which does not. *Economics*, the authenticity of which is questioned, examines the role of economic science in founding and maintaining a household.

An economic approach to historical phenomena arises through a complex interaction between philosophy and economics around the time of the great Industrial Revolution. Modern economics arises out of, and retains a link to, early modern philosophy. Later modern philosophy relies on modern economics in relating economics to history. Among the key names are Thomas Hobbes (1588–1679), the English philosopher, Adam Smith (1723–90), the Scottish philosopher and economist, and such German "idealist philosophers" as Hegel and Marx.

Modern economics, or more precisely modern political economy—that is, economics understood as situated within, hence dependent on, the social context—emerges in the writings of Smith and other members of the Scottish school early in the Industrial Revolution.[19] The Industrial Revolution, which began in England after 1750 and later spread to the entire industrialized world, produced deep and permanent changes in modern life. The rapid expansion of industrial manufacture, which occurred in both agriculture and industry, brought together modern science and capital to satisfy increasing demands for such conveniences as cotton cloth from India, earthenware dishes, iron pots and pans, and so on. This expansion depended on the development of various industries through a series of inventions. It also increased demand that affected the textile and iron industries. For instance, the invention of the steam engine[20] increased demand for coal mining, since coal was used in the newly invented smelting furnaces and steam engines. The textile industries typically flourished through the invention of various spinning machines and weaving machines. The iron industry passed through a series of phases, leading from smelting ore with coke rather than charcoal. Although the changes in industry greatly enriched some people, increasing their living standards, for others living standards were greatly lowered, especially for factory workers, impoverished by large-scale business depressions between the end of the eighteenth and the middle of the nineteenth centuries.

It is often noted that John Locke (1632–1704) is the great philosopher of modern capitalism and Adam Smith is its great economist. Locke provides an explicit justification of private property, or the private ownership of the means of production, which several hundred years later remains as the central institution of modern capitalism.[21] According to Locke, private property is justified since an individual has an absolute right, which cannot be abridged,[22] to whatever one "mixes" one's labor with. "Whatsoever he . . . removes . . . he hath mixed his Labour with, and joyned it to something that is his own [,] thereby making it his Property." This view remains influential. It is, for instance, the basis of Robert Nozick's libertarian social theory.[23] We owe to Smith the justification of the idea, as alive today as in his own time, that the mere functioning of modern society is sufficient to bring about a better world for all of us, in fact the best world that is possible in practice.

Thomas Hobbes, the first great English political philosopher and the author of *Leviathan* (1650), argues that differences in individual interest generate what he famously calls a war of all against all (*bellum omnes contra omnes*). He even more famously describes human life as "nasty, brutish and short."[24] Hobbes, like Smith, analyzes modern society in terms of the egotism of individuals. Hobbes's point, which later became the basis of Smith's view of political economy, is that the individual pursues only his own private (or enlightened) self-interest. Smith drew a far more optimistic conclusion than Hobbes on the grounds that private interests result in public benefits. Hegel, arguably more realistic about social life than either Hobbes or Smith, later agreed that individuals pursue their own interests while omitting any claim that to do so is useful for everyone.[25] Marx contends that, not immediately but in the long run, the development of the means of production has beneficial effects for everyone, while recommending revolution to hasten capitalism's "inevitable" demise. Contemporary European socialists, with some exceptions, have generally abandoned belief in capitalism's inevitable demise as well as in social revolution and the corresponding rhetoric. They mainly depend on state intervention to do what, according to Smith, mere economic activity should have done.[26]

The argument leading to Smith's conclusion is set out in his great work, *The Wealth of Nations*, which appeared in 1776 as the Industrial Revolution was beginning to take hold. Smith offers a coherent account, giving order and meaning to the newly emerging world of commerce and industry issuing from the Industrial Revolution, by providing the foundations of modern economic thought, foundations that have remained basically unaltered ever since.

It is widely believed that Smith explains modern economic thought in terms of only three main principles.[27] To begin with, self-interest, the main psychological drive in individuals, is easily verified in practice. Individuals, with many exceptions, are mainly egotistical, concerned with themselves. Next, there is a natural order in the universe. For this reason, naked egotism, expressed in different ways by what we do, nonetheless, and certainly unintentionally, furthers the general social good. This principle, held on faith, apparently cannot be verified in practice. But it is obviously "comforting" to those who receive a more than equal share of economic wealth to believe that wealth also "trickles down" to others. Finally, it follows that the best program is to leave the economic process alone. This conclusion is expressed through such closely synonymous terms as economic *laissez-faire*, economic liberalism, or economic noninterventionism. In practice, this principle is more often discussed than invoked. When it has been applied, for instance when Margaret Thatcher was British prime minister (1979–90), the result has been an unregulated, individualistic form of capitalism approximating what the English historian Thomas Carlyle (1795–1881) strikingly described: "government" as anarchy *plus* a street-constable."[28]

Smith was both a philosopher as well as an economist. He occupied the chair of Moral Philosophy in Glasgow where his lectures covered the fields of ethics, rhetoric, jurisprudence, political economy and "police and revenue." Smith's crucial difficulty lies in showing that capitalism is good for everyone, hence in justifying the beneficent effects of what is sometimes called *enlightened self-interest.* The problem lies in forging a link between economic self-interest and the interests of all concerned, or, between economics and morality.

Smith addresses this concern by developing ideas borrowed from Gottfried Wilhelm Leibniz (1646–1716) and Bernard Mandeville (1630–1733). In the *Monadology* (1714), Leibniz suggests that nothing occurs contingently or gratuitously.[29] When applied to theology, this insight leads to the idea that this is the best of all possible worlds. In *The Fable of the Bees; Or Private Vices, Public Virtues* (1705, 6th edition 1729), Mandeville argues that virtue, or altruism, is socially harmful, while vice, or actions taken only with oneself in view, are socially beneficial.[30]

Smith in turn contends that the effort of each individual improves his own condition[31] as well as (unintentionally) improving the public good. In a justly famous passage, he writes:

> As every individual, therefore, endeavors as much as he can both to employ his capital in the support of domestic industry, and so to direct that industry that its produce may be of the greatest value; every individual necessarily labors to render the annual revenue of society as great as he can. He generally, indeed, neither intends to promote the public interest, nor knows how much he is promoting it. By preferring the support of domestic to that of foreign industry, he intends only his own security; and by directing that industry in such a manner as its produce may be of the greatest value, he intends only his own gain, and he is in this, as in many other cases, led by an invisible hand to promote an end that was not part of it.[32]

Hegel's view of political economy is rather unlike the current view of economics, according to which an economist is limited to merely charting, but also on occasion intervening in, the dynamic functioning of the modern economy mainly without regard to its social consequences.[33] Hegel, like Aristotle before and Marx after him, detects an indissoluble link between economics and ethics. As a political realist, Hegel is under no illusions about the effect of modern society on individuals. He was skeptical about the fact that capitalism helps everyone. He was uneasy about the modern tendency toward inequality. He was also uneasy about the social consequences of the apparent failure to solve the problem of poverty, which he regards as morally unjust. He further points to the social consequences of reducing the poor to the state of what he calls the "rabble" (Pöbel)[34] But unlike Smith and other Scottish economists on whom he relies, he is not mainly concerned with providing an accurate formulation of the foundations of political economy.

Hegel is also a profoundly historical thinker. He is one of the first thinkers to apply economic ideas to understanding history. He bases his analysis of the modern state in *The Philosophy of Right* (1821) on the concept of the will, more generally on a conception of individuals as active within the legal framework of a social context. In a famous passage in "The System of Needs," he analyzes the economic foundations of modern liberal society as a social system that responds on an economic level to the eminently practical problem of meeting real human needs.[35]

Hegel's sophisticated theory of modern society, including its contribution to the realization of natural and unnatural or social human needs, is based on a conception of human beings as social actors.[36] Individuals, in meeting their needs, produce a web of relations, specifically including economic relations, between themselves, things, and others. It is often mistakenly thought that philosophers, particularly Hegel, are uninterested in concrete social phenomena.[37] On the contrary, his focus in the "System of Needs" lies squarely on how and to what extent modern liberal capitalism in fact satisfies human needs. This will be Marx's project as well.

Marx, Economics, and History

Hegel is a profoundly historical thinker deeply interested in economics, which he incorporates into his theories. He draws attention to, lays the foundation for, but does not work out in any detail, the link between economics (including modern capitalism) and history. Marx, writing in Hegel's wake, is arguably the first major thinker to develop a large-scale analysis of history on an economic basis.

Marx combines a "horizontal" analysis of modern industrial society and a "vertical" analysis of history to formulate a broadly-based theory englobing an enormous series of social phenomena arising primarily through the evolution of an underlying economic framework. He acknowledges a long series of factors influencing the social context, while he contends that, in the final analysis, all other phenomena in capitalism can be understood as a function of its economic basis.[38]

Marx sums up his view in a famous, difficult passage that deserves to be cited at length, since it provides a strong argument for an economic approach to historical phenomena of all kinds:[39]

> In the social production of their existence, men inevitably enter into definite relations, which are independent of their will, namely relations of production appropriate to a given stage of development of their material forces of production. The totality of these relations of production constitutes the economic structure of society, the real foundation, on which arises a legal and political superstructure and to which correspond definite forms of social consciousness. The mode of production of material life conditions the general process of social, political and intellectual life. It is not the consciousness of men that determines their existence,

> but their social existence that determines their consciousness. At a certain stage of development, the material productive forces of society come into conflict with the existing relations of production or—this merely expresses the same thing in legal terms—with the property relations within the framework of which they have operated hitherto. From forms of development of the productive forces these relations turn into their fetters. Then begins an era of social revolution. The changes in the economic foundation lead sooner or later to the transformation of the whole immense superstructure.

This passage raises two very difficult questions, which have been frequently discussed but never resolved: What does it mean to assert the primacy of economics over other social factors? And how does economics relate to human history? There are two main lines of interpretation concerning the "absolute" or the "relative" primacy of economics. Either the economic factor is primary and all other factors secondary, in some way dependent on it, or there is an interaction between economic and other causal factors. In the former case, literally everything can be explained through the causal influence of the economic basis. This approach has the advantage of explaining all social phenomena of whatever kind through the "reductionist" maneuver of invoking a single economic cause at the evident cost of depriving human beings of any capacity for rational, goal-directed action. From this perspective, the only causal factor, hence the only factor we ever need to take into account to understand any given human society, is its economic structure. Exaggerating only slightly, if according to this model we know who owns what in a particular society, then we can in principle explain on purely economic grounds what will happen and how individuals will understand these events. In the latter case, economic and other factors depend on the primacy given to the economic basis in influencing other factors. Yet, there is no way to understand what economic "primacy" means in general. Through concrete analysis of specific cases one can at most understand the relationship between various factors. Hence, the better way to understand the relationship between economic and other factors is as an interaction in which, by virtue of their priority and greater explanatory weight, economic factors are relatively more important.

In the cited passage and elsewhere in his writings, Marx applies his view of the explanatory primacy of economics—that is, the need to give more explanatory weight to economics than to other factors—in order to understand the production and interpretation of historical phenomena. There are many problems with Marx's position, which has given rise to an immense literature. Notwithstanding, this position marks a significant advance in the application of economics thinking to historical phenomena, hence an approach that should not be "blocked" by the tendency to reject Marx's position on political grounds.

Max Weber, Economics, and the Explanation of Social Behavior

Marx links the economic dimension of human history to the teleological development of human beings. He thinks that, in normal circumstances, the profit motive prevents most people from developing as individuals. Yet, at this late date, even after the decline and disappearance of Soviet-style socialism, it is difficult to be sanguine about his proposed "solution." Marx believes that capitalism will give way to Communism, leading to a change from what he perhaps over-optimistically considers as human prehistory to human history—the latter being a period in which human beings will finally be able to individualize themselves by developing their human capacities.

This vision is perhaps overly romantic. The jury is still out about the teleological component that Marx believes is embedded in capitalism. To acknowledge the importance of taking seriously the economic component of historical phenomena, we need not adopt the conclusions Marx draws. We can disagree with Marx's conviction about the future evolution of modern industrial society from capitalism to Communism, while still acknowledging the importance of analyzing the effect of its central economic dimension on the lives and activities of individuals and groups. The result provides a powerful conceptual tool to understand the modern world. In his study of the relationship of religion and capitalism, the great German sociologist Max Weber shows how to make use of an economic perspective that is largely shorn of its romantic trappings.

Weber applies economic analysis to sociological phenomena in interesting, influential, and often novel ways. For Weber, who criticizes the views of the founders of the historical school of political economy (Wilhelm Roscher, Karl Knies, and Bruno Hildebrand), no form of human activity is purely economic, but all activities have an economic aspect. Social activity cannot be reduced solely to economic factors, which need to be supplemented by other factors or values. Weber, like Wilhelm Dilthey, distinguishes between understanding (*verstehen*) and causal explanation (*erklären*). Social phenomena arise through the actions of individuals. In their role as agents, individuals give a meaning (*Sinn*) to what they do, which sociology seeks in turn to understand. Weber relies on both understanding and causal explanation in invoking, as explanatory models, what he calls "ideal types."

Marx, who has been read from many different angles of vision, can be interpreted reductively, or as reducing all social phenomena to economic phenomena. Though he acknowledges other factors, he argues that, in the final analysis, the rise of capitalism can be understood in purely economic terms. Weber rejects Marxian economic reductionism. In *The Protestant Ethic and the Spirit of Capitalism*, Weber invokes a thesis borrowed from Puritanism in arguing that the successful emergence of capitalism cannot be accounted for solely through economic factors. Human institutions, including religion, do not solely derive from economic foundations. On the contrary, the economic foundations of capitalism were fostered by, and can be understood in relation to, the ascetic secular morality associated with the twin emphases in Calvinistic theology: predestination and salvation. According to Weber, the emergence of capitalism must be attributed to a kind of religion that arose in the Renaissance as a by-product of Luther's revolt against Roman Catholicism and led to a way of life shared by large groups of people.[40]

This claim can be put more simply by calling attention to two points. First, Weber contends that certain types of Protestantism favor the rational pursuit of economic gain (central to capitalism) as giving meaning to life in this world, to the *hic et nunc*, as opposed to salvation. Aspects of Protestantism favorable to capitalism include rational planning and self-denial, or asceticism. Second, Weber argues that social factors such as capitalism should be understood in terms of economics but also in relation to other factors such as jurisprudence, mathematics, types of government, and so on. In effect he denies a reductionist form of economics approach to social phenomena in what amounts to an interactionist interpretation of Marx's thesis about the relation of superstructure and economic base in modern capitalism.

Economics, Globalization, and Historical Phenomena

In the familiar religious approach to history, the historical subject is not the finite human being but God. In the *Iliad*, composed at the dawn of the Western literary tradition, Homer, usually considered its author, describes the intervention of gods and goddesses in the daily round. The idea that history must be understood in terms of a divine element is present in later religious approaches to history until early in the modern Western tradition, when the view emerges that history is neither a divine nor a natural phenomenon, but rather a specifically human phenomenon that we need to understand in terms of human beings; and, at least since the rise of capitalism, economics is acknowledged as including an "ineliminable" historical dimension.

Since it is not possible to return to a precapitalist form of society, there is no going back before an economic approach to understanding historical events. It follows that it is an important error to omit the economic dimension in considering historical events. Yet, it would be an equally important error to attempt directly or indirectly to "reduce" all social phenomena to economics. The proper approach lies somewhere in between, identifying and evaluating the economic dimension as one among several explanatory factors, and as being particularly important, but not the only dimension of an acceptable account of the history of modern industrial society.

Roughly since the Industrial Revolution, capitalism has become the dominant economic form in the industrialized world, but all forms of capitalism are not the same. Capitalism plays out in different ways in different times and places.[41] Different kinds of capitalism in different parts of the world tend to be associated with different forms of national economies.[42] Scholars study the problem of how to classify types of capitalism. Some contend national economies are characterized by distinct institutional configurations that generate a particular systematic "logic" of economic action. For instance, Chinese capitalism, officially decided on by Deng Xiaoping, is now developing under the strong central control of the Chinese Communist Party, which at the time of this writing was being led by Hu Jintao.[43] It is sometimes suggested that the countries of the largely capitalist West tend, on the basis of shared interests, to act in a certain way with respect to noncapitalist regions of the world.[44]

I will be concentrating here on economic globalization. Events prior to, during, and after 9/11 have occurred, are occurring, and presumably will continue to occur in the context of the increasing extension of contemporary capitalism—what is now widely called (economic) *globalization* (also globalism). This term did not appear in standard dictionaries until recently.[45] But the relentless global extension of capitalism on the way to encompassing the entire planet, the phenomenon to which globalization refers, is much older. Globalization can be understood as going back to the beginnings of modern capitalism, which since its inception has been steadily expanding in every country throughout the entire world. Globalization has become identified with a number of trends, many of which have developed since World War II, including greater international movement of among other things commodities, money, information, and people; and the development of technology, organizations, legal systems, and infrastructures to allow this movement.

There is a difference between the worldwide spread of inventions, discoveries, and information, for instance, in mathematics (e.g., the concept of zero) and the natural sciences (e.g., how to make gunpowder or paper), and economic globalization. Globalization, which has no precise meaning, is understood in very different ways. Amartya Sen calls attention to two rival interpretations of globalization: as a useful Western product, the gift of the West to everyone else; and, on the contrary, as a form of Western domination of everyone else through an extension of Western imperialism.[46] Each understanding identifies an aspect of the present situation. But neither focuses on the economic component of globalization, including its relationship to capitalism and its many-sided impact on economic, political, religious, and other factors.

By globalization I mean the integration, in different ways, of national economies into an international economy.[47] I further have in mind two related phenomena: First, there is the tendency in capitalism (which needs constantly expanding markets) to develop ceaselessly, continuing to extend itself throughout the world. Capitalist expansion occurs in different ways, including geographical expansion and the expansion of markets by creating new needs within an existing market. One example is the currently expanding desire for what are called "smart phones," now spreading rapidly throughout the world. The process of expanding old markets and creating new ones has no clear limit. It is always possible to create a new desire by inventing a product, such as the "i-phone," which enough consumers will want to buy to justify its manufacture. The process of geographical expansion of markets has a natural limit. This process has already culminated, or will one day culminate, at a point in which nothing is left untouched. When that point is reached, the geographical aspect of the process of economic expansion characteristic of capitalism will come up against its natural limit, its *terminus ad quem*, beyond which there is no further possibility for development. Further, there is the effect of globalization, the way in which capitalism, in the course of maximizing profit, encroaches upon, adheres to, and transforms everything with which it comes into contact. This aspect of globalization, presupposed by the ceaseless expansion of capitalism in search of further markets, displacing, whenever possible, other types of economic organization, is by no means benign. It is rather extremely menacing, even a deadly threat for all (indigenous) forms of social "organization," including, but not limited to, local customs, traditions, and economic structures, for which it tends to substitute a version of itself.

A full account of globalization, which is fast becoming a special area of research, lies beyond the scope of this book.[48] I will be interested here in the social and historical impact of economic globalization, or the near- and long-term consequences of the incessant extension of capitalism. One way to put the point is to note that globalization is economically useful—although on occasion socially malignant and harmful in various ways—in fact very useful in increasing the standard of living for many people.

One cannot deny the positive side of globalization, its vast contribution to the improvement in the standard of living around the world for rich and poor alike, which results from increased trade. Yet there is also a negative side, which necessarily accompanies the positive side of globalization. One problem is, as Sen points out, to find a way to share more fairly the immense potential benefits of globalization. It is clearly not enough for everyone to benefit; everyone must benefit in a "fair" manner.[49] One wonders, then, if the South China workers manufacturing computers for the entire world are benefiting fairly from the demand for their labor.

Opinions on this basic point vary widely. Jagdish Bhagwati, resists the proposition that globalization is economically beneficent but socially malignant.[50] His view is partly supported, but partly rejected, by Paul Collier, who believes globalization is responsible for rapidly falling poverty rates in 80 per cent of the world. [51] Yet, Collier also believes that despite globalization, but in part because of it, some fifty countries are sinking deeper into ever more hopeless forms of poverty.[52] A second difficulty is to respond to such consequences of globalization as the weakening of the middle class, the loss of job protection, and the downward pressure on wages.[53] These difficulties have been exacerbated by the great global recession of 2008. As mentioned above, another problem, which concerns us here, is avoiding the strongly negative impact of economic globalization on traditional forms of life. In its crudest form, this impact is the "uprooting" of everything that stands in the way of the expansion of capitalism.

Globalization is a slippery adversary, difficult to defeat for long or even to hold at bay. It is simply incompatible with differences of any kind. Economic globalism impedes, undermines, and destroys economic and cultural differences of all kinds by creating economic and cultural sameness. Just as there are different kinds of capitalism, there are different approaches to concrete economic problems. Dell focuses on distribution, while outsourcing everything else, but Samsung manufactures everything itself.[54] Yet these and other differences are less important than the underlying similarity pervading different kinds of capitalism, which is accompanied by a kind of bland international culture that is the same, or nearly the same, everywhere and is in the process of encircling the globe.

The effect of capitalism on European economies is at present very clear in the form of opposition between two competing systems. One is what is widely understood as an American-style economy, where the few remaining social entitlements, such as health care and pensions, are routinely sacrificed to economic imperatives. The other is the more social orientation of national economies that underwrite entitlements such as free, or nearly free, education from kindergarten through the universities, free or nearly free universal health care, and a strong system of unemployment insurance. This is common, for instance, throughout most of Europe. The great recession that began in 2008 has added additional financial pressure, suggesting that Europe has arrived at a crossroads where it will need to choose.[55] Either it will pursue the path it has so far taken of protecting these entitlements at the cost of consistently lower economic growth, or it will reduce, perhaps considerably reduce, and even finally abandon them for economic purposes.[56] To put the same point otherwise: either Europe will continue to resist the laissez-faire pressure of a form of capitalism devoid of any overriding social interest other than itself, or it will maintain at least a recognizable form of its social capitalism while accepting the economic consequences.

It is not important for present purposes to predict the evolution of European health care. Yet, I suspect that over time, and on strictly economic grounds, the countries in the European community will be forced into progressive abandonment of long-term entitlements. This is already happening, for instance in efforts to pass part of the health-care burden from the state to the individual. Various forms of medical care are now only partially reimbursed in France. While there still is universal health care, a two-tier system is increasingly in evidence in which more money creates access to better and faster health care. The effect of the increasing penetration of American-style, laissez-faire capitalism is even more obvious. An American who goes abroad at present is likely to feel very much at home in increasingly larger parts of the world, now including Kabul and Baghdad, which are among the many regions "penetrated" by the very same economics that rule the roost at home. It is not by accident that people all over the world speak English to the point where it is becoming, if it has not already become, the world language. The spread of the English language has nothing at all to do with alleged, but linguistically nonexistent, advantages for communication or other qualities. It rather derives from its link to the American economy. This economic reason accounts for the fact that the traveler today will find the same McDonalds in Beijing as in Boston, and the same Burger King in Paris as in Pittsburgh, since these and other visible symbols of the American economy are spreading throughout the world.

The Chinese have not decided to abandon their language for English, and Italian cuisine has not been overtaken by American hamburgers. It is rather that, on a series of different levels and in as many different ways, capitalism, as represented by the US and its advanced, mainly Western, industrial allies—Japan is the big exception to this rule—is increasingly penetrating local economies everywhere and as a by-product destroying their autonomy. As part of this process, other forms of culture around the world are being transformed into so many similar examples of the same thing. A century and a half ago, this tendency was clearly anticipated by Marx and Engels in a famous passage in "The Communist Manifesto." In discussing what they call the "bourgeois" period, in which capitalism has become the single most important social force, Marx and Engels write: "All fixed, fast-frozen relations, with their train of ancient and venerable prejudices and opinions, are swept away, all new-formed ones become antiquated before they can ossify. All that is solid melts into air, all that is holy is profaned, and man is at last compelled to face with sober senses, his real conditions of life, and his relations with his kind."[57]

The Austrian economist, Joseph Schumpeter, proposes a related idea, and the German sociologist, Werner Sombart, uses the term "creative destruction" in his own economic theory of innovation and progress. Schumpeter, who thinks that creative innovation is the lifeblood of capitalism, popularized this term, "creative destruction," in *Capitalism, Socialism and Democracy* (1942) to refer to the process of radical innovation. He speaks of "the opening up of new markets, foreign or domestic . . . that incessantly revolutionizes the economic structure *from within*, incessantly destroying the old one, incessantly creating a new one. This process of Creative Destruction is the essential fact about capitalism."[58] The only thing to add is that capitalism, in expanding, destroys not only its former economic models, but also everything else that stands in its path.

Economic Globalization and the Islamic World

It is not clear that we fully understand the consequences of economic globalization, about which there is a wide swath of opinions. Some identify difficulties following from incessant capitalist expansion. William Greider, a political journalist, believes globalization is leading the world down the path to a major economic and political crisis.[59] Dany Rodrik, an economist whose view is more moderate, discerns tensions between social stability and globalization, which tend to undermine it.[60] For Rodrik, globalization results in increased demands for the state to provide social insurance, while reducing its ability to do so, at least to do so effectively. He detects a contradiction between globalization and the requirements of maintaining the social legitimacy of trade, which on occasion turns against globalization and toward protectionism.[61] Rodrik sees two main dangers engendered by globalization: the political backlash against trade, in protectionism; social disintegration provoked by the realignment of nations along lines of national income.[62] Jagdish Bhagwati, another economist, is an unabashed cheerleader for globalization, whose problems are to his mind never more than illusory. His general view of globalization is followed by still another economist, Deepak Lal, who is concerned that the US, the central player in the global economy, will fail to take its "imperial" responsibilities seriously. He contends that the global economy grows best through periods of high international trade, requiring order and security, hence empires to provide them. He is amenable to a Pax Britannica as well as to a Pax Americana. In the interests of economic efficiency, he recommends closing ineffective international organizations intended to support international economic and political intervention—such as the World Bank, the IMF, and the United Nations—to let America get on with the job.[63]

It would go beyond the present focus to consider in detail the economic advantages or difficulties, real or imagined, engendered by globalization. Yet, it is important to direct attention to its social consequences not only within, but also outside of, Western capitalism. Economic globalization is a crucial factor in the ongoing contest between the Islamic world and the West, including in the intra-Islamic division between Muslim modernizers and Muslim fundamentalists, which turns the latter against the capitalist West. Opposition between Islam and the Christian world preceded capitalism. But the formerly uneasy coexistence between these two main forms of Abrahamic religion was later transformed by the emergence of capitalism.

Like capitalism, of which it is a phase, or a stage, economic globalization is a mixed blessing, good in that it is useful to develop the economy, but also bad in that development at any cost is not necessarily desirable. With this in mind, it is useful to distinguish between the process of globalization (as an economic reality), and its impact (both economic and noneconomic) on non-Western societies, particularly in the Islamic world. Globalization assumes steadily increasing importance in the contemporary world, even in an officially Marxist country like China, where in the wake of the Cultural Revolution capitalism has been officially anointed by the Communist Party as the only way forward.

Globalization is obviously the extension, to its limit, of the tendency for capitalism to spread throughout society. There is a long list of figures and organizations that are either pro- or contra-globalization. Early opponents of what later became global capitalism include the Luddites, early nineteenth-century English textile artisans and followers of Ned Ludd, whose existence is apparently uncertain, but who was opposed to the spread of machines. Opposition to globalization, which often assumes a political form, has no particular correlation to politics. The many contemporary opponents of globalization are spread widely throughout the political spectrum. They include rightwing economic nationalists like the American political commentator, Patrick Buchanan, and leftwing "antiglobalists" (so-called "alter-mondialistes") such as the French peasant labor leader, José Bové.

One difficulty in thinking about globalization is that the term seems to have been coined only recently, and to have become popular even more recently. There is at present no agreement on its precise meaning. In general, globalization refers to global capitalism, or capitalism that has spread internationally around the globe. This obvious point is understood in different ways, and different interpretations and strategies of interpretation have been proposed. The French politician and novelist, Erik Orsenna, who never defines his terms, studies the general phenomenon of globalization through the development of the exploitation of cotton at various times and places.[64] George Soros, the widely known hedge fund manager, takes it to mean "the development of global financial markets, the growth of transnational corporations, and their increasing domination over national economies."[65] His emphasis lies in promoting what, following Karl Popper, he calls "open societies." Soros criticizes so-called "market fundamentalists" as well as antiglobalists. He acknowledges that existing international financial and trade institutions create wealth, while he complains they are deficient with respect to providing other public goods. According to George Stiglitz, the Nobel prize-winning economist, "the phenomenon of globalization . . . is the closer integration of the countries and peoples of the world which has been brought about by the enormous reduction of costs of transportation and communication, and the breaking down of artificial barriers to the flow of goods, services, capital, knowledge, and (to a lesser extent) people across borders . . . accompanied by the creation of new institutions that have joined with existing ones to work across borders."[66] The World Bank and the IMF both emerged as the result of the UN Monetary and Financial Conference at Bretton Woods, New Hampshire, in July 1944. Both institutions are still dominated by the US; and both reflect a uniform American approach to economic problems, on the assumption that it is universally valid, which, Stiglitz objects, often makes the situation worse. In pointing to problems in the latest stage of capitalism, Soros and Stiglitz both raise questions about Adam Smith's conception of the "invisible hand," according to which the proper development of enlightened self-interest, or psychological egotism, is in everyone's interest.

In considering the political consequences of a global economy, Michael Hardt and Antonio Negri propose a different approach, suggesting that economic empire throughout the world is the irreversible consequence of the global expansion of capitalism.[67] Colonialism and the nation-state are linked economic phenomena. In general, colonialism can be characterized as the effective control by a nation-state over a dependent area and its people. For example, though the countries of French West Africa are all independent, France continues to exert strong political, cultural, and economic influence on them, an influence roughly equivalent to when they were part of the "mother" country.

At present, we have entered a period in which the nation-state is increasingly superseded in different ways. It is, in part, weakened by the emergence of supranational entities, such as the United Nations or the European Union, which, as they grow stronger, inevitably weaken national sovereignty. Also, the nation-state increasingly needs to contend with enormously powerful international corporations, such as Microsoft, or giant economic entities, earlier such as Long-Term Capital Management, which failed in the 1990s, and at present The Goldman Sachs Group, Inc., with their steadily increasing financial muscle—often financially more important than individual countries. Indeed, roughly half the world's largest economies are not governments, but giant companies.

The different views of globalization are complementary. Soros and Stiglitz focus on evaluating the success of economic globalization in meeting human needs. It is, for example, stunning to realize that poverty in the US was actually increasing before the great recession of 2008. Hardt and Negri are rather concerned with an equally important theme: the effect of economic globalization on local economic environments.

There seem to be only two main possibilities, with many variations. Either these environments take on, and become part of, a familiar Western form; or they give way to stronger economic forces, which in turn create the potential for conflict between various local non-Western societies and the West, conflict centered around what can be called the economic "contradiction" between very different types of societies. The point is not that the global extension of capitalism is bad, as such. It is, rather, that globalization comes with a "price tag": the simultaneous generation of problems that, in extreme cases like 9/11, have the potential of tearing apart what it creates.

In part, the situation confronting the Islamic regions of the world is similar to that of other regions confronted with the reality of advanced industrial capitalism. In certain ways it is specific to the situation of Islamic countries. Surprisingly, in virtue of its importance, insufficient attention is devoted to the specific economic impact of the globalized economy on Islamic countries.[68] There is a clear tension between development and traditional identity. Islamic countries are both fertile ground for Western-style economic development as well as for nation-states whose specificity as traditional or even non-traditional Islamic societies is threatened by the growth of international capitalism.

Economic contradiction is an increasingly prominent fault line between Western capitalism and non-Western, noncapitalist societies. Benjamin Barber describes the opposition between the Arab world and the West under the heading of *jihad* and what he calls "McWorld."[69] Barber focuses on the opposition between Western capitalism and the Muslim population instead of analyzing the effect of the former on the latter. He discerns an opposition between processes working in different directions, between Islamic tradition and industrial capitalism.

> The tendencies of what I am here calling the forces of Jihad and the forces of McWorld operate with equal strength in opposite directions, the one driven by parochial hatreds, the other by universalizing markets, the one re-creating ancient subnational and ethnic borders from within, the other making national borders porous from without. They have one thing in common: neither offers much hope to citizens looking for practical ways to govern themselves democratically. If the global future is to pit Jihad's centrifugal whirlwind against McWorld's centripetal black hole, the outcome is unlikely to be democratic. . . .[70]

Barber is insightful in pointing to the opposition between strongly capitalist and other societies. He is less insightful in his failure to see that capitalism generates its own "other," an opposition to itself that cannot merely be ascribed to the bad manners supposedly arising from traditional Islamic culture. Yet, Barber at least acknowledges the Islamic point of view, which other observers, including even specialists from the Islamic world, sometimes simply dismiss.

Even John Gray, one of the most interesting current commentators, fails to grasp that the "contradiction" between the Western pursuit of economic expansion and the Muslim pursuit of the kind of life prescribed in the Qur'an is a leading cause of problems the West now faces. Gray notes that al Qaeda uses the internet and other modern means of communication, trains and airplanes, employs sophisticated explosives, and so on. He correctly claims it is a product of modernity, hence is modern, even, depending on what this trendy term means, postmodern. But he overlooks the deeper point that the increasing importance of the economic dimension of society only exacerbates the contradiction, hence the social conflict, between the West and those rare non-Western countries that thrive on modern capitalism, on the one hand, and everything else, on the other. Al Qaeda is modern for at least two reasons: first, as Gray notes, by virtue of its employment of a wide array of modern tools; and, second, because it is the "other" of capitalism—capitalism's negation, which, far from being a mere accident, is called forth and produced through global capitalism's own development in the modern period.

Excursus: Hegel, Marx, and Social Contradiction

The intentions of individuals and groups are often motivated by, and hence can be understood in relation to, what I call "social contradictions." The idea of social contradiction, which is complex, requires a separate discussion. We can begin by calling attention to the difference between contradictories and contradiction. Two propositions are contradictories if, and only if, one is true and the other is false. In the propositional and predicate calculus, the conjunction of a proposition and its denial is always false.

Contradictions can be logical, formal, subjective, objective, and so on. According to Aristotle, a violation of the law of noncontradiction prevents rational discourse.[71] Hegel, who discusses many different types of contradiction, distinguishes explicitly between subjective and objective contradiction. A contradiction is subjective if it concerns no more than our way of talking about the world, but not about the mind-independent world itself. A contradiction is objective if it does not concern our way of talking about the world, but concerns the world itself. According to Hegel, Kant's *antinomies*, or contradictions of reason, are only subjective or "within" subjectivity, but are not located within the world.

The concept of contradiction is sometimes used for explanatory purposes. Zeno of Elea (about 490–430 BCE) identifies subjective contradictions in arguing that motion is impossible. Heraclitus of Ephesus (540–475 BCE) identifies objective contradictions in arguing that the "tension of opposites"—he had no word for contradiction—provides the unity as well as the change of the world. Hegel and Marx rely on contradiction to understand history.

For Hegel, negation leads to contradiction, which in turn leads to change. In the *Encyclopedia*, he obscurely claims, "Generally speaking, it is contradiction that moves the world, and it is ridiculous to say that contradiction cannot be thought."[72] In the *Philosophy of History*, he applies the concept of contradiction to historical phenomena. In discussion of ancient Egypt, he remarks that its task was to unite opposing elements (Babylonian, Syrian, and so on).[73] He sees Egypt as a previous unity, as an unresolved contradiction between nature and spirit.[74] He further detects a series of unresolved contradictions in the Church during the Middle Ages: in subjective spirit as witnessing absolute spirit, and as finite and existential; in the relationship in the Church, as such, in which the true spirit exists in people, whereas the Church has only the relationship of a teacher of this cult; and in the Church, which is immensely rich, but also despises wealth.[75]

Marx builds on Hegel's conception of objective contradiction to analyze modern industrial society. In working out a theory of economic contradiction, Marx is influenced by Adam Smith and Hegel. Smith devotes two chapters to commodities, in *The Wealth of Nations.* In *Philosophy of Right*, discussing the "Use of the Thing," Hegel distinguishes quantity and quality with respect to a thing, and further specifies that this quantity concerns the amount of money for which a product can be exchanged.[76] This Hegelian distinction, which Marx repeats at the beginning of *Capital*, exactly captures Marx's own distinction between use-value and exchange-value. In his analysis of commodities, Marx describes the contradiction between use-value and exchange value that he regards as central to capitalism. In Marx's opinion, the distinction between use-value and exchange-value, with respect to the commodity, corresponds to a further distinction between (in his words) the two-fold nature of labor contained in the commodity. Use-value is the product of one kind of labor, which is so to speak contained in the thing in a way that meets a human need, and (if one abstracts from use-value) exchange-value is also contained in the thing as the average amount of labor power for which it can be exchanged.

Marx's interest in economic contradiction in modern industrial society runs throughout his writings, beginning in the *Paris Manuscripts* (1844). Here, Marx identifies contradictions between capitalists and workers, or basically opposed interests that express themselves in relation to wages, profit, and rent. In the *Grundrisse* (1857–58), he elaborates on the familiar claim that the inherent contradictions of modern industrial society will lead to overproduction crises and eventually to its economic collapse. In *A Contribution to the Critique of Political Economy* he identifies a basic contradiction between use-value and exchange-value within the commodity, a contradiction situated at the heart of modern industrial society. Analyzing commodities in *Capital*, Marx describes an objective contradiction found in the deepest recesses of capitalism itself. Capitalism depends on the institution of private property, which supposes the accumulation of capital, and which in turn depends on the sale of commodities in the market. Commodities contain an objective contradiction between use-value and exchange-value, between quality and quantity, between the use of the thing, which results from the process of production, and what can be had for it when it is exchanged in the market. A transformation of one type of society into another, of capitalism into Communism, will supposedly follow upon the ripening of contradictions situated in the commodity.

Hegel detects contradictions in all kinds of change, including history. Marx discusses contradiction within economic phenomena. In discussing 9/11, I will be focusing on a contradiction between economics and religion, more precisely between the capitalist tendency toward economic globalization, and fundamentalist Islam.

Contexts, Contradictions, and "Causes" of Human Actions

We bring this chapter to a close by briefly sketching an approach I will be applying to understand the events before, during, and after 9/11. Historical events are not ends in themselves but rather means to realize selected human ends. Understanding historical events requires understanding the desires motivating individuals and groups, as well as understanding the conditions under which they choose their course of action. It is basic to capitalism that economics tends to change from a means into an end, in becoming an end in itself as the possession of various forms of capital becomes a central goal of human life. To overlook economic constraints and economic goals (as do Bush, Huntington, and Lewis) makes it more difficult to understand the current confrontation between radical Islamic elements and much of the rest of the world.

Economics is peculiarly important, and never more so than at present. It is sometimes thought that, in the final analysis, politics is just a disguised form of economics. While everything cannot be reduced to economics—for instance the view that unrestricted support of Israel is God's politics is based on Christian fundamentalism—the economic dimension of the modern world is clearly pervasive. Economics "generates" the surroundings in which we live out our lives, the situations in which we either prosper or falter, and the context in which we are able or, more often unable, to choose actions that we can reliably expect to help meet our goals. It follows that to understand human events we will need to provide a plausible reconstruction of the wishes or desires as well as of the situation, or context, within which human beings arrive at and act on their choices.

What we identify as important, and how we interpret particular events, depends on an interpretive framework. There is no obvious way around the kind of cognitive relativism that follows from the need to "index," or link, our interpretations of historical phenomena to prior conceptual frameworks. Heidegger's well-known inability to distinguish between agricultural technology and the Holocaust, derives from his lofty focus on being itself as distinguished from beings, including human beings.[77] The conflict over many years between Protestants and Catholics in Northern Ireland created a situation in which it was literally the case that one person's terrorist was another person's freedom fighter.[78] Iraqis fighting the US occupation regard it as an unjust invasion leading to the usurpation of their rights. The US government and its allies regard the same conflict as being justified by US self-interest as well as a self-assigned mandate to spread America's concept of democracy around the world.

The point is, emphatically, not to pass moral judgment, but rather to identify the outlines of a conceptual framework that will enable us to understand, or better understand, historical events. Now, some frameworks are obviously better than others. The obvious deficiency of the analyses of 9/11 attributable to Bush, Huntington, and Lewis is that none pays more than the most cursory attention to economic factors. On the contrary, I believe the very economic dimension that Bush, Huntington, and Lewis lightly pass over needs to be taken very seriously to understand radical Muslims as well as those to whom they are opposed. The interaction between economic globalization and conservative Islam can be usefully understood as creating a social contradiction between partisans of continued economic expansion and partisans of maintaining, or of reproducing without change, a favored interpretation of traditional Islam. This contradiction is not new. If economic globalization is intrinsic to capitalism, then this contradiction has existed in different forms ever since capitalism began to emerge. But it has recently reached a critical stage through a series of events, opposing fundamentalist Muslims to the largely non-Muslim, capitalist West.

Notes

1. See, for the "rationality" of madmen, Remo Bodei, *Le logiche del delirio. Ragione, affetti, follia*, Roma-Bari, Laterza, 2000. For the rationality of irrationality, see Marco Sgarbi, *La Logica dell'irrazionale. Studio sull significato e sui problemi della Kritik der Urteilskraft*, Milano-Udine: Mimesis, 2010.
2. See Maurice Merleau-Ponty, *Phenomenology of Perception*, translated by Colin Smith, London: Routledge, 2003, p. 198, n 19.
3. See Friedrich A. Hayek, *The Road to Serfdom: A classic warning against the danger to freedom inherent in social planning*, Chicago: University of Chicago Press, 1972.
4. See David Hume, *Dialogues Concerning Natural Religion*, in Dialogues Concerning Natural Religion And Other Writings, edited by Dorothy Coleman, New York: Cambridge University Press, 2007.
5. See Alain Besançon, *The Rise of the Gulag : Intellectual Origins of Leninism*, translated by Sarah Matthews, New York: Continuum, 1981.
6. Francis Fukuyama, *The End of History and the Last Man*, p. xii.
7. Niall Ferguson, *Colossus: The Price of America's Empire*, New York: Penguin, 2004.
8. See Chalmers Johnson, *Nemesis: The Last Days of the American Empire*, New York: Metropolitan Books, 2006.
9. According to Schumpeter, "an aggressiveness, the true reasons for which do not lie in the aims which are temporarily being pursued . . . an aggressiveness for its own sake, as reflected in such terms as 'hegemony,' 'world dominion,' and so forth . . . expansion for the sake of expanding. . . . This determination cannot be explained by any of the pretexts that bring it into action, by any of the aims for which it seems to be struggling at the time. . . . Such expansion is in a sense its

own 'object'" Joseph Schumpeter, *Imperialism and the Social Classes*, translated by Heinz Norden, A.M. Kelly, 1951, pp. 5–6.

10. See *Deus Caritas Est*, p. 26: "Historically, the issue of the just ordering of the collectivity had taken a new dimension with the industrialization of society in the nineteenth century. The rise of modern industry caused the old social structures to collapse, while the growth of a class of salaried workers provoked radical changes in the fabric of society. The relationship between capital and labour now became the decisive issue—an issue which in that form was previously unknown. Capital and the means of production were now the new source of power which, concentrated in the hands of a few, led to the suppression of the rights of the working classes, against which they had to rebel."
11. See, for discussion, Tom Rockmore, *Marx After Marxism: The Philosophy of Karl Marx*, Oxford: Blackwell, 2002.
12. See Michel Henry, *Marx: A Philosophy of Human Reality*, translated by Kathleen McLaughlin, Bloomington : Indiana University Press, 1983.
13. See Ernest Barker, *Greek Political Theory: Plato and His Predecessors*, London: Methuen, 1961, pp. 190–92.
14. See Plato, *Republic* 417A, in *Plato: Complete Works*, edited by John M. Cooper, Indianapolis: Hackett, 1997, p. 1052.
15. See Plato, *Republic* 423D, in *Plato: Complete Works*, p. 1056.
16. See Plato, *Laws* 742E–743A, *Plato: Complete Works*, p. 1423.
17. See Aristotle, *Nicomachean Ethics* V, 5, in *The Complete Works of Aristotle*, II, pp. 1787–89.
18. See Aristotle, *Politics* I, 8–11, in *The Complete Works of Aristotle*, II, pp. 1992–98.
19. Marx studies the Industrial Revolution in detail under the heading of "Machinery and modern industry" in *Capital*, translated by Edward Moore and Samuel Aveling, edited by Friedrich Engels, New York: International Publishers, 1967, 3 vols., I, chapter XV, pp. 371–507.
20. Marx correctly claims that the steam engine did not cause the Industrial Revolution, whose machines required its amelioration. See Karl Marx, *Capital* I, chapter 15, p. 375. See Karl Marx, *Capital: A Critique of Political Economy*, introduced by Ernest Mandel, translated by Ben Fowkes, Penguin: London, 1990, chapter 15, p. 497.
21. Locke's view still has many defenders. A recent example is Robert Nozick, *Anarchy, State and Utopia*, Cambridge: Blackwell, 1984.
22. Locke's idea that the right to property is absolute contradicts the ancient Greek view that the right to property is merely a social creation, but neither absolute nor inherent. See Barker, *Greek Political Theory*, p. 371.
23. See Robert Nozick, *Anarchy, State and Utopia*, Oxford: Blackwell, 1974.
24. The full passage reads as follows: "And the life of man, solitary, poore, nasty, brutish, and short." Thomas Hobbes, *Leviathan*, edited by C.B. Macpherson, Harmondsworth: Penguin, 1974, part I, chapter 13, p. 186.

25. See G. W. F. Hegel, *Elements of the Philosophy of Right*, edited by Allen W. Wood, translated by H. B. Nisbet, New York: Cambridge University Press, 2005, § 187, p. 124.
26. For discussion, see chapter XI: "The Social Democratic Movement," in Judt, *Postwar*, pp. 360–89.
27. See Adam Smith, *An Inquiry into the Nature and Causes of the Wealth of Nations*, edited, with an introduction, by Edwin Cannan, New York: Modern Library, 1937, Introduction, p. viii.
28. Cited in *A Carlyle Reader: Selections from the Writings of Thomas Carlyle*, edited by G.B. Tennyson, Berkeley: University of California Press, 1984, p. 437.
29. For various statements of this principle, see § 31, pp. 113–15; § 32 (pp. 116–20), § 33 (pp. 120–24), § 36 (pp. 128–34, in Nicholas Rescher, *G.W. Leibniz's Monadology: An Edition for Students*, Pittsburgh: University of Pittsburgh Press, 1991.
30. See Bernard Mandeville, *The Fable of the Bees and Other Writings*, edited by E.J. Hundert, Indianapolis: Hackett, 1997.
31. See Smith, *The Wealth of Nations*, p. 508.
32. Smith, *The Wealth of Nations*, p. 423.
33. This approach is dominant but not universal. For a more socially responsive approach, see, e.g. Amartya Sen, *Poverty and Famines*, New Delhi: Oxford University Press, 1999.
34. See Hegel, *Elements of the Philosophy of Right*, p. 244, p. 266.
35. See "The System of Needs," in Hegel, *Elements of the Philosophy of Right*, pp. 189–208, pp. 227–39.
36. Hegel's theory of action is currently attracting increasing attention. See, e.g., Robert B. Pippin, *Hegel'sPractical Philosophy: Rational Agency as Ethical Life*, New York: Cambridge University Press, 2008.
37. According to Bottomore and Rubel, following the standard Marxist view, Hegel was uninterested in and not able to explain real social phenomena. See Karl Marx, *Selected Writings in Sociology and Social Philosophy*, edited by Thomas Bottomore and Maximilien Rubel, p. 6. It is at least arguable that this was not Hegel's immediate intention.
38. See, for a functional approach to Marx, G.A. Cohen, *Karl Marx's Theory of History: A Defense*, New York: Oxford University Press, 2000.
39. Karl Marx, *A Contribution to the Critique of Political Economy*, edited, with an Introduction by Maurice Dobb, translated from the German by S.W. Ryazanskaya, New York: International Publishers, 1989, pp. 20–21.
40. See Max Weber, *The Protestant Ethic and the Spirit of Capitalism and Other Writings*, edited by Peter Baehr and Gordon C. Wells, New York: Penguin, 2002.
41. See, e.g., Bruno Amable, *The Diversity of Modern Capitalism*, New York: Oxford University Press, 2003.
42. See, e.g., Peter A. Hall and Daniel W. Gingerich [2004], "Varieties of Capitalism and Institutional Complementarities in the Macroeconomy: An Empirical Analysis," in *British Journal of Political Science*, vol. 39, pp. 449–82.

43. See, e.g., Michel Aglietta and Yves Landry, *La Chine vers la superpuissance*, Paris: Editions Economica-Groupama, 2007.
44. See Gregory Jackson and Richard Deeg, "How Many Varieties of Capitalism? Comparing the Comparative Institutional Analyses of Capitalist Diversity," April 11, 2006, MPIfG Discussion Paper No. 06/2
45. According to the OED, it dates back only to 1959, when it appeared in *The Economist*.
46. See Amartya Sen, *Identity and Violence: The Illusion of Destiny*, New York: Norton, 2006, p. 125.
47. See Jagdish Bhagwati, *In Defense of Globalization*, New York: Oxford University Press, 2004, p. 3.
48. For an overview, see Manfred B. Steger, *Globalism: The New Market Ideology*, Lanham: Rowman and Littlefield, 2002.
49. See Sen, *Identity and Violence: The Illusion of Destiny*, p. 132.
50. In a recent book, Bhagwati, who is one of the best known defenders of globalization, examines the proposition that globalization is economically beneficial but socially malignant. He argues strongly that the former but not the latter is correct. See Jagdish Bhagwati, *In Defense of Globalization*, New York: Oxford University Press, 2004.
51. See Paul Collier, *The Bottom Billion: Why the Poorest Countries Are Failing and What Can Be Done About It*, Oxford: Oxford University Press, 2007.
52. See Collier, *The Bottom Billion: Why the Poorest Countries Are Failing and What Can Be Done About It*, chapter 6: "On Missing the Boat: The Marginalization of the Bottom Billion in the World Economy," pp. 79–98.
53. For discussion, see Joseph Stiglitz, "A Progressive Response to Globalization," in *The Nation*, April 2, 2006, in *Economist's Voice*.
54. This example is borrowed from Gray's review of recent work by Suzanne Berger. See John Gray, "The Global Delusion," in *The New York Review of Books*, volume LIII, Number 7, April 27, 2006, pp. 20–23.
55. For an analysis of the great recession in terms of capital flow, see David Harvey, *The Enigma of Capital and the Crises of Capitalism*, New York: Oxford University Press, 2010. For a study of the great recession and democracy, see Richard Posner, *The Crisis of Capitalist Democracy*, Cambridge: Harvard University Press, 2010. For a comparative study of the great depression and the great recession, see Paul Krugman, *The Return of Depression Economics and the Crisis of 2008*, New York: W.W. Norton, 2009.
56. This difficulty seemed to be at stake in the election of Nicholas Sarkozy as president of France. Sarkozy, who is enamored of all things American, appears to be taking steps to roll back the social protections traditionally enjoyed in France.
57. Marx and Engels, "Manifesto of the Communist Party," in *Classics of Moral and Political Theory*, edited by Michael L. Morgan, Indianapolis: Hackett, 1992, p. 1194.
58. Joseph Schumpeter, *Capitalism, Socialism and Democracy*, New York: Harper and Row, 1976, p. 83.

59. See William Greider, *One World, Ready or Not—The Manic Logic of Global Capitalism*, New York: Simon and Schuster, 1997. For criticism of Greider, see See Dani Rodrik, *Has Globalization Gone Too Far?*, Washington, D.C.: Institute for International Economics, 1997, pp. 74–75.
60. See Rodrik, *Has Globalization Gone Too Far?*, p. 73.
61. See Rodrik, *Has Globalization Gone Too Far?*, pp. 53, 64–65.
62. See Rodrik, *Has Globalization Gone Too Far?*, pp. 69, 70.
63. See Deepak Lal, *In Praise of Empires: Globalization and Order*, New York: Palgrave Macmillan, 2004.
64. See Erik Orsenna, *Voyages aux pays du cotton. Petit Précis de mondialisation*, Paris: Fayard, 2006.
65. George Soros, *On Globalization*, New York: Public Affairs, 2002, p. 1.
66. Joseph E. Stiglitz, *Globalization and Its Discontents*, New York: Norton, 2002, p. 9.
67. "Empire is materializing before our very eyes. Over the past several decades, as colonial regimes were overthrown and then precipitously after the Soviet barriers to the capitalist world market finally collapsed, we have witnessed an irresistible and irreversible globalization of economic and cultural exchanges. Along with the global market and global circuits of production has emerged a global order, a new logic and structure of rule—in short, a new form of sovereignty. Empire is the political subject that effectively regulates these global exchanges, the sovereign power that governs the world." Michael Hardt and Antonio Negri, *Empire*, Cambridge: Harvard University Press, 2000, p. xi.
68. A recent collection of papers on globalization includes no mention of its impact on the Arab world. See Alan Freeman and Boris Kagarlitsky, *The Politics of Empire: Globalisation in Crisis*, London: Pluto, 2004.
69. He describes the latter as "being borne in on us by the onrush of economic and ecological forces that demand integration and uniformity and that mesmerize the world with fast music, fast computers, and fast food—with MTV, Macintosh, and McDonald's, pressing nations into one commercially homogenous global network: one McWorld tied together by technology, ecology, communications, and commerce. The planet is falling precipitantly [sic] apart AND coming reluctantly together at the very same moment." Benjamin Barber, "Jihad vs. McWorld," in *Atlantic Monthly*, 1992, no. 269, p. 53.
70. Barber, "Jihad vs. McWorld," in *The Atlantic Monthly*, March 1992.
71. See Aristotle, *Metaphysics* IV (gamma), 4–5, in *The Complete Works of Aristotle*, II, pp. 1588–96.
72. G.W.F. Hegel, *The Encyclopedia Logic: Part 1 of the Encyclopedia of the Philosophical Sciences with the Zusätze*, trans. T.F. Geraets, W.A. Suchting and H.S. Harris, Indianapolis: Hackett, 1991, p. 119, Addition 2, p. 187.
73. See G. W. F. Hegel, *Philosophy of History*, trans. J. Sibree, New York: American Home Library, 1902, pp. 271ff.
74. See Hegel, *Philosophy of History*, pp. 295–96.
75. See Hegel, *Philosophy of History*, pp. 480–82.
76. See Hegel, *Philosophy of Right*, pp. 59–64, pp. 88–94.

77. See the original version of the "Question concerning Technology," in Wolfgang Schirmacher, *Technik und Gelassenheit: Zeitkritik nach Heidegger*, Freiburg i. B.: Alber, 1983, p. 25. See, for discussion, chapter 6: "Nazism and Technology," in Tom Rockmore, *On Heidegger's Nazism and Philosophy*, Berkeley: University of California Press, 1997, pp. 204–43.
78. According to Walzer, this is an impossible situation, since one could not then choose to defend innocent people. See Michael Walzer, *Arguing About War*, New Haven: Yale University Press, 2004, p. 13.

CHAPTER SIX

Globalization and Terrorism: Modernity or Jihad?

Hegemony at the level of the entire globe is a recurrent theme in American neoconservative political thought. There are different ways to arrive at planetary domination. Some might include the spread of a particular religion, military conquest, or political hegemony. But in our time the most effective way still seems to be the continued economic expansion of capitalism, the latest form of which is now being discussed with increasing frequency under the heading of globalization.

Conceptual models formulated to explain experience are constrained by their cognitive objects. We need to determine as best we can the factor or factors that drive the dispute between the largely non-capitalist Islamic world and the largely non-Islamic capitalist West to explain the crisis stage reached on and after 9/11. Is it, as Bush (at least publicly) appeared to believe, that our enemies feel called upon to act since they are simply evil? Is the main cause a religious difference, as Lewis claims? Is it the very existence of differences in civilization (or culture) as Huntington suggests? Or is it something less often mentioned in connection with 9/11: economic globalization? Could it be there is a social contradiction between different views of the good life, from the divergent perspectives of economic globalization, and conservative Islam?

Lewis, who diagnoses the conflict between the traditional Islamic world and the non-Islamic West as deriving from Islam's failure to modernize, seems to understand the modern world, or modernity, hence modernization, as a phase of human development that can only be attained by adopting liberal capitalism. This approach, which is tantamount to comprehending the modern world in solely economic terms, is obviously too narrow. Capitalism is a basic dimension of the modern world, one which cannot, however, merely be reduced to, nor understood solely in terms of, its economic framework. There are numerous other aspects of modernity that are not derivable from or reducible to economics; for example, religion, on which Lewis focuses. In the case of Islam, but not of the West, to modernize along capitalist lines implies renouncing an inherent identification of politics and religion—an identification that has long been a central feature of Islamic culture and which has no clear counterpart in the West. For Muslim countries to succeed in modernizing in the way Lewis has in mind would require them to give up central aspects of traditional Islam, hence willingly to forfeit vitally relevant differences, at least from the Islamic side, between Islam and the West.

Muslim and Western views of the conflict that has placed them in opposition derive from incompatible commitments on the part of the various participants. This is the first of two chapters that consider Muslim, and then Western, attitudes toward their complex series of interactions. I have already described and criticized explanatory models associated with Bush, Huntington, and Lewis. In the remaining chapters, I will sketch the outlines of an alternative interpretation of the three-cornered conflict among fundamentalist Muslims, less radical Muslims, and the mainly non-Islamic West. Like Lewis, I believe Islam is pluralistic. I will, for this purpose, be presupposing basic distinctions between conservative, more traditional forms of Islam, and more moderate, less traditional forms. I will have in mind how Islam is interpreted by different believing Muslims (which is reflected in their actions) as opposed to what may be found in Islamic texts.[1]

Religious fundamentalism is pluralistic. As one of many different types of fundamentalism, Islamic fundamentalism in the wider sense includes Islamic conservatism as well as a more narrow form of Islamic fundamentalism. Both conservatives and fundamentalists are committed to very traditional views of Islam. Yet, in practice the effects are very different. There is a crucial difference between conservative Muslims, who desire a religious life without change but are unwilling to resort to such extreme measures as terrorism, and more radical Muslim fundamentalists, who do not eschew, and on occasion even embrace, such measures.

The term Islamic "fundamentalism," which is primarily used in the West, is borrowed from Protestant fundamentalism. As applied to Islam, fundamentalism refers to the concern to adhere to and reproduce unchanged a traditional but perhaps mythical Islamic way of life. In the present context, I will take Islamic fundamentalism to describe two related but distinct phenomena: first, the proper attitude toward, and interpretation of, the sacred texts; second, the political usage of that interpretation in preserving or, as the case may be, in returning to the original, unaltered form of a life according to the favored interpretation of the principles of Islam as identified long ago by the Prophet.

This distinction can be described in different vocabulary, for instance as a difference between a "revealed" religion and "Islamism," the latter term having, in English, largely replaced "fundamentalist Islam." "Islamism" is understood as a set of political ideologies that hold that Islam is not only a religion but also a political system; that it is not (or not only) a revealed religion, but also a political ideology. A Western analogy might be "born-again," or evangelical Protestantism, which supposes unwavering acceptance of a particular religious view, sometimes leading, as in the case of George W. Bush, to a closely related neoconservative form of politics.

There are different ways to understand Islamic fundamentalism. Olivier Roy, one of the most interesting contemporary Western commentators on Islam, understands what he calls Islamic neofundamentalism along Salifist lines, hence on the model of the Saudi Arabian branch of Islam.[2] Islamic fundamentalism, which is not necessarily ideological, becomes ideological if it is combined with an effort to impose it on others. It is important to note that Islamic fundamentalism, perhaps like all religious fundamentalisms, is not basically ideological, but turns on the question of identity. Those concerned with fundamentalist forms of Islam are interested in recovering an identity that, for various historical reasons, has been weakened or even usurped by other considerations, such as the need to compromise with other, more flexible, more adaptable forms of Islam, keen on coming to grips with the modern world. In such cases, the concern of Islamic fundamentalists in hewing as close as possible to an imaginary line laid down by the Prophet, is to recover an imaginary view of religious perfection, which perhaps lies at the basis of all religion.

Radical and moderate forms of Islam differ in their respective interpretations of Islam. They feature different, clearly incompatible, strategies for coping with modern capitalism. The result is not, as is often suggested, a simple dichotomy between Islam and Christianity, or between Islam and the West. Islam and capitalism are not as such incompatible. A claim for their incompatibility in principle would be inexact for at least two reasons. First, any focus on an opposition between Islam and other religions masks a deep, abiding, intra-Islamic conflict beginning soon after the Prophet's death in 632 and continuing ever since. Sunnis and Shi'ites are at least as opposed to each other as they are to non-Muslims. Bin Laden, a Shi'ite of Saudi Arabian origin, is known to reject the Wahabite form of Shi'ite Islam, dominant in Saudi Arabia, at least as strongly as he does the other main Abrahamic religions. Second, Islam as such is not opposed to the West, although elements of Islam are. Capitalism flourishes in varying degrees in Malaysia, in parts of Turkey, and in several other Islamic countries. A very well known example is the combination of Islam and capitalism in central Anatolia, in what is called sometimes Calvinist Islam. In Kayseri or Hacilar, for instance, where one speaks of the "Anatolian tiger," prayer breaks have replaced coffee breaks. Still, this is an exception in the antagonism of traditional Islam to modern capitalism.

Conversely, the "West" functions here not only as a geographical location. What I am calling the "West" is in fact a complex entity that cannot simply be assimilated by, or "transposed on," the other two main Abrahamic religions. In fact, in varying degrees Western countries include all the major as well as minor religions, thus, Christians, Jews, Muslims, and all other faiths. France, for instance, a middle size European country with a population of slightly more than 60 million, currently has some five million Muslims. More generally, the West cannot simply be understood as the "other" of Islam, if for no other reason than that it also includes the full range of Muslim elements. It is well known that a number of the most radical Islamists are not Islamic but rather Western in origin.[3] The London suicide bombings in July 2005 were apparently carried out by four Muslims who were born and grew up in England.

Some might object, asserting that the problem is Islam itself, which is intrinsically conservative, and which jealously responds to any effort to modernize. Yet, the idea that civilization can only be defended by adhering to a strict religious code is by no means restricted to Islam, or even to the most conservative form of Islam.

This struggle between a religious equivalent of the quarrel between the ancients and the moderns, between those concerned with maintaining a particular faith intact and those who wish to update it, was notoriously played out in France in the last century. An instance is *Action française*, founded by Charles Maurras, for whom Roman Catholicism was reputedly the sole factor capable of defending civilization, and whose political desires were realized by Franco, Salazar, and Pinochet. Maurras was answered by Jacques Maritain.[4] Other French Catholics, more liberal, have tried to bring Catholicism into line with the modern world in resisting supposed excesses of papal power, in moving toward a more open form of socially-engaged, liberal form of Christianity, in linking the gospels to the resistance to totalitarianism, and in creating such social groups as *Action catholique*, *Jeunesse agricole*, and worker-priests. Suffice it to say, as this example shows, that over the centuries the problem of adapting a given religion to the modern world or, on the contrary, of maintaining it unaltered, continues to run throughout all the Abrahamic religions.

Inequality and the Relationship of Master and Slave

Events leading up to, including, and leading away from 9/11 feature a number of sharp-edged confrontations, often related to economic inequality dominated by capitalism. Like colonialism or imperialism, economic globalization is an inherently unequal process. In the same way as there are those who colonize and those who are colonized, the continued expansion of capitalism unequally empowers some and clearly "disempowers" others, while generating often very serious social tensions born of economic inequality.

The deepest, most general, and certainly the most interesting treatment of social inequality I know of is Hegel's famous analysis of the master-slave relationship.[5] This analysis provides a useful framework to interpret the complex, three-sided contradiction I believe is working itself out in 9/11. This section will, in very simple form, briefly sketch Hegel's analysis of social inequality prior to applying that analysis to understanding the conflict now under way.

In his analysis of inequality, Hegel builds on the view of Jean-Jacques Rousseau. In *The Social Contract* (1762), Rousseau famously writes: "Man is born free, and everywhere he is in chains. Many a one believes himself the master of others, and yet he is a greater slave than they."[6] According to Rousseau, when all people are subjected to, or subjugated by, the whim of a single individual, then by implication no one is free and, for that reason, everyone is "unfree" since, as he influentially notes, there is only a master and his slaves.[7]

Hegel follows Rousseau in stressing the nature and significance of inequality in modern society. He accepts the literal reality of inequality as a fundamental social dimension. In a highly original analysis, he depicts the slave as the "truth" of this inequality in pointing toward a revolutionary solution, seemingly anticipating the liberation movements of our own historical period. It has already been noted that Hegel was well versed in the economic theories of his time. He anticipates the complex relationship of force between what Marx will later call the bourgeoisie and the proletariat, roughly between those who own the means of production and those who own nothing more than their own capacity to work. Through the continuing extension of the global economic framework, the capitalist West increasingly plays the role of the owner of the means of production in "exploiting," for economic gain, a vast proletariat scattered throughout the world.

This relationship now takes many forms, some of which differ greatly from Marx's vision, in the middle of the nineteenth century, of the effects of British capitalism on the British population. The desperate nature of social inequality—in which the total absence of child labor laws sent little children to work at the crack of dawn, and infants were sent to jail and even executed for, say, stealing spoons—has for the most part given way to a "softer" form of capitalism in the West. Yet, significant inequality remains. The current "outsourcing" of labor-intensive forms of production to the Third and Fourth Worlds, above all to China, later perhaps to Vietnam, India, and Bangladesh, represents the extension of an unequal relationship among individuals, a relationship Hegel describes within the worldwide economic framework of modern capitalism. It is, then, no accident that the deplorable labor conditions in South China, in a country that is still officially Marxist but which, since Deng Xiaoping, clearly embraces a Chinese variant of capitalism, illustrate many of the same problems: subsistence wages, insufficient health care, social alienation of various kinds, and so on, problems Marx already discussed in the middle of the nineteenth century.

Hegel's analysis of the relationship of masters and slaves depends on the concept of recognition. This can take many forms, including a prize in the workplace, a distinction in the university, an expression of public thanks for heroism or service to the community, and so on. The basic human need to be recognized, or acknowledged, by others creates a double dependency. According to Hegel, a relationship to another person, to someone who can, should, will later, or can be "forced" in different ways to acknowledge me mediates my relation to myself. This relationship takes shape as a double opposition in which each person strives to achieve, and if necessary to force, or even to extort, recognition from the other. This relationship is obviously two-sided. To put the point simply, if the relationship is unequal, then individuals realize (or satisfy) their desires, including the desire of recognition, at the expense of others, who in turn do the same. This leads to an unromantic, but "realistic" view of modern social life in which, more often than not, as Smith already suggests for modern economic life, one "exploits" others to satisfy one's own needs.

Exploitation presupposes inequality. An unequal relationship between individuals often leads to conflict. The opposition between two individuals, understood as instances of self-consciousness, manifests itself in a conflict or struggle that can take many forms, but that invariably opposes each to the other. Each seeks recognition, or acknowledgment from the other, at the expense of the other in what, in extreme situations, can even take the form of a struggle to the death.

In an ideal world devoid of the tensions that pervade existing societies, each person would fully acknowledge the other through any one of numerous forms of mutual recognition.[8] Perhaps the most elementary form of mutual recognition in modern society is equality before the law. Yet, legal equality is a formal form of equality that holds only in theory, not in practice. In practice, legal representation, hence the degree of protection actually afforded by the law, depends on the financial means at one's disposal. After several thousand years of effort, we have still not arrived at the point of practical legal equality. Many places and many situations continue to feature important inequalities. In its most extreme form, opposition between individuals takes the form of a struggle in which each desires nothing more than the physical demise of the other.

One might think of a dictator who extorts recognition by threatening the other with death, for instance in our time in various forms of the cult of personality in totalitarian regimes. According to Hegel, it is only when we run the risk of death, in short when we very literally place our lives in the balance, that it is possible to receive meaningful recognition surpassing its general form, for instance acknowledgment in the "anonymous" juridical form widespread in contemporary Western society. Yet, there is a contradiction: recognition obtained at the price of the death of the other, which is self-stultifying, is, hence, not recognition at all. To suppress the other is at the same stroke also to suppress the possibility of recognition one seeks to wrest from the other.

The first possibility, which ends in death precluding any possible satisfaction through recognition, is also the most extreme outcome of this struggle. Hegel further analyzes a second possibility, more easily tolerated and certainly more widespread: the relationship of master and slave that does not lead to physical death but rather to numerous forms of inequality in which one person subjugates the other. In the modern world, for the most part, there is no question of doing away with, or actually killing, the other. The result is an enduring inequality, which often becomes stable, hence permanent. This type of relationship is illustrated virtually throughout modern society. Capitalism, arguably the most important "social force" in modern society, presupposes, not only in caricature, but also in fact, a basic inequality between those who own the means of production and those who work for them. Modern industrial society simply cannot function without a steady supply of labor, which comes from those who are willing, or at least able, to earn a living by producing a nearly endless list of commodities for the market places of the world.

Enduring inequality can either be stable or, with the passage of time, finally unstable. An unequal situation that loses its stability can become violent. For Hegel the domination masters exert on slaves is not only theoretical but also practical. Hegel specifically envisages the "development" of this relationship (which is subject to change, hence unstable) as always in principle capable of assuming another form. An example might be the change in the relationship between those who work in a factory and those who own it.

In practice, the "development" of this inequality tends to invert, hence subvert, the relationship of force between the one who dominates, the master, and the one who is dominated, the slave. It is as if the workers in the factory were to change their relationship to the owners, for instance by going on strike and withdrawing their labor, or by somehow acquiring a majority share in, or control of, the factory so that the workers replace the former management team, and so on.

Hegel entertains the idea that the transformation of the relationship of master and slave tends toward the transfer of power from the former to the latter. The result is an inversion in their relationship. The "truth" of this relationship is the opposite of what one might expect. In point of fact, through a "dialectical reversal" it is not the slave who depends on the master but the master who depends on the slave. This consequence follows from the inability of the master, the stronger of the two individuals, simply to "crush" or otherwise bring about the demise of the slave without thereby losing sight of the end in view: recognition. Or to put the point otherwise, factory owners simply cannot do without workers, without those who manufacture the products, since the work would grind to a halt.

Hegel's brilliant analysis of the master-slave relationship is widely influential. Hegel is routinely, but mistakenly, described as a conservative thinker, as someone one who identifies with, and is satisfied by, the status quo. Marxists traditionally criticize him for allegedly identifying with the Prussian restoration of his time.[9] But this is neither an accurate description of his own conviction nor of the main thrust of his position. On the contrary, his analysis suggests that though modern society appears stable, a deep potential for social transformation is permanently lodged at the center of modern capitalism.

To begin with, fear of the master, of the person or persons in authority, transforms what is in principle a neutral, impersonal relationship between workers and their bosses into a relationship of dependency. Yet, according to Hegel the slave, or dependent individual, becomes self-aware through work. Since self-consciousness is essentially liberating, self-awareness in and through work transforms the relationship of the slave to the master and, in the process, at least potentially and on occasion even actually (for instance through some sort of act that changes the relationship between the boss and the workers) frees the "slave." We see this occur not only in the work place but also in the family. An example might be a woman who is employed outside the house and, as a consequence of her new role becomes aware of herself and as a result demands equal rights in the family and society. In the ordinary situation, she would not be able to assert herself, which becomes possible by virtue of her participation in the economic process. In other words, participation in the capitalist version of the daily round results in undoing the fear emanating from the relationship of domination by the other. According to Hegel, when someone who is dominated within such a relationship becomes self-aware, this very awareness creates the possibility of social transformation.[10] In framing this transformation of the master-slave relationship through the struggle for recognition, Hegel anticipates Marx's later analysis of modern society from a more narrow economic perspective.[11] Though Marxists often detect in Hegel one who merely supports the status quo, the young Marx, though critical of Hegel, understood the revolutionary potential in the latter's analysis of the relationship between master and slave.

Intra-Muslim Rivalry and Islamic Fundamentalism

Hegel's brilliant analysis of the relationship of master and slave can serve as a metaphor for the unequal economic situation currently setting the Muslim world and the West in opposition. There are more than two hundred countries in the world, but from the economic perspective only a few count more than marginally. What is now called the G8, or Group of 8, is the successor to an economic forum created by France in 1975 that originally included France, Germany, Italy, Japan, the United Kingdom, and the United States, and currently includes Canada and Russia as well. It is fair to say that with the obvious additions of India, perhaps Brazil, and, above all China, the world's economy is currently mainly under the control of only a few countries. China and India are growing economies that aspire to the status of First-world countries, but are not yet there. This means the US and a handful of other First-world countries exert economic, military, political, and other forms of domination on the great majority of countries, with the clear exception of China, whose economic relation to the rest of the world is exceedingly complex.

This is particularly the case in the so-called Third or Fourth Worlds that play no more than a subordinate role in the current period of advanced industrial capitalism. An illustration is how, by exerting economic muscle and a variety of more or less veiled threats, President George W. Bush was able to assemble what he called the "coalition of the willing" to invade Iraq and prosecute the ensuing war. I come back to this point in the next chapter. This section will sketch a simple picture of Islam as the basis for an analysis of its relationship to the West.

The struggle between the competing parties turns on an ongoing struggle for economic "recognition" in a contest the terms of which terms are dictated by "financial masters" to "financial slaves." Much of the Islamic world is poor, hence dependent on the advanced industrial countries. Even exceptions, such as Qatar and Brunei, which are hardly typical—the GDP in Qatar, estimated at $39,607 for 2005, compared well at the time with those of Western European nations; the GDP in Brunei for 2003 was estimated at $23,600—depend on Western capitalist markets to buy their crude oil and natural gas.

The economic relationship between the masters and slaves of the world economy makes itself felt on different levels. These include the intra-Muslim rivalry around the identity of Islam; the earlier struggle of Islam against Christendom that, after the rise of capitalism, has increasingly been transformed into a defensive struggle against the economic encroachments of the West; and the Western reaction to the Islamic world. The intra-Islamic struggle, as well as the long-standing Islamic struggle against the West, will be discussed in this chapter.

Intra-Islamic rivalry arose quickly after Muhammad's death in 632. As in other Abrahamic religions, perhaps as in all religions, the struggle for the founder's mantle took the guise of the interpretation of the religion this individual founded. This complex struggle, which has never ceased, is still a central feature of contemporary Islam. It concerns the "correct" interpretation of a leading religion, including various facets of its relationship to the modern world. In respect to religion, this includes a number of factors. One is a struggle for political and religious hegemony in the Islamic world. Another is a conceptual quarrel around the normative nature of Islam, a struggle between strict, purist readings, linked to maintaining or recovering the original impulse without regard to later history, which is simply bracketed,[12] or to rethinking and transforming Islam in reaction to later developments, specifically including an ongoing dispute between Muslims about how they should be interacting with the mainly non-Muslim West.

Religions are often founded by charismatic figures (Buddha, Mohammed, Jesus). After the founder's passing, they are routinely, often substantially, transformed during the ensuing period of consolidation, development, and adaptation. The struggle for the soul of the Muslim religion, which broke out immediately after Muhammad's death, was unrelated to capitalism, which had not yet emerged, and only later became concerned with Christianity in reaction to the Crusades during the eleventh, twelfth, and thirteenth centuries. After capitalism arose, it became increasingly important to the interaction between Islam and the West.

It is useful to distinguish between the evolution of Islam after the death of the Prophet and the relations between Islam and the West. The Islamic world is large and very varied. There are at present more than fifty Muslim countries, which contain roughly 20 per cent of the world's population, as opposed to nearly 30 per cent among Christians. According to some estimates the Muslim population is growing at about 2.9 per cent annually, whereas the population of the world grows at 2.3 per cent annually. It is projected that by 2025 Christians will represent 25 per cent, but Muslims will represent 30 per cent of the population of the entire world.

There are legitimate questions about how to interpret Islam, hence how to interpret the relationship between Islam and the West. Edward Said famously suggested that the view of Orient favored in Western intellectual circles was largely imaginary.[13] This perspective has recently been applied to the present struggle between the largely non-Islamic West and militant Islam. In his review of a number of important thinkers (e.g. Burke, Tocqueville, the Mills, and Marx), Michael Curtis points out that their view of the Orient should now be nuanced.[14] Certainly the relationship between Islam and the West is more complex than is often thought. There may well be a point to Henri Pirenne's famous claim that feudalism in the West resulted from rapid economic advances in the Orient. It is possible, as Pirenne thinks, that without Islam the Holy Roman Empire, whose leadership Charlemagne assumed, would never have existed.[15]

In the present context, it is more important to understand the effect of the West on Islam than the Islamic contribution to the West. In simplifying greatly, the relations between Islam and the West record rapid growth after the death of Muhammad, later followed by a long, slow decline, and an inability, depending on the individual country, to adapt to capitalism as it took shape in the largely non-Muslim West. Within a century after the death of Muhammad, a great Islamic empire arose, stretching from Spain to the Great Wall of China. The golden age of

Islam was a period of Muslim dominance, which lasted until a decline set in beginning in the twelfth century. For several hundred years, Arabic was the most important scientific language, and Muslims made important advances in mathematics, astronomy, medicine, literature, architecture, and other fields. Beginning in the ninth century, the works of the Greeks were translated into Arabic. This was also an important period of trade, as Muslim countries developed and expanded mercantile relations.

The specifically Muslim view of economics later became a factor in the interaction between mercantilist Islam and the capitalist West. The ancient Greek thinkers were already concerned with economic themes. Plato, who rejected private property, favored exchange. Aristotle defended private property but rejected exchange. By the time we arrive at the Muslim thinkers, the situation has greatly changed. Both the Qur'an and the *hadith*, or the traditions compiled early in Islam about the Prophet's words and deeds, are favorable to wealth and profit as the result of exchange and productive activity. At about the same time, the medieval Christian church adopted the position that no Christian should be a merchant. The Prophet is said to have indicated that the role of the state should be limited in economic matters. Standard sources recount the highly developed character of mercantile activity in medieval Islamic society. This included such themes as fiscal and monetary policies, deficit financing, taxation to encourage production, credit and credit instruments for checking and savings accounts, banks, rules concerning partnerships, contracts, and monopolies. Various forms of economic activity were codified as early as the ninth century.[16] A series of Muslim writers praised economic activity and the accumulation of wealth, understood human beings as acquisitive, and denounced poverty. They also discussed division of labor, as well as barter and money, and the forces of supply and demand in fixing prices.

The problem of how to interpret the Prophet's heritage began very early. Over the centuries, this has taken the form of an answer to the question, which in different ways occurs in all religions: what should a Muslim believe and do? As in other religions, but also in such domains as literature, philosophy, and so on, there is a tension, or quarrel, between the ancients and the moderns. In religion, this takes the form of a dispute between those who favor strict adherence to the founder's view, or the view they attribute to that person, and those who favor adapting it to changing circumstances. The former are religious fundamentalists, who reject as such any and all efforts to abandon or to adapt the religion to changing circumstances, and the latter, who either seek to adapt or simply abandon the religion, turn away from fundamentalism in the direction of secularism.

In Islam, the problem of interpretation is complicated by several factors, including the composition of the only sacred text, the Qur'an, in formal Arabic, which is becoming steadily more archaic, and the question of the authenticity (or inauthenticity) of the hadith. As in other religions, further problems arise because of the difference between literal and nonliteral interpretation. It is usual that the founding texts of a major religion are either ambiguous or sufficiently vague to lend themselves to different interpretations, depending on what one wants to find there. Like other religions, the major divisions of Islam represent different interpretations of the same or a selection of the same texts.

Islam, is mainly, but not exclusively Arab. Iranians, Malians, Turks, Pakistanis, Indonesians, Indians, Nigerians and Somalis are non-Arab Muslims. Although not necessarily connected ethnically, Muslims are linked through a shared religious vision as component parts of a single religious community, or *umma*. The two main Islamic sects are the Sunnis, who comprise some 90 per cent of all Muslims, and the Shia, a small, but sometimes very powerful minority, especially in the Middle East in Iran, Iraq, and Lebanon. All Muslims agree in principle on five claims: *shahadah*, or the view that Muhammad is the messenger of God, who alone is worthy of worship; *salah*, or the five daily prayers; *zakat*, or the giving of charity (*zakaah*), which is distributed among the poor; *ramadhan*, or fasting from dawn to dusk during the month of *Ramadan*; and *hajj*, or the pilgrimage to Mecca, which is compulsory at least once during one's lifetime.

After this minimal core of agreement, there is the usual wide area of disagreement characteristic of other religions. There is, for instance, a range of different opinions concerning the Qur'an. Muslims believe the Qur'an was revealed to the Prophet by the Angel Gabriel between 610 and 632, and that the text available today is the same as that revealed to Mohammad and by him to his followers. Scholars believe the version of the Qur'an currently in use was compiled before 750 by the third caliph, Uthman ibn Affan. There is considerable controversy about the verses composing the Qur'an, including even their order. Since the Qur'an was written down in script without vowels, there is further controversy about the exact reading of many verses. As early as the eighth century, a split developed between the Mu'tazilis, who claimed the Qur'an was created in time and is not eternal, and those who, as in Ashari theology, claim it is perfect and eternal, since it existed in heaven before it was revealed to Muhammad.

This difference of opinion within Islam is sharpest between Islamic fundamentalists and more moderate Muslims. In general, Muslim religious and political conservatives, above all Muslim fundamentalists, are opposed to religious and political liberals. Muslim religious fundamentalism, which insists on the permanent, unchangeable character of Islam, is opposed to Islamic religious modernism, whose adherents take a more flexible, evolutionary approach to Islam, to which they are committed, but which they seek to adapt to changing circumstances. Islamic fundamentalism encompasses traditional Muslims, who restrict themselves to literal (or at least traditional) interpretations of the sacred texts, and who may be entirely apolitical, as well as Muslim groups advocating Islamism, including the replacement of secular state laws with *shari'a*, or Islamic law. Shari'a, which has a long and complicated tradition, is the sacred law of Islam, binding on all Muslims, and which is derived from two main primary sources: the revelations in the Qur'an and the sayings and examples of the Prophet in the Sunnah, or sayings and practices of Muhammad.

Fundamentalism, which is religiously extremely conservative, is antimodern, opposed to modernization, and associated with literal readings of the sacred texts as well as efforts to impose Islamic law. It is opposed by liberal movements, which are friendlier to modernity, and well disposed, or at least better disposed, to a modernization of Islam.

The struggle within Islam between fundamentalists and other conservatives as well as modernists arose soon after Muhammad died. An early, but important view was formulated by the legal philosopher ibn Taymiyya (1268–1328), who denied any distinction between religion and politics in refusing the subordination of religion to the state. According to ibn Taymiyya, the role of the ruler is to enforce shari'a and exhibit personal piety. Ibn Taymiyya was concerned with purifying the faith by distinguishing between true Muslims and others, and by restoring the place of jihad to the center of Muslim life. His work later was taken up by ibn Abd al-Wahhab (1703–1792) who strove to recover an authentic, unadulterated Islam, in the process inspiring the very puritanical Saudi brand of Islam known as Wahabism. Rashid Rida (1866–1935) later argued that Islam must be purged of impurities and Western influences in order to resist subordination to colonial powers. According to Rida, only a return to authentic Islam would bring Muslims political and economic power. He was succeeded in the last century by the multi-national Muslim Brotherhood, a Sunni fundamentalist group founded in Egypt in 1928 by Hosn al Banna. The credo of the Muslim Brotherhood points to an uncompromising adherence to conservative religious and political views, leading directly to armed struggle: "God is our goal. The Prophet is our leader. The Qur'an is our constitution. Struggle is our way. Death in the service of God is the loftiest of our wishes."[17]

This view was further elaborated by its most important adherent, Sayyid Qutb (1906–66). Qutb, the most important theological thinker in the Muslim Brotherhood, fused the core elements of modern Islam into a single coherent position. Qutb, who denied the legitimacy of human rule, considered the Egyptian government, which features human rule, as a legitimate target of jihad. He was a partisan of permanent revolution through jihad in order to destroy *jahili* or pre-Islamic, barbarous rule with a view to making possible the emergence of a pure Islamic society. He further rethought *jahiliyya*, a term that before Qutb was used to refer to pre-Muslim Arab society. Qutb, who thought in typically Manichean, dualistic categories, and who rejected the entire modern world in both Islamic and non-Islamic versions, reconfigured this term to refer to the barbarous nature of the contemporary world as such. According to Qutb: "Islam cannot accept any compromise with jahiliyya, either in its concept or in its modes of living derived from this concept. Either Islam will remain, or jahiliyya; Islam cannot accept or agree to a situation which is half-Islam and half-*jahiliyya*. In this respect Islam's stand is very clear. It says that truth is one and cannot be divided; if it is not the truth, than it must be falsehood. The mixing and coexistence of the truth and falsehood is impossible. Command belongs to Allah, or else to jahiliyya. The Shari'ah of Allah will prevail, or else people's desires."[18]

Qutb's reformulation of Islam as the rejection of modernity is one of the most extreme forms of fundamentalist Islam. This kind of neo-Islamic fundamentalism, with deep roots in the Islamic past, has proven very influential in recent years. As Roy points out, under the pressure of economic globalization, the wholesale destruction of traditional societies has strengthened the counter effort to reestablish the imaginary original Muslim community.[19]

There is an obvious analogy between the return to sources in Islam, which resists all changes, and its philosophical counterpart in Heidegger's aptly named fundamental ontology. The latter is fundamental in at least two senses: in a quasi-religious sense, which resists change of all kinds, and in the further sense that it is the supposed foundation of any real philosophy, in the same way as the most original form of Islam is the foundation of a certain view of an Islamic life. Islamic fundamentalism is an effort to recover Islam as it originally arose, which is as imaginary as the Heideggerian effort to recover the problem of the meaning of being, as it was initially raised in ancient Greece. The problem is the same. It is no more possible to go back before the later tradition to recover the original meaning of Islam than it is possible to go back before the philosophical tradition to recover early Greek philosophy as it initially emerged.

Since Islam is pluralist, it has many other strains as well. Islamic fundamentalism should not be allowed to obscure Islamic modernism. Jamal al-Din al-Afghani (1838–97), often regarded as the father of Islamic modernism, is particularly important. He argued, on the basis of the Holy Qur'an, the central religious text in Islam, in favor of *ijtihad*, or independent judgment and interpretation. He believed human beings must apply the principles of the Qur'an afresh to the problems of the time. He was extremely critical of *ulama*, religious scholars, who discouraged any new and creative thought. He was convinced this type of medieval mentality was primarily responsible for the decline of Muslim power and influence in the world. He denied the distinction between Muslim knowledge and European knowledge in insisting on the importance of acquiring Western knowledge to improve the lives of Muslims. He was followed by Muhammad Abduh (1849–1905), who insisted that Muslims could improve their lives by carefully studying the Qur'an in the light of reason and rationality. He taught that the Qur'an gives all Muslims the right to differ, even with the ulama, if the latter were unreasonable or irrational. There are also Islamic sects that strive to adapt the Muslim faith to the modern world. For instance, the Daudi Bohras, who claim a direct relationship to the Prophet through his daughter, and who live mainly in India and Yemen, were traditionally traders. Today they are increasingly doctors or allied with the medical profession.

Islam, Islamic Fundamentalism, Economics, and the West

Long before Qutb, for Muslim fundamentalists the encounter with the modern world took the form of a struggle between partisans of the return to, and defense of, a purified, original form of their religion, and everyone else, including followers of a more modern form of Islam, which fundamentalists reject, as they also reject the largely non-Muslim West. The starkly binary worldview of Muslim fundamentalists like Qutb turns them against the modern world, both within and without Islam. And it simply equates contemporary Islam and the extra-Islamic world, both of which, from the perspective of Muslim fundamentalists, fall short of the goal of a life as organized according to the principles of the supposed original version of Islam.

The contemporary Muslim encounter with the West, which cannot merely be reduced to economics, but which also cannot be severed from it, is very complex. This encounter occurs on different levels. As concerns economics, it pits mercantilism, the form of economics authorized by the Islamic religion, against postmercantilist, largely Western capitalism, an economic form which, although once fostered, aided, and abetted by religion, is by now largely independent of it.

Mercantilism is an approach to the entire range of economic activity that, in the West and in parts of the non-West (including portions of the Muslim world such as Turkey and Malaysia) later developed into capitalism.[20] Mercantilism can be roughly defined as an economic system for the distribution of goods in order to realize a profit. Goods are bought at one site for a certain price and then moved to another site and sold at a higher price. Mercantilism features strict government control, which developed during the decay of feudalism in order to accumulate bullion and is sometimes identified as its defining characteristic: to bring about a favorable balance of trade, to develop agriculture and manufacturing, and to establish foreign trade monopolies.

Capitalism shares with mercantilism the general aim of realizing profits by acquiring goods for lower prices and selling them for higher prices. It differs from mercantilism in three further characteristics: First, there is the accumulation of the various means of production (materials, land, tools), termed capital in the form of property, into a few hands, those of the "capitalists" or property owners, or the owners of the means of production. Second, productive labor—the human work necessary to produce and distribute goods—takes the form of wage labor. That is, individuals work for wages rather than for products they produce. It follows that the worker, who in effect sells a quantity of wage labor (or more precisely labor time) for a wage, in turn provides a product that is sold in the market. Labor also becomes "efficient" in that it becomes defined by its "productivity." Capitalism increases individual productivity through "the division of labor," which divides productive labor into its smallest components. In a famous passage, Adam Smith discusses how workers make pins in a pin factory in arguing that division of labor greatly increases productivity:[21]

> But in the way in which this business is now carried on, not only the whole work is a particular trade, but is divided into a number of branches, of which the greater part are likewise peculiar trades. One man draws out the wire, another straights it, a fourth points it, a fifth grinds it at the top for receiving the head; to make the head requires two or three distinct operations; to put it on, is a particular

> business, to whiten the pins is another; it is even a trade by itself to put them in the paper; and the important business of making a pin is, in this manner, divided into about eighteen distinct operations, which, in some manufactories, are all performed by distinct hands, though in some others the same man will sometimes perform two or three of them. I have seen a small manufactory of this kind where only ten men were employed, and where some of them consequently performed two or three distinct operations. But though they were very poor, and therefore but indifferently accommodated with the necessary machinery, they could, when they exerted themselves, make among them about twelve pounds of pins in a day. There are in a pound about four thousand pins of a middling size. Those ten persons, therefore, could make among them upwards of forty-eight thousand pins in a day. But if they had all wrought separately and independently, and without any of them having been educated to this particular business, they certainly could not each of them have made twenty, perhaps not one pin a day; that is, certainly, not the two hundred fortieth, perhaps not the four thousand eight hundredth part of what they are at present capable of performing, in consequence of a proper division and combination of their different operations.

The result of the division of labor is to lower the value (in terms of skill and wages) of the individual worker. Third, the means of production and labor are both "manipulated" by the capitalist, or owner of the means of production, who uses rational calculation in order to realize a profit.

Traditional Muslims often favor mercantilism, but not full-blown capitalism, for religious reasons. It is not difficult to see why. Capitalism reflects Smith's view that individuals should freely pursue their own interests in featuring economic freedom for the fortunate few on the assumption that society as a whole will benefit. In capitalism, the production and distribution of goods and services are understood as independent endeavors that exist apart from such other concerns as politics, ethics, and religion. The "mechanical" capitalist model is organized around predictable laws that are the basis of rational calculations carried out with the aim of increasing (national) wealth, which is understood as leading to happiness.

Capitalism separates church and state in the belief that the "rational" way to respond to human needs is through economic activity. This separation does not exist in Islam, which presupposes that the only "rational" way to meet human needs is through the rigorous observance of God's laws. While capitalism depends on relative scarcity in fixing prices, in Islam, at least in principle, all basic needs are guaranteed by the state and market price is simply ignored. This leads to numerous specific differences with respect to ordinary capitalist practices. In capitalism (which features laissez-faire), as a result of the separation between economics and ethics, money can in practice be earned by any legal means. But in Islam, which does not distinguish between economics and ethics, though wealth is not discouraged, wealth is not, as is so often the case in capitalism, an end in itself. Weight is further placed on the distinction between just, or *halal*, and unjust earnings. Money, which must be earned according to the ethical standards prescribed by religion, must not be allowed to eclipse such religious duties as prayer or pilgrimage. Muslims must reject opportunities to earn money through interest, gambling, pornography, and liquor, all of which are proscribed, or *haram*, off limits to the observant individual. Money is redistributed through regular charity to those in need. Other differences include rejection of all forms of insurance, as well as cooperatives, monopolies, and any form of price-fixing, and speculation in gold and silver. Islamic law famously prohibits usury and perhaps, though this is controversial, even interest. In 1991, in a landmark decision the Federal Shari'a Court of Pakistan declared that the concept of interest was repugnant to Islam. In contemporary Islam many banks claim not to charge interest, but it is, however, hidden in different ways, for instance through charging a premium. Investment funds are allowed. But instead of paying a fixed return linked to face value, they carry a prorated profit actually earned by the fund, the pooled return from which must be invested in a business acceptable to shari'a.

Muslim History, Western Religion, and Capitalism

There is an obvious dissimilarity between Western (largely Christian) and Islamic (largely non-Western) views of Islam's role in the contemporary world, in which economic globalization increasingly holds sway. The US, still the leading Western industrialized nation, is the focal point of the Western attitude toward Islam. The US is a comparatively young country, with a relatively short history, which enables many things to happen because it is not mired in tradition, which often impedes the much older European nations. Yet the same lack of long tradition, which makes so many things possible, is an obstacle for a historical grasp of the modern world and of the American place in the wider international arena. The Islamic view of its role is the result of a much longer history dating back to the 700s. Many Muslims believe they have often been humiliated by the Christian West. Instances include the Crusades, as well as numerous military conflicts, many of which the Islamic side lost, and, more recently, increasing economic encroachments of Western capitalism into the Muslim geographical space. With the advent of capitalism, these economic battles have become more and more unequal. From the Islamic side, those engaged in jihad, the *mujahideen*, are ready to sacrifice themselves to preserve their view of the good life based on Islam. At stake from the Western perspective is continued and ever-increasing economic domination. This reaches a new peak in the sacrifice of Western soldiers for what the administrations of George W. Bush, continuing a long tradition, which has obvious roots in Woodrow Wilson's espousal of an activist foreign policy to spread American values, called democracy[22] and freedom. This dual objective was publicly justified during the Iraq War in both secular and religious terms. In the former, it was described as the necessary struggle against Islamic terrorists. It was characterized more subtly in the latter as the struggle for the democratic way of life rooted in, and justified by, Christianity.

From the Islamic side, the interaction between the Islamic countries and the West is a result of Western incursions in, and effective rule of, a large number of countries. Muslims often believe the nineteenth century was a century of political oppression during which powerful Western nations effectively "enslaved" most of the Asian and African nations, including many Muslim countries.

Recent interactions between Islam and the West have been marked by a series of hostilities in Palestine, Afghanistan, Chechnya, Bosnia, Iraq, and Lebanon, as well as wars in Afghanistan sandwiched between two wars concerning Iraq, and the so-called global war on terror. These are all cases in which a besieged, generally poor, and often discouraged Muslim population is pitted against an enormously more powerful Western foe. The global war on terror, in principle directed against terrorists everywhere, often appears to Muslims to be directed mainly against Muslims. These wars belong to an ongoing process, lasting numerous centuries, that, in Muslim eyes, has been largely unfavorable to them. Further, there is the issue, significant both for Western policies toward Arab countries as well as for Muslims impacted by them, that economic sanctions on Iraq resulted in many deaths, including hundreds of thousands of Iraqi children.[23] Another relevant theme is what Muslims everywhere—as well as not a few non-Muslim Westerners—regard as basically unfair US policies toward the Palestinians. This includes inordinate American tolerance of Israeli "misconduct" in relations with Muslims, over many years in Palestine,[24] including in Gaza, in Lebanon, and elsewhere. Iraqi Sunnis have a similar view of the close American relationship with Iraqi Shi'ites after the American-led invasion and occupation of their country.

These specific circumstances are the visible face of a perhaps more insidious phenomenon. This consists in the economic "penetration" and subsequent transformation of Islamic society, at all levels, as part of the transformation of colonialism into economic domination with obvious political and military aspects. In the Islamic world, the latter currently includes American bases in such countries as Saudi Arabia and Qatar as well as throughout the old Silk Road as part of continuing economic expansion. This expansion has given rise in the Islamic world to what looks very much like a counter-effort, less to conquer Western countries, which no one has so far suggested, than to "defend" the continued existence of Islam against Western economic incursions. One of the main "defensive" mechanisms, very much in evidence in current Islamic terrorism, is a transformation of the concept of jihad into an instrument of terror.

Terror as a political instrument is certainly not a Muslim invention. It was already practiced much earlier, for instance by Russian anarchist groups in the nineteenth century. It was later introduced into the Middle East in the 1940s by Jewish insurgents in what was then occupied Palestine. The Irgun, the Stern Gang, and the Hagana began bombing crowded Arab areas to terrorize the population and force the British to withdraw from Palestine.

To understand the appeal of terrorism in the Islamic context, it is necessary to comprehend, at least in barest outline, the history of Islam's interaction with (and eventual humiliation by) the West. This history is one of Islamic strength followed by increasing decline and fall to a point where Islam now plays the role of a strategically important, but relatively helpless, giant community. When Muhammad died in 632, he and his followers controlled the entire Arabian Peninsula. Within a hundred years of his death, Islam had become a vast empire, spreading from the Atlantic to the gates of Central Asia.

There followed two Islamic civil wars, or *fitna*. The First Fitna, or first Islamic Civil War, also called the Fitna of the Killing of Uthman, began as a struggle over who had the right to become the caliph, supreme ruler of the caliphate, the Islamic realm. This war, which began with the assassination of Uthman Ibn Affan, resulted in a permanent division of Islam into Shi'a and Sunni sects. The Second Fitna, the dates of which are uncertain, was a period of political and military unrest in the entire Islamic empire. A main event during this period was the Battle of Karbala on *Muharram* 10 in the year 61 of the Islamic calendar (October 10, 680) at Karbala, now in Iraq. The battle involved supporters and relatives of Muhammad's grandson Hussein ibn Ali against the forces of Yazid I, the Umayyad caliph. This battle, still commemorated by the Shi'a and many Sunnis, is often cited as the definitive break between the two sects.

These fitna were followed by the invasion and later final defeat of the Turks, who were in turn followed by the Mongols, and then the Ottoman Turks, who conquered the Byzantines. The Ottomans expanded until their decisive defeat in the Battle of Vienna in 1683, after which they withdrew from Eastern Europe and much of the Balkans. During the eighteenth century, there were still three great Muslim empires. The Ottoman Empire, ruling from Turkey, lasted from 1299 to 1923 and at the height of its power in the sixteenth and seventeenth centuries encompassed parts of three continents (West Asia, Southeast Europe, and North Africa), and was for some six centuries at the center of exchanges between the East and the West. The Safavids, who were Shi'a, were one of the most significant ruling dynasties in Iran, establishing the greatest Iranian empire since the Islamic conquest of Persia. The Safavid empire, which began to arise in the fifteenth century—the Safavids were a native Iranian dynasty from Iranian Azerbaijan—included at its peak Iran, Georgia, Afghanistan, Azerbaijan, and parts of other countries. The Safavids, who ruled Iran from 1501 to 1722, spread the Shi'a sect into major parts of the Caucasus and West Asia. To the east, the Mughal (Mogul) empire was founded by Zahir ud-din Muhammed Babur, a Muslim conqueror from Central Asia. He was a direct descendent of Timur through his father and a descendant of Genghis Khan through his mother. The Mughal empire ruled a large part of the Indian subcontinent, beginning in 1526 and expanding into much of South Asia by the late seventeenth and early eighteenth centuries.

All three great Muslim empires were destroyed as the result of contact with the West. The Safavid state came to an end in 1760 with the fall of Ismail III. The Mughal empire, which lasted a century and a half, included most of the Indian subcontinent, as well as parts of what is now Afghanistan and Western Pakistan. It was finally dissolved by the British capture of Delhi in 1857, when the last king,

Bahadur Zara Shah II, was exiled. During the First World War, as part of the defeat of Ottoman forces in the Middle Eastern theater, most territories of the Ottoman Empire were captured by the Allies. This led indirectly to the Treaty of Lausanne in 1923, after which modern Turkey emerged.

Islamic relations with the West were initially determined by religious and later by economic objectives. The Crusades were a series of military campaigns (usually sanctioned by the papacy) that occurred from the eleventh through the thirteenth centuries. The Crusades were waged against infidels, including Muslims, pagans, heretics, and those who had been excommunicated. Their original purpose was to capture the Holy Land from the Muslims, but there were also other objectives, such as that of the Fourth Crusade (1202–04), directed against Constantinople. The First Crusade (1095–99), which resulted in the capture of Jerusalem and the massacre of its Jewish and Muslim inhabitants, was an important turning point in the expansion of the West at Muslim expense.

In general, Islam has been in steady territorial retreat since the Turkish defeat in the 1683 Battle of Vienna, usually taken as marking the end of Ottoman expansion into Europe. As a result of the Treaty of Berlin in 1879, the Ottoman Empire lost roughly four fifths of its territory. In 1882, the British occupied Egypt. In 1901, the French occupied Morocco. In 1928, Turkey became a secular state. In 1946, Jordan, Lebanon, and Syria were granted independence by Britain and France. In 1947, Pakistan was created as India became independent, leading to a series of conflicts among Muslim or partly Muslim states. In 1948, Israel became a state over Arab objections. In 1967, Israel won the Six Day War, defeating combined Arab forces, and in the process seizing control of Jerusalem, the West Bank of Jordan, the Gaza Strip and Sinai Peninsula from Egypt, and the Golan Heights from Syria. In 1980, Iraq (with US encouragement) invaded Iran in a war lasting eight years. In 1991, a US-led military coalition liberated Kuwait from Iraqi occupation. In 1987, Palestinians began their first *intifada*, a popular uprising against Israeli rule, which lasted until 1993. On September 11, 2001, members of al Qaeda, a radical Islamic organization, launched attacks on the US, and the US and its allies declared a war on terrorism and invaded Afghanistan. Finally, on March 20, 2003, the US and its allies invaded Iraq.

This brief outline points to the conclusion that Islamic civilization, which reached a relative highpoint within a century after Muhammad's death, has been on the decline ever since. Religious unity among Muslims has been increasingly fractured by strife among Islamic countries as well as by the inability of the Islamic community either to find its place within the wider community of nations or to resist the encroachments of Western power. The steady extension of the West into Islamic space has resulted in a much-weakened Islamic world, which is substantially dominated economically, hence politically and militarily, at virtually every turn in the road.

Overwhelming and steadily increasing Western economic power has reduced the Islamic countries, despite their great proven oil and gas reserves, to the status of weakened role players. The two-fold Islamic response has been either cooperation or resistance, both of which take many forms. A number of Islamic countries, including Egypt, Pakistan, and Saudi Arabia have cooperated to varying degrees with the West, especially the US. The other response running throughout countries in the Islamic world, and which has mainly manifested itself on the religious plane, features religious fundamentalism. Islamic fundamentalism has proliferated in response to perceived Muslim weakness, frequently through aggressive and novel use of jihad. Jihad, which over the centuries has evolved within Islam, now increasingly takes the form of a defensive, terrorist response, a reaction of the weak against the strong, in answer to Western domination.

Jihad and the Defense of Islam

There is widespread ignorance in non-Islamic circles about jihad. According to Fukuyama, *jihadism* is a product of modernization and globalism.[25] In fact, jihad is deeply rooted in the Islamic tradition.

Jihad, a verbal noun that means to struggle or to strive (from the verb *jahada*, exerting oneself or striving), is difficult to grasp. The frequent Western rendering of this term as "holy war" is arguably a simplistic misrendering for a more subtle and flexible doctrine, which may, but need not, lead to bloodshed. Jihad has a long and complicated history that goes back to the Qur'an.[26] The first detailed studies of the concept were written during the second half of the eighth century,[27] and complex debate about it has continued ever since. Since the texts are ambiguous and can be taken to support different lines of interpretation, there is no real prospect of arising at a definitive interpretation, which changes as the situation changes.

Muslims generally distinguish between "greater jihad," which concerns the struggle against oneself, including one's bad inclinations, roughly like the Platonic struggle against one's base impulses, and "lesser jihad," which involves war and other forms of physical struggle. Muslim scholars further distinguish other forms of jihad. According to Maxime Rodinson, "Jihad is a propagandistic device which, as need be, resorts to armed struggle—two ingredients common to many ideological movements."[28] Jihad generally includes all forms of struggle as concerns God. Such struggle, which may or may not be political, also includes many other things, such as pilgrimage or even taking care of elderly parents. President Habib Bourguiba of Tunisia issued an economic jihad in 1960, requiring his subjects to work harder to remedy the economic backwardness of the country. His idea was that fasting was not religiously obligatory during Ramadan. Another form is the so-called "educational jihad," either within Muslim society, as a kind of home mission, or among unbelievers through argument and demonstration, much as the Mormons proselytize, as a kind of external mission. The Qur'an regards jihad, which can, but need not, take the form of holy war, and which is often understood in a military sense, as the greatest deed of a Muslim.

Ibn Taymiyya situated jihad on the same level as the five pillars of Islam. He transformed it into a weapon against other Muslims as well as infidels, including

Crusaders and Mongols, in arguing for jihad against apostates within Islam. The result was to create the potential for revolutionary violence at the heart of Islam by overturning the principle that war against other Muslims was never justified, or is justified only by denying them status as Muslims, for instance in classifying them as apostates.

Prior to modern times, jihad took three main forms. These include a classical, legal view of jihad as a compulsory effort to defend and expand Islam; Ibn Tamiyya's idea of "active jihad" as belonging to legitimate rule; and the Sufi doctrine of greater jihad, or the internal struggle of the soul. In the modern period, jihad has evolved in opposing directions linked to Islamic modernism and fundamentalism.

Modernists and fundamentalists employ jihad in different ways for the dual purposes of instructing and mobilizing the people. In general, Islamic modernists are "realists" who strive to come to grips with the changing world as it exists at a given time. This includes finding a way to coexist with the modern world outside Islam. In contrast, Islamic fundamentalists are "idealists," who reject a modern world (in which coexistence is both possible and even desirable) in favor of an entirely traditional Islamic world in which it will be neither necessary nor desirable to compromise with those who reject Islam. They reject change in favor of an unchanging, starkly traditional, uncompromising Islamic view of the world seen as closely as possible through the eyes of the Prophet.

Both Muslim modernists and Muslim fundamentalists are reacting to relentless Western economic penetration, the modernists defensively in compromising with, and in adapting Islam to, Western practices and values, and the fundamentalists also defensively in reasserting traditional Islamic practices and values against Western alternatives, which they reject. Islamic modernists emphasize the defensive aspect of jihad, which is permitted outside of Islam if, and only if, a Muslim proselytizing among nonbelievers is being hindered, or again if Muslims situated outside the Islamic world are being oppressed. This is a modern version of the traditional Muslim "expansionist" view. Sayyid Ahmad Khan, a modernist writing in the nineteenth century, argued that, since jihad only means defensive war, it could not justify further resistance to British rule if the British did not interfere with the practice of Islam. Similarly, Rashid Rida positioned jihad as a defensive doctrine in claiming the Qur'an regards fighting as defense against those opposed to Muslims because of their religion.[29]

While emphasizing the defensive aspect of jihad, Muslim fundamentalists place more weight on its function in propagating a traditional version of Islam. They are particularly concerned with preventing domination over others through human law by turning to shari'a, literally the "way" or the "path," which is God's law, the sacred law of Islam. In this sense, jihad functions to promote liberation in the here and now, hence human happiness, at the cost of submitting to God's law. Thus Abul A'ala Mawdudi (1903–79), an Indian and later Pakistani Muslim theologian, apparently the first Islamic writer to provide a systematic account of jihad, presents it as warfare to expand Islamic political dominance in view of establishing a just rule, including freedom of religion. For Mawdudi, jihad takes the form of a war of liberation, and Islamic rule means freedom and justice for Muslims and non-Muslims alike. His approach creates the possibility of joining forces with anti-colonialist, national liberation movements, as well Arab resistance to Zionism and Israel. His conception of jihad is amenable to secular as well as nationalist interpretations. Hasan al-Banna and Sayyid Qutb both build on Mawdudi's view of jihad as an instrument to establish truly Islamic government. They argue, like Ibn Taymiyya, that jihad includes armed struggle against all governments that fail to enforce shari'a law. Qutb maintains that Islam must, in the course of establishing a different social, political and economic order, liberate human beings from something that is not God. Similarly, al-Daqa argues that it is only in capitulating to the pressures of "Orientalists"[30] that Muslim scholars accept a merely defensive reading of jihad.[31] Another way to put the same point is that Muslim modernists accept coexistence between the non-Islamic and the Islamic worlds, but Muslim fundamentalists accept only the universal victory of Islam.

The appeal to jihad is hardly novel. It is the application of an instrument already studied centuries ago by Ibn Taymiyya in different circumstances. According to scholars, it is unclear if the Qur'an authorizes Muslims to fight unbelievers only in response to aggression or in all circumstances. In early Islam, it was regarded as the duty of the umma to expand, with the aim, by eradicating unbelief, of eventually bringing the whole world under Islamic sway. In this sense, jihad functioned as an instrument of expansionist policy not dissimilar to similar policies in the other Abrahamic religions.[32] In modern times, at least for Muslim fundamentalists, who regard their religion as under attack, jihad has become an adaptive mechanism of Islam that is confronted with an increasingly secular world. It is the weapon of the weak against the strong, wielded mainly, but not exclusively, by relatively powerless but deeply religious Muslim fundamentalists. In resorting to terrorism, they are reacting against more powerful but, in their view, secular or overly secular Muslims and unbelievers of all kinds to defeat or at least destabilize the enemy while winning new recruits. Terror is also increasingly a weapon employed by Muslims living outside the Islamic countries, [33] with which fundamentalist Muslims may or may not have direct contact, as already noted in the Muslim terrorist attack in London.

There is an increasing tendency to interpret jihad as an individual's obligation. In April 1948 the *mufti* of Egypt, Hasanayn Muhammad Makhluf, issued a *fatwa*, or Muslim legal opinion, to the effect that all Muslims were individually obliged to contribute financially to the struggle against the efforts of Zionists to establish a Jewish state by force. The Zionist aim, according to Makhluf, is "take possession of Palestine, but also to dominate all Islamic states and to eliminate their Arabic character and their Islamic culture."[34] Anyone participating in this jihad must respect the rules as drawn up by the Arab League. Similarly, in November 1977 the Congress of the Academy of Islamic Research—it had previously issued fatwas regarding the duty of all Muslims to realize the aims of the Palestinians in destroying Israel in order to establish in its place a Palestinian state—issued a fatwa to liberate the territories occupied in 1967, to establish an independent Palestinian state, and to return to Jerusalem.

Roughly since the defeat of the Arab countries by Israel in 1967, jihad has been revived as Muslim fundamentalists sought to make their presence felt. Jihad is not a weapon of the powerful but of the powerless against those who wield or who are thought of as wielding power. It is a means to strike back against the richer and more powerful countries and their representatives as well as against Muslims who fail to live up to the requirements of their religion.

In the hands of a Muslim fundamentalist, jihad is a terrorist weapon, but it is not irrational. In the Islamic world terror is the weapon of choice of militant organizations which have no other weapons. In a way similar to ETA, the IRA, and other terrorist organizations, fundamentalist Muslims who engage in terrorism have a specific religious goal. Unlike, say, such secular terrorist groups as the RAF or ETA, their aim is not simply to disrupt public life, nor to undermine institutions, but rather to bring about a return to Islam as it originally emerged.[35]

Muslim fundamentalists have been encouraged by a number of developments, for instance in Egypt, even before this war on terrorism. Fundamentalists were opposed to the Egyptian government, because it was insufficiently Islamic. It did not rely on shari'a instead of human laws, and it negotiated a peace treaty with Israel. The Muslim Brotherhood tried but failed to assassinate Egyptian president Gamal Abdel Nasser, who favored a secular approach to Islam. The Brotherhood was later repressed and Qutb, its leading theoretician, who was especially important in transforming jihad into a terrorist rationale, was imprisoned and in 1966 executed. After the 1979 Camp David agreements between Egypt and Israel, President Anwar Sadat continued on Nasser's secularist path by allowing the clearer emergence of class distinctions between the rich and the poor. A contradiction arose as the government simultaneously encouraged a rapprochement with the West and the Islamization of public life and discourse through various groups (e.g. Jamat Islamiyya, al-Dawa) promoting the ideal of an Islamic state by peaceful means. After Sadat cracked down on fundamentalist groups like the Muslim Brotherhood, others committed to similar aims arose in their place. They included the Military Academy Organization, which was implicated in a failed assassination attempt, The Association of Muslims, which kidnapped and assassinated a minister, and the Jihad Organization, which assassinated Sadat in October 1981.

The revolutionary violence that has erupted in Egypt and elsewhere in the Arab world since the 1970s is not a mere historical aberration. Nor is it simply attributable, as the administration of George W. Bush claimed, to a small fringe group of fanatics outside the Muslim mainstream. It is, rather, a reaction to events in which fundamentalist Muslims have been rethinking Islam and jihad's role within it. Thus Hosn Al-Banna, the leader of the Muslim Brotherhood, was in the 1940s already maintaining that the teachings of Islam must govern all facets of life for everyone. He supported the use of force as a last resort against the Egyptian government to realize God's plan everywhere.[36] Similarly, Ayatollah Ruhollah Khomenei, who led the Iranian Revolution, affirmed as early as 1942 that Islam does not counsel against, but rather for, war.[37] Qutb extended this notion by contending that everything in this world, including Islamic thinking and culture of all kinds, is simply barbaric, or jahiliyya.

According to Qutb, "Islam must defend itself against aggressors" in the course of replacing human rule with divine rule.[38]

For Qutb and others influenced by him, jihad becomes an instrument for redressing the failure of Islamic states, such as Egypt, to conform to the fundamentalist Islamic understanding of shari'a, but also for reacting against the perceived aggression of the West. The view that Islam is justified in waging war against Western aggression, hence in employing jihad as a defensive measure, is a constant theme in recent writings of important Muslim figures. In a speech delivered at the opening ceremonies of the Eighth Organization of the Islamic Conference [OIC] Summit Meeting in Tehran in 1979 —the OIC, which has 57 member states, is a permanent delegation to the UN—, Ali al-Husseini al-Khamenei, Iran's spiritual guide after the 1979 Iranian revolution, maintained that the Iranian revolution and Islam are incorrectly depicted in the West. He complained about "colonialism, neocolonialism, and recently the extensive and all-out political, economic, propagandistic, and even military invasion by previous colonizers and their heirs."[39] According to Khamenei, "The West, in its all-rounded invasion, has also targeted our Islamic faith and character."[40]

There is a difference between the declarations of religious and spiritual figures, and those of revolutionaries. In 2002, when Ayman al-Zawahiri, an al Qaeda leader, addressed the importance of the Afghan war for the Islamic revolution, he distinguished between foreign and domestic enemies: "This situation led the homeland to the brink of the abyss of domestic ruin and surrender to the foreign enemy, exactly like the current situation of the majority of our [Arab] countries under the aegis of the new world order. . . ."[41] A more detailed public statement of grievances in the form of a fatwa calling for jihad on the part of each individual Muslim in response to the American waging of war against Islam exhorted Muslims to kill Americans and their allies. In this fatwa, published on February 23, 1998 in *Al-Quds al-'Arabi*, an Arabic newspaper in London, a long list of prominent leaders of jihad groups, including Osama bin Laden, complained, in reference to the 1991 Gulf War, that for seven years the US had been occupying and plundering Arab lands in view of fighting against Islam. Significantly, they also complained, before the onset of the 2003 war in Iraq, that the US was engaged in aggression against the Iraqi people in what was described as a Crusader-Jewish alliance. They further stated, "While the purposes of the Americans in these wars are religious and economic, they also serve the petty state of the Jews," and "There is no better proof of this than their eagerness to destroy Iraq . . . and their attempt to dismember all the states of the region[, which] would ensure the survival of Israel and the continuation of the calamitous Crusader occupation of the lands of Arabia."[42]

Notes

1. In claiming there is no difference between moderate and fundamentalist Muslims Harris simply obviates any distinction between how Muslims understand their religion and what the texts can be read as saying. See chapter 4: "The Problem

with Islam," in Sam Harris, *The End of Faith: Religion, Terror and the Future of Reason*, New York: W.W. Norton, 2004, pp. 108–52.

2. See Olivier Roy, *L'Islam mondialisé*, Paris: Editions du Seuil, 2002, pp. 145–78.
3. See Ladan and Roya Bouroumand, "Terrorism, Islam and Democracy," *Journal of Democracy* 13, no. 2, pp. 5–20.
4. See Jacques Maritain, *Integral Humanism: Temporal and Spiritual Problems of a New Christendom*, trans. by Joseph W. Evans, New York: Charles Scribner's Sons, 1968.
5. "Master" and "slave" are widely accepted English translations of Hegel's terms: "Herr" is a courtesy title used in ordinary German in the way "Lord," "Mister," or "Sir" are used in English, and "Knecht," an older term, with a pejorative meaning, to refer to a "servant," originally the servant of a knight, and that by extension as a verb (knechten) means "to subjugate."
6. Jean-Jacques Rousseau, *The Social Contract and Discourse on the Origin of Inequality*, edited by Lester Crocker, New York: Washington Square Press, 1971, p. 7.
7. See Rousseau, *The Social Contract and Discourse on the Origin of Inequality*, p. 16.
8. For an analysis of this ideal relationship, see Hegel, *Encyclopedia of the Philosophical Sciences*, pp. 436–37, pp. 176–78.
9. For a treatment more sensitive to Hegel's thought by a leading Marxist, see Georg Lukács, *The Young Hegel: Studies in the Relations between Dialectics and Economics*, translated by Rodney Livingstone, Cambridge, MA: MIT Press, 1976.
10. For a theory of the practical potential of class consciousness, see "Class Consciousness," in Lukács, *History and Class Consciousness*, pp. 46–82.
11. See Hegel, *Encyclopedia of the Philosophical Sciences*, p. 433, pp. 173–74.
12. Heidegger undertakes to carry out what looks like the same effort with respect to recovering the original impulse of early Greek philosophy. See Martin Heidegger, *Being and Time*, translated by John Macquarrie and Edward Robinson, Evanston: Harper and Row, 1962.
13. See Edward Said, *Orientalism*, New York: Vintage, 1978.
14. See Michael Curtis, *Orientalism and Islam: Thinkers on Muslim Government in the Middle East and India*, New York: Cambridge University Press, 2009.
15. See Henri Pirenne, *Mohammed and Charlemagne*, New York: Norton, 1939.
16. See H. S. Hosseini, "Contributions of Medieval Muslim Scholars to the History of Economics and their Impact: A Refutation of the Schumpeterian Great Gap," in *A Companion to the History of Economic Thought*, edited by Warren J. Samuels, Jeff E. Biddle, and John B. Davis, Oxford: Blackwell, 2003, pp. 32–33.
17. Richard P. Mitchell, *The Society of the Muslim Brotherhood*, New York: Oxford University Press, 1993, pp. 193–94.
18. Sayyid Qutb, *Milestones* (*Ma'alim fil Tariq*) English Translation, Indianapolis: American Trust Publications, 1990, pp. 101–2, 112, cited in David Zeidan, "The Islamic Fundamentalist View of Life as a Perennial Battle," in *Middle East Review of International Affairs*, vol. 5, no. 4, p. 5.

19. Roy, *L'Islam mondialisé*, p. 156: "L'extension du néo-fondamentalise s'explique parce qu'il correspond précisément aux phénomènes de globalization contemporaine: destruction des sociétés traditionnelles, refondation de communautés imaginaires à partir de l'individu."
20. Mercantilism is widely studied in Western economics. For Smith's view, see Adam Smith, *The Wealth of Nations*, bk. Iv, chapter 1, 398–419, and chapter 8, pp. 607–26.
21. Smith, *The Wealth of Nations*, pp. 4–5.
22. The concept of "democracy" is routinely taken as an undefined presupposition in political debate. For a recent detailed study by an opponent of the war in Iraq, see Amartya Sen, *The Idea of Justice*, Cambridge: Harvard University Press, 2009. Sen, who is a critic of Rawls, is especially interested in the link between democracy and public reason. See chapter 15: "Democracy as public reason," in Sen, op. cit, pp. 321–37.
23. Though Western sanctions led to this result, to be fair one must also mention the way Saddam Hussein diverted money intended to finance the food for oil program meant to feed the population.
24. Mearsheimer and Walt argue that the imbalance in US policy that tilts towards Israel and against the Palestinians puts the US at risk in a number ways, such as increasing Muslim terrorism, increasing the spread of nuclear weapons in the Arab world, and putting American access to oil in the Persian Gulf at risk. See John J. Mearsheimer and Stephen M. Walt, *The Israel Lobby and US Foreign Policy*, New York: Farrar, Straus & Giroux, 2007.
25. See Fukuyama, *America At the Crossroads: Democracy, Power and the Neoconservative Legacy*, pp. 74, 186.
26. See, e.g., Rudolph Peters, *Jihad in Classical and Modern Islam*, Princeton: Markus Wiener Publications, 1996.
27. These were due to al-Awza'i (d. 774) and Muhammad al-Shaybani (d. 804).
28. Maxime Rodinson, *Muhammad*, New York: Random House, 2002, p. 351
29. See Rashid Rida, 1912, p. 35, cited in Peters, *Jihad in Classical and Modern Islam*, p. 188, n. 58.
30. See, for a critical analysis, Edward Said, *Orientalism*, New York: Vintage Books, 1979.
31. See al-Daqs, 1972, cited in Peters, *Jihad in Classical and Modern Islam*, p. 130.
32. According to Shaltus, in early Islam Muslims only attacked those who showed "a spirit of hostility, opposition and resistance against the Mission and contempt for it." See Mahmud Shaltut, "Koran and Fighting," in Peters, *Jihad in Classical and Modern Islam*, pp. 99–100.
33. For Roy, jihadism is not an attempt to establish a genuine earlier form of Islam but rather the product of the isolation of individual Muslims from authentic local tradition. See Olivier Roy, *Globalized Islam: The Search for the New Ummah*, New York: Columbia University Press, 2004.
34. Cited in Peters, *Jihad in Classical and Modern Islam*, p. 105.

35. On the idea that terrorism is not irrational, see Tony Judt, *Postwar: A History of Europe Since 1945*, London: Penguin, 2005, pp. 469, 471.
36. See Barry Rubin and Judith Colp Rubin, eds., *Anti-American Terrorism and the Middle East: A Documentary Reader*, New York: Oxford University Press, 2002, pp. 27–28.
37. See Rubin and Rubin, *Anti-American Terrorism and the Middle East: A Documentary Reader*, p. 29.
38. Rubin and Rubin, *Anti-American Terrorism and the Middle East: A Documentary Reader*, p. 31.
39. Rubin and Rubin, *Anti-American Terrorism and the Middle East: A Documentary Reader*, pp. 38–39.
40. Rubin and Rubin, *Anti-American Terrorism and the Middle East: A Documentary Reader*, p. 39.
41. Rubin and Rubin, *Anti-American Terrorism and the Middle East: A Documentary Reader*, p. 48.
42. Cited in Bernard Lewis, *The Crisis of Islam: Holy War and Unholy Terror*, New York: Modern Library, 2003, pp. xxiv–xxvii.

CHAPTER SEVEN

Economic Globalization and Empire

The preceding chapter discussed the Islamic view of the relationship between Islam and the West, with special emphasis on adaptation of the traditional concept of jihad to the present situation, which is characterized by ever increasing Western economic penetration of Islamic space as part of the steady, unremitting expansion of capitalism. This chapter will focus on Western views of the Western relationship to the Islamic world. The innovation will lie in stressing the specific importance of the economic dimension of social reality for the present conflict between Islam and the West.

On the Western View of the Western World

It will be helpful, as a first step, to distinguish between how the West depicts itself and how others view it. Opinions about the proper role of the US, the most advanced industrial and military power the world has ever seen, and currently with China one of the two central players in the global world economy, vary widely. Just in terms of square miles, the US is one of the largest countries, with numerous regional differences, a nation where many often very different views compete for attention. Nonetheless, like citizens of other modern states, Americans in general have certain entrenched ideas about themselves. One that is particularly compelling may even agree with a certain neoconservative concern in establishing international hegemony. It is the image of the US as a basically well-intentioned, sometimes ill-mannered, very strong but inept friend, who invariably means well, and whose actions are, on the whole beneficial, not only for Americans, but for everyone else.

In the wake of 9/11, international terrorism has apparently become a permanent menace with which the world will have to learn to live. Paradoxically, and despite enormous efforts to root it out (including a series of foreign wars entered into by the US and its allies in the wake of 9/11), terrorism today seems not less but more likely, something that, like the weather, no one can change, that one must endure, that cannot be foreseen with any accuracy, that is unlikely to improve over time, and that may even worsen with "climate change." No one can take heart from recent events showing that economic and military forces greater than the world has ever seen are apparently no match, despite public claims to the contrary, for the havoc that can be wrought by a determined foe of a new kind, such as al Qaeda, for internecine religious struggle in Iraq, or even, as Hurricane Katrina reminds us, simply for the vagaries of mother nature.

Increased resistance to US leadership around the world is a byproduct of the US response to 9/11. This is a direct, foreseeable result of other countries, ostensibly part of the so-called "coalition of the willing," being "coerced" into actions they would not otherwise have undertaken in the wars started by the US after 9/11. The term, "coalition of the willing," which is a clear misnomer, was used after 1990 to describe those interventions for which, since agreement did not exist among all parties, the UN was unable to mount a full-scale peacekeeping operation. As used by George W. Bush, it refers to some 49 countries who were supposedly in favor of the US led invasion of Iraq, to which a grand total of four contributed combat troops (United Kingdom, Australia, Denmark, and Poland) and 33 contributed occupation forces.

This list is less than meets the eye. For instance, six of the "coalition" countries have no military. It is known that threats of various kinds—often economic, sometimes military—were made to secure cooperation. Pervez Musharraf, the Pakistani president at the time, reported a threat to bomb Pakistan if it did not agree to cooperate with American demands.[1] It is further alleged that, to secure the cooperation of Germany and Belgium, threats were made to remove American military personnel from Germany and NATO headquarters from Brussels. Such threats are merely one aspect of the ongoing effort to impose American values and goals on everyone else. The consequence is that the very success in carrying out US foreign policy under the very public show of unity bought and paid for, or as the case may be, coerced, by the US generates not less but rather increasing resistance to America and Americans, even among close allies. The resistance of Prime Minister Tony Blair, George W. Bush's closest ally throughout the aftermath of 9/11 (including the Iraq war), to the American military "surge" in response to and rejection of the so-called Baker-Hamilton report[2] and so on, already indicated that Great Britain, over the centuries America's staunchest friend through thick and thin, after approximately a decade of war stood ready to distance itself from American hegemony. This became increasingly likely under Prime Minister Gordon Brown. David Cameron, his successor, nearly immediately announced that all British troops would be withdrawn before the next general election. One can speculate that, should the US choose at some later time to take military action under the cover of the war on terror or on any other ground against Iran, Syria, North Korea, or a large number of other countries, there would not be more than minimal support from traditional European allies.

In the interval since the break-up of the Soviet Union, wealth in advanced industrial countries has enormously increased even as the disparities between the rich and the poor have widened. This has created a situation in which it is unclear how to understand "democracy." If we understand this term etymologically as meaning power to the people, and if we interpret power as economic power, then it is clearly false that the people in general have "power," especially of the economic variety. However we construe what has been happening since the end of the cold war, it is clear that increasingly wealth is accruing disproportionately to that small fraction of the population that was already wealthy. In such a rich country as the US, it remained a scandal that until March 2010, when the Patient Protection and Affordable Care Act and the Health Care and Education Reconciliation Act of 2010 were signed into law by President Obama, at any given time almost 50 million people did not have basic health insurance. The recent decision to provide most residents of the US with health care did nothing to alleviate such other problems as the fact that about a quarter of the population is functionally illiterate, that according to standard measurements large minorities, including African-Americans and Hispanics, have never been integrated into the social mainstream, and that access to higher education is still largely based on social class. The current decline of financial support for public universities suggests access to higher education will not improve and may well worsen in the near future. There is no easy alternative to saying that in these and many other ways democracy remains a theoretical concept that has not yet been realized in a more than marginal way in the US.

One wonders to what extent the US, which has made democracy a centerpiece of the global war on terror, really desires to bring about anything recognizably resembling it elsewhere. It is certainly does not seem to be a main, or even a significant objective in the link to such archconservative Middle Eastern countries as Saudi Arabia and Kuwait. These countries are not important in the US scheme of things because they were or currently are even potentially fertile terrain for the spread of democracy—they are not—but rather because they are sources of fossil fuel, sources whose political stability precisely depends on the fact that they are not democratic. It is because they are not democratic, because the vast majority of the population does not have real power in running these countries, that, despite their official Islamic religious commitments, they have been reliably integrated into the Western economic framework. Nor is "democracy," as it is normally understood, something the US seems to be seeking with such former Soviet republics situated on the old Silk Road. And it is apparently not part of the complex American relations with Pakistan.

The increasing "weakness" of the US is also apparent in a different way, which can be described as a relative decline and contrasts sharply with current American hegemonic ambitions. Some are attracted to the analogy between the US, ostensibly on the decline, and ancient Rome.[3] The historian Paul Kennedy points to the fact that the global interests and obligations of the US exceed its capacity to defend them simultaneously.[4] Writing in the late 1980s, Kennedy was understandably concerned with such themes as nuclear annihilation, a theme that, since the end of the cold war, seems to be less pressing. The fact that the Bush and Obama administrations and their allies have recently been concerned about the potential nuclear threat actually posed by Iran and North Korea, Iran increasingly more than North Korea, is a difference that seems to be regularly overlooked in American governmental rhetoric. Almost two decades after the breakup of the Soviet Union, other issues have came to the fore. The reality, or perhaps better suspicion, of a relative decline is arguably one of the reasons why during the presidency of George W. Bush the US was striking out in such uncontrolled ways against enemies real and imagined everywhere in the world.

The issue Kennedy identifies about whether the US has the financial muscle to realize its hegemonic international ambitions remains a serious concern. In different ways, a number of important observers, some of whom are sympathetic to the concept of an American empire (Niall Ferguson) and some who are opposed to it (Immanuel Wallerstein), argue on strictly financial grounds that this ambition is unrealistic.[5] Support for this inference can be drawn from the balance of payments problem, or the inability over many years to balance the value of exports and imports, for the American economy. Since the value of imports increasingly exceeds the value of exports, the US has increasingly come to depend on an important daily infusion of foreign capital to prop up its economy, which would literally be unable to function at anything like current levels without that infusion. Rather than becoming less dependent and more independent, as its aggressive foreign policy suggests, the US has recently become steadily more dependent on other countries, especially China.

Another theme is the preservation or forfeiture of "democracy," however defined, which when George W. Bush was in office became an official excuse to create a contemporary American empire by in effect colonizing not one country or another but the entire world. There is a difference between an ideal concept of democracy, which exists only in the mind of the political theorist, and the many ways in which democracy takes shape in practice. It seems as if the brand of democracy that was current in the US before 9/11 was incompatible with the global war on terror as the administration of George W. Bush conceived it. Thus Bob Brecher , who is concerned with what is called the ticking bomb argument, contends that we can justify torture on utilitarian grounds, but that it should be prohibited on moral grounds. Left unclear is how to distinguish utilitarianism and morality.[6]

Paradoxically the Patriot Act, signed by President George W. Bush on October 26, 2001, severely reduced civil liberties with the aim of protecting democracy, hence the very civil liberties it restricts. This includes even habeas corpus, a cornerstone of the Anglo-Saxon legal system, hence of democracy in the US. Then there are a series of troubling measures concerning prisoners suspected of terrorist activities, or even of a variable, imprecise relationship to terrorism, however defined, who are arrested and held incommunicado, abused, tortured,[7] even tortured to death,[8] in prisons such as Abu Ghraib,[9] perhaps at Guantanamo Bay, and others known and perhaps even still unknown scattered around the world. Changes in the law that legalized such practices reduced the possibility that those responsible, such as the CIA, can later be charged with crimes.[10] But such changes do not counter the impression that democracy worthy of the name was and still is increasingly being honored in the breech. Other measures include the massive diversion of available funds to projects concerning the global war on terror. In part because of the great recession that began in 2008, but also in part because of the financial demands of the war on terror, normally available funds were becoming unavailable for ordinary purposes, such as federal emergencies, including massive hurricanes (for example, Katrina), but also for schools, highways, civil rights enforcement, and other tasks governments normally assume. It is not as if there were a temporary state of emergency. Toward the end of George W. Bush's second term, it was already beginning to look as if the state of emergency would later, or perhaps had already, become permanent. Barack Obama, who came into office stressing his differences with George W. Bush, has so far not done nearly enough to distance his administration from its predecessor. I come back to this point below.

It would be an error to claim that a meaningful democracy cannot be realized, or that it is incompatible with the larger countries such as the US. There is no reason to infer the American democratic "experiment" has failed or is inconclusive. Yet, as a result of the form taken by the response to 9/11, there is an increasingly real danger of being obliged to forfeit a significant part of what we understand as democracy as the price to maintain it as it existed prior to 9/11. Apparently, the challenge the US is now facing has increasingly forced it into an antidemocratic stance, for instance as concerns the steady erosion of the rule of law that, however understood, is intrinsic to democracy. The rule of law is perhaps the single most important cultural advance in modern times. Its prevalence in American society separates it from such countries as Russia that, having left institutionalized Communism behind, has not yet reached this stage. The result is the decline of democracy, even as its triumph is still being celebrated in the highest places.

A further factor is the increasing attention accorded to military figures and civilian-military links in wartime. Military figures not surprisingly, loom large, sometimes very large, in times of war. General David Petraeus, who commanded the Multi-National Force—Iraq from January 2007, to September 2008, during which he directed the so-called troop surge, quickly became a national figure. His importance continued to grow after the dismissal by President Obama in June 2010 of Stanley McChrystal, who was in charge of the American effort in Afghanistan, after imprudent comments in *Rolling Stone* magazine. Petraeus immediately replaced McChrystal as the US continued to prosecute the war according to roughly the same plan.

The idea that politics and the military must come together in the triumph of democracy on a legal basis is one of the most dangerous myths now afoot in the land. Dwight D. Eisenhower came to prominence because of his role in the Second World War, when he was Supreme Commander of the Allied Forces in Europe. In his farewell speech many years ago, then President Eisenhower denounced what he called the military-industrial complex.[11] He was worried about the acquisition of unwarranted influence by representatives of the military and related businesses, which would distort the relationship between security and liberty. An obvious instance is the influence of big business on government, illustrated during the Iraqi war through the close relationship of Vice President Cheney with Halliburton, the company that he had earlier directed.

Economics, Politics and War since 9/11

My claim that economics is a central factor in the interaction between the capitalist West and the Islamic world is illustrated through the complex Western reaction, led by the US, to 9/11. This reaction features a series of no less than three, and, depending on how one counts, as many as four wars (Afghanistan, Iraq, the so-called global war on terror, and perhaps even the Israeli invasion of Lebanon), which cannot be reduced to, but also cannot be understood without, consideration of economic interests. The US (and allied) response to 9/11 is arguably driven by cultural, political, religious, historical, economic, and other considerations that do not hinder, and are not neutral to but rather reinforce, economic expansion in the Middle East. They also, as is often the case when wars are waged, help to expand the economy, which in turn makes them, when combined with other conditions, such as limiting the number of American casualties, politically "tolerable."

The events of 9/11, which featured an unusual terrorist attack in the US, were followed by traditional, but otherwise dissimilar wars, pitting nation against nation, in Afghanistan and Iraq. The US had been attacked by al Qaeda, a Muslim fundamentalist group apparently then mainly located in Afghanistan, and which was supported by the Taliban, a fundamentalist Islamic group in power at the time in Kabul. The US and its allies responded by attacking the latter group as well as that country in general. In Iraq, in a very different situation, the US and its allies attacked the Iraqi people, who had not in any way attacked them. At the time, Iraq was ruled with an iron fist by a former American ally, Saddam Hussein, who had been supported in various ways by the US for many years until he seized power in 1979, and even later, including in his war against Iran, and up until the first Gulf War. From all indications, when the US went to war against Iraq, that country was not then embarked on, or even likely to embark on, preparations to attack the US, its allies, or apparently even to act in a significant way against their interests.

The ongoing Western reaction to 9/11 reflects a variety of political, economic, military and other considerations. The war in Afghanistan met the felt need to act, after the break up of the Soviet Union, on the part of the world's only remaining superpower by doing something quickly in the face of a massive attack on a series of American symbols. One can wonder if the later reaction leading to a series of other wars was not disproportionate to the real threat, even exaggerated or "hyped" for partisan domestic political reasons linked to neoconservative political ideology. Yet, this initial war was at least initially comparatively less controversial than later conflicts. On political grounds it was obviously important for the American government to move rapidly and decisively in a variety of highly visible ways to defend the US in showing with no ambiguity it was ready and able to resist an attack of this kind. It was further psychologically important that the US, which had been dealt a massive blow, deal an even more massive one in return. Whether it was justified in destroying Afghanistan depends on whether one believes that an appropriate way to get back at al Qaeda was to "burn down the house" in which it was hiding so to speak.

Because of obvious time constraints, the war in Afghanistan was very quickly undertaken in the immediate aftermath of 9/11. The time factor was very different for the Iraq war, which did not officially begin until March 20, 2003. Yet this war was underway long before it was officially declared. Even before the shooting started Iraq had been subjected to an important embargo, and there was a large no-fly zone with considerable, often daily, bombing from the US and allies. The transition from an undeclared, but ongoing, state of war to declared war was a question of a difference of degree but not a difference in kind.

Causes of war are often hard to assess. Paul Collier points to the difficulty of ascertaining the causes of civil wars.[12] Historians have notoriously never been able to agree on what caused the First World War. In assessing the war in Iraq, it is useful to distinguish among many possible causes of the conflict. They include the "official," public, exoteric justifications, other possible "unofficial," public, exoteric reasons, and at least one covert, esoteric reason based on political ideology.

As part of the "official," public, exoteric justification, during the first administration of George W. Bush much effort went into preparing the American public to accept two related points. First, it was alleged there was not merely a hypothetical, or possible, but a "real" threat to American interests, something approaching a clear and present danger calling for the rapid use of deadly force. This same view in scarcely more muted form was later floated with respect to North Korea's, and then Iran's, nuclear capacities. In each case the argument took the form of the unsupported and unverifiable claim that time was running out and we were faced with a situation in which we were called upon to act in a decisive way. Second, it was argued that, since the US had in fact done all one could reasonably expect it to do in the diplomatic arena before undertaking overt military action, war with Iraq could not reasonably be avoided. This argument tended to make war sound reasonable, and anything less than war simply unreasonable.

The decision to begin an openly declared war in Iraq was accompanied by a great deal of public posturing on both sides. This included resolutions in the UN Security Council, resolutions in NATO, renewed efforts by the International Atomic Energy Agency to ascertain the state of Iraq's nuclear weapons capabilities, discussions with friendly and less friendly states, the process of assembling a group of "friendly" nations, willing, bribed, or at least coerced into participating in this action, and other activities.

The overt, exoteric justification of this war from the US side was undertaken on a series of levels, including the revision of a key national security doctrine, the interpretation of that revision, the gathering and interpretation of intelligence about the nature and extent of the Iraqi menace to US interests, a similar evaluation concerning the likely response to a US attack on and occupation of Iraq, and so on.

In preparation for this war, and perhaps in the minds of the neoconservatives who were keen on revising security policy for others like it, the National Security Strategy of the United States was basically revised. It is perhaps not well known that the revision of the National Security Strategy in 2002 (NSS 2002) authorized first-strike, or preventive, military action under the guise of providing a new and (substantially) different meaning to the term "preemptive" warfare. In standard usage in policy and scholarly circles, the term "preemption" (unlike "prevention") refers to a military strike intended to stop an adversary from carrying out an attack that is imminent. A good analogy comes from martial arts. An attacker begins an attack, say through launching a punch to the jaw; and the person about to be struck preempts the blow with a kick to the stomach of the attacker. To continue the analogy, a preventive attack is one in which an attack is not expected in the immediate future. For example, if the United States launched a "surgical strike" against North Korea targeting its nuclear facilities and weapons (on the grounds that it expected a nuclear attack from North Korea in six months), the US attack would be considered preventive, not preemptive. Since in both cases the adversary possesses the relevant military capacity and presumably desires to launch an attack, one important difference between military preemption and military prevention concerns whether the attack is imminent or only extremely likely in the near future. The result of that NSS revision is to suppress any distinction between an attack that is now taking place, one that is likely to take place in the future, and one that might never take place. From the perspective of NS 2002, these were henceforth simply distinctions without a difference. It follows that as a result of this revision of the NSS it was legally possible for the US to go into any country at any time for any reason whatsoever in claiming in its defense that, not now but at some indeterminate time in the future, that country might conceivably represent a threat to American security.

The effect of NSS 2002 was to equip the US with a legal basis sufficient to justify any and all cases of preemptive war, specifically including the Iraq war. Indeed, it is not impossible, or even far-fetched to infer, since plans for so-called regime change were underway even before George W. Bush's first term, that the NSS was revised in 2002 with this invasion in mind. Military preemption was certainly also something that others, for instance such US allies as Israel, were thinking about as well at roughly the same time.[13]

Preemptive war is understood in this doctrine as preventive war, which is illegal under the UN Charter, but after the revision of national defense policy became legal under US law, though still illegal under international law. In spite of the new formulation in NSS 2002, it is at least arguable that preemptive war is never legally and morally justified. Though the decision to wage preemptive war was sometimes taken on political and/or military grounds, as it was in the war in Iraq, there is no moral, and perhaps there ought not to be any legal, way to justify attacking a country that has neither attacked nor is manifestly about to attack another country. Yet, whether NSS 2002 is morally or legally justified is different from its practical effect.

This doctrine, promulgated after 9/11 as part of the response to that series of events, was extremely useful for George W. Bush's foreign policy. NS 2002 offered retroactive cover, so to speak, for the war in Afghanistan and prospective cover for the war in Iraq. It provided what amounted to a blank check, if not under international law, at least under US law. This means there were no restrictions whatsoever against "legally" waging war on any number of other countries without limit, including Iraq, as specifically justified by US defense doctrine. This doctrine rendered legal this particular conflict and any other claimed preemptive war. While an open-ended justification of this kind might be sufficient in providing "legal cover" for military personnel and others closely associated with the US government, it was not sufficient to convince either the American public or American allies. The American public was unaware of, and unlikely to be interested in, the subtleties of defense doctrine. With this in mind, the government headed by George W. Bush hit on the idea of the possession of weapons of mass destruction (WMD) as its central exoteric, public justification for military action in Iraq.[14]

This concept is problematic on several levels. First, the meaning of the term is unclear. The term "WMD" seemingly appears for the first time in an article in *The Times* of London on December 28, 1937, to refer to the bombing of Guernica during the Spanish Civil War by the German Luftwaffe. In recent times, this same term is usually understood to refer to nuclear, biological, or chemical weapons. But the presence of WMD, the meaning of which term is usually left undefined, is hence difficult, perhaps impossible, to verify in practice. One problem is determining when a weapon becomes a weapon of mass destruction. By definition a weapon is able to inflict grave bodily harm and to kill. Under the right conditions that is possible for almost any weapon, but it would not make sense to say that a kitchen knife falls into that category. A second problem is whether the term refers only to the quality of the weapons, or further refers to who possesses them. If it refers to the quality of the weaponry, then as the world's only superpower the US obviously has more and probably more lethal WMD than any other country. But the US does not object to such weapons possessed by itself or its allies. If it refers to who possesses such weapons, then it is merely a disguised way of referring to a certain, but undefined level of weapons under the control of a possible foe.

Before the beginning of the official invasion and occupation of Iraq, that country's alleged possession of WMD was publicly identified as the official excuse warranting overt military action. Yet, a zealous search over months for WMD, both before and after the invasion, never turned up such weapons. This had the unanticipated effect of discrediting the public political justification of this war, which in this way was retrospectively exposed as no more than a political pretext, in a word as a mere sham.[15] In fact, Paul Wolfowitz, who from 2001 to 2005 was deputy director of defense reporting to Donald Rumsfeld, hence a main architect of the war in Iraq, publicly conceded in the July 2003 issue of *Vanity Fair* that the appeal to WMD was no more than an excuse.[16] This meant that those who had even more publicly made the case to go to war because of the existence of WMD, but who were now exposed as having utilized a mere unfounded pretext, needed to run for cover. An example is George Tenet, director of the Central Intelligence Agency from 1997 until 2004, who allegedly told George Bush that it was a "slam-dunk" that Saddam Hussein possessed WMD.[17] Perhaps not surprisingly, since he appeared to be a team player, Tenet was awarded the Presidential Medal of Freedom in 2004. Yet, after he resigned, Tenet lashed out against Vice President Dick Cheney and other Bush administration officials by saying they pushed the country to war in Iraq without ever conducting a "serious debate" about whether Saddam Hussein posed an imminent threat to the United States.[18]

Democracy Through Force in Iraq

Complex events such as wars are usually determined by a wide variety of factors, each of which influences the decision to enter into, prosecute, and terminate armed conflict. If the public justification of WMD were all one had to go on, it would be difficult, perhaps not possible, to understand why the US went to war in Iraq. Yet there is no reason to think this is the whole story, since there are obviously other reasons as well. Beyond reacting to nonexistent WMD, or even responding sympathetically to the plight of the Iraqi people, the Iraq war was, when declared by President Bush, arguably intended to accomplish a number of other related goals. At a minimum, these include:

(1) spreading "democracy," however this term is understood;
(2) securing access to oil;
(3) maintaining a special relationship to Israel;
(4) supposedly stabilizing the situation in the Middle East;
(5) at least in principle redrawing the map of the Middle East;
(6) removing a potential source of further trouble;
(7) warning other potential foes about US resolve, and
(8) bringing about what is often called "regime change."

As concerns the last goal, one must distinguish between expressions of sympathy for the Iraqi people and what is euphemistically called regime change. No one denies the very real suffering of the Iraqi people under Saddam Hussein, a people who have again suffered greatly under the occupation of its American and allied self-appointed (Western) saviors. Though it plays well in the evening news, it is doubtful that sympathy for Iraqis was ever high on anyone's list as an important rationale for the war in Iraq. The obvious, large-scale trauma inflicted on ordinary Iraqis in the course of the war counts as a strong counterargument to the claim the US undertook this war for the Iraqis' benefit.

The announced American desire to bring democracy to Iraq (through overwhelming military force) is understandable, but, if anything, even less credible. Democracy, as already noted, means different things to different observers. Hence, there is room for legitimate difference of opinion about how to understand it. There can be different tests of whether it has been achieved, or if a situation likely to lead to it was in place, or was ever later plausibly in the process of being put in place.

Democracy is a form of political organization. Clearly different "democratic" countries offer different political models. Democracy in England is different from democracy in Italy, not to mention the United States. Theoreticians of democracy understand it in widely different ways. Amartya Sen touts democracy as a goal agreed on during the twentieth century by all parties, as the so-called "normal" form of government. He suggests that democracy cannot (merely) be identified with "majority rule," but must also include voting and respect for election results, the protection of various forms of freedom, respect for legal entitlements, uncensored distribution of news, and so on.[19]

This list is not exhaustive. One might want to add other characteristics, such as universal suffrage, which is still not universally permitted even in Switzerland, a reputedly democratic country. Another characteristic might be multiparty politics, which is the case everywhere in Europe, including the United Kingdom, but which has never caught on in the US. In thinking about democracy, it makes sense to aim for a reasonably robust model, a more than minimal conception that offers the best aspects of what can loosely be called a democratic political system. Yet, sometimes, when a more developed form of democracy is not possible, one must accept a less developed form. The least developed form of democracy seems to be the reality of majority rule as suggested by the etymology of the term. It is arguable that if the people as a whole cannot decide through free and fair elections who rules the country, then democracy worthy of the name does not exist.

Marcus Aurelius, an important philosopher, was Roman emperor from 161 until 180. Yet, except in Platonic dialogues, governments are not often directed by philosophers or others concerned with conceptual distinctions.[20] It is scarcely surprising that the administrations of George W. Bush, which insisted on democracy for Iraq and Afghanistan, never went on record about what it took this crucial term to mean. This administration, hardly prone to introspection, and which had good political reasons to avoid making any statements that could be precisely evaluated, claimed to be interested in bringing democracy to Iraq and more generally to the entire world.

Yet, unless we know what democracy means, there is no way to ascertain whether it has been achieved. We are meant to infer that democracy is of such enormous importance that even a large number of American deaths, a total considerably more than the nearly 3,000 deaths on 9/11, and an untold number of Iraqi deaths—at the time of this writing there is as yet no reliable account of how many Iraqis have so far died, though estimates, which vary widely, earlier ranged up to some 600,000 deaths, which, if confirmed, would be a strong indication that this war is a form of genocide—and the eventual expenditure of several trillion dollars, are justified to achieve it. Yet, despite the public rhetoric, democracy in Iraq was probably not a central priority for the Bush government. One suspects that, if it had its choice, the US would prefer an Iraq "friendly" to the US, certainly willing to provide its oil to America under stable and favorable conditions, before one committed to democracy.

Condoleezza Rice, secretary of state in Bush's second term, was for democracy in the Middle East in theory but opposed to it in practice. As secretary of state, she introduced a policy of transformational diplomacy focusing on democracy in the Middle East. "Transformational Diplomacy," Rice said, entails "work[ing] with our many partners around the world [and] build[ing] and sustain[ing] democratic, well-governed states that will respond to the needs of their people and conduct themselves responsibly in the international system."[21] These noble sentiments call for equally noble actions. Yet, she failed to respond favorably when Hamas captured a popular majority in Palestinian elections while continuing to support Islamist militants. And she failed to oppose Saudi Arabia and Egypt, which maintained authoritarian systems with US support while flouting democracy of any kind.

Let us suppose the US was committed to bringing democracy to Iraq, and that we knew what the term meant. Why should one believe this project was likely to succeed? The main argument seems to be that—like the ancient Greek view of incompatible qualities, which cannot co-exist—democracy replaces tyranny, its opposite, which was widespread in the Middle East. Thus, a democratic country can impart democracy to another country lacking democracy, such as a dictatorship like Iraq, if necessary by violent means, in virtue of the idea that democracy is "transmissible," perhaps even "catching." According to this view, democracy simply displaces anything else, in this case the brutal Iraqi dictatorship, as soon as it appears or, if we take political reality into account, at least in a reasonable interval.

As concerns the real possibility of bringing about democratic Iraq in a reasonable period of time, this argument rests on at least four dubious premises simply too weak to sustain it. These include the supposition that the US is itself still a democracy, or at least still a meaningful form of democracy; the further claim that democracy can be brought about through force, imposed from the outside, or again, in top-down fashion, specifically through war; the claim that Iraq, when freed from the dictatorship of Saddam Hussein through regime change, suddenly became, or could be induced to become, fertile territory for democracy, waiting to be transformed through outside intervention in its internal affairs; and, finally, the implicit suggestion that a unified Iraq is viable. All these assumptions must be true for the US to be able to transform Iraq, through war, into a modern democracy on a Western model. If any were false, then the effort set in motion by the US and allied attack on that country would be implausible, likely to fail, or at least unlikely to succeed. If any of the four reasons for bringing democracy to Iraq were questionable, then the very idea that the US was about to transform a dictatorship into democracy through war would be no more than an enticing political myth.

Democracy, which the US was officially supporting even as it went to war in Iraq, is increasingly under attack. The same American system Tocqueville thought was full of promise in the nineteenth century now seems to many either to have failed in practice or at the very least to be problematic, replete with unresolved difficulties, difficulties that apparently cannot be solved by normal means. An example among many is the polarization between the two main American political parties around the great recession of 2008, a polarization that means the most important obstacle to economic recovery was not simply economic but political as well. This points to a form of political paralysis, a sign that the democratic political process is not able to meet its challenges, hence is not functioning normally.

Critics of democracy, such as Julius Nyere, the former president of Tanzania, point to a wide variety of practical problems in realizing a meaningful version of democracy. In ancient Greece, when the concept of democracy was still relatively young, the majority of the population, including slaves, women, and noncitizens had no say in running the state. The American Declaration of Independence proclaims that all men are created equal and endowed with inalienable rights, although slaves were denied the status of human being, hence denied the protection afforded by such rights. This contradiction, which led to the Civil War and the Emancipation Proclamation, has still not been fully resolved. The British touted democracy at the same time as they ruled over a colonial empire in which the colonizers had different rights than those they colonized.[22] Many other examples could be given pointing to the difference between the idea and the reality of democracy around the world.

Is the US a democracy? The US is certainly is not a democracy in the sense the word had when the country became a republic in the eighteenth century and the model was direct participation in a New England town meeting. Nowadays, not only is democracy in the US representative, but most people, at least those without a private fortune, are incapable of waging a competitive electoral campaign, hence simply unable to be elected. This suggests that in the course of time even in the US the meaning of "democracy" has changed.

One central theme in democracy, however defined, is that the people are empowered, for instance to choose their own government. If democracy requires a significant degree of participation in the electoral process, then its realization is a question of degree. When Tocqueville came to the US in the 1830s, many, including those without property, all blacks, and all women, could not vote. The situation was then not very different from that in ancient Greece, where women, slaves, and children , in a word all noncitizens, were also denied the vote.

It is plausible that there can be degrees of democracy. The US became more democratic after the Civil War, when black males acquired voting rights and the possession of property as a prerequisite to voting was progressively dropped. It became still more democratic when, after the First World War and as a result of the eleventh amendment to the US Constitution, women acquired the right to vote. But it became less democratic when George W. Bush was "appointed" as president by the U. S. Supreme Court in a way that apparently circumvented, hence thwarted, the popular electoral process.

Philosophers have very different views of democracy. Plato, who was committed to excellence as a political criterion, favored aristocracy, as famously illustrated by his conception of the philosopher king. He opposed the idea of democracy, considering it rule of the mediocre. Hegel and Marx were attracted to the promise of the young American democracy. Tocqueville discussed American civilization in *Democracy in America* (*De la démocratie en Amérique,* 2 vols., 1835, 1840). In *The Old Regime and the French Revolution* (*L'Ancien régime et la Révolution,* 1856), he later suggested that the danger of equality in a Christian form of democracy lies in the despotism of the majority, which can only be avoided through freedom of the press and an independent judiciary.

Both of these remedies were called into question after 9/11 by actions of Bush and his colleagues. In the aftermath of the terrorist attacks, the US government exerted pressure on the media to present the administration's view of events following the terrorist attacks in September 2001. I. Lewis Libby, chief of staff for vice-president Cheney, was later indicted and sentenced to prison,though Bush commuted the sentence, for presenting a false view, by utilizing classified information, tending to justify government foreign policy, and then lying about it. This is consistent with recent efforts to name justices to the Supreme Court who will not decide important legal questions on their legal merits, but rather in terms of a prior, known commitment to conservative ideology. This theme was central in the nomination of Harriet Meiers, which was later withdrawn, and of Samuel Alito, who was later nominated and confirmed. It is at least arguable that Tocqueville would regard these and similar events as dangerous to democracy. The judicial appointment of George W. Bush, which circumvented the usual democratic electoral process, and is for that reason arguably an abuse, opened the door for further abuses of all kinds. It effectively nullified the carefully crafted system of checks and balances among the judiciary, executive, and legislature, which is central to the American form of government. The result was a persistent unwillingness to respect the rule of law on various levels in substituting for it a modern version of the ancient view that might makes right. This view was refuted by Plato long ago in the first book of the *Republic*. Thrasymachus argues that "justice is the advantage of the stronger."[23] He is answered by Socrates, who affirms the importance of wisdom over strength in ruling the city.

Instances during the administrations of George W. Bush in which the US arguably rejected or attempted to circumvent the rule of law in favor of the ancient view that might makes right include the rejection of international law by refusing to participate in the World Court; the decision to denounce treaties signed and ratified by previous US administrations; conduct of a war against Iraq that, since it was never authorized by the UN Security Council, was illegal under international law; the practice of detaining citizens of the US and other countries indefinitely in a kind of legal limbo and in defiance of the Geneva Convention without their being charged and without access to proper legal representation, which was later justified, hence retrospectively "legalized," by Congressional action; the restriction of basic civil liberties in the name of antiterrorism, and so on.

In the wake of 9/11 democracy in America was in danger, but perhaps less from terrorism, which had, has and will never have any prospect of "defeating" the US, than from those who claim to oppose it. There is an obvious contradiction between the expressed idea of bringing democracy to Iraq by importing as leaders a series of Iraqi exiles, individuals such as Ahmed Chalabi whom the Bush administration regarded as reliable proxies, and the will of the Iraqi people. Nobody has ever explained why such initiatives as appointing US military rulers, including retired general Jay Garner, later Jerry Bremer, a diplomat specialized in anti-terrorism, or the proposed division of the country into three districts governed by the US, Great Britain, and Poland, or even the imposition of Iraqi exiles friendly to the US, successfully represented the expressed desire of the Iraqi population, as established through the normal functioning of the electoral process, which a meaningful form of democracy arguably requires.

As conservative Muslims, many Iraqis, like their Iranian neighbors, clearly prefer theocracy, which the US "officially" opposes, to democracy. By geography, religion, history, and even inclination, Iraq belongs to a deeply conservative Islamic part of the world, situated next door to the Islamic Republic of Iran. The latter, which is hardly democratic, emerged as the expression of the will of the people through a revolution against the former Shah Reza Pahlevi, at the time supported by the US. The Shi'ite majority in Iraq, which cannot help but be aware of the Iranian theocracy, which is some 89 per cent Shi'ite, seems increasingly to identify with it. Though when George W. Bush was president, the US spoke of liberating the Iraqi people, and though the Shi'ites are in the majority in Iraq, the US attitude toward the Shi'ites during the Bush and the Obama administrations is perhaps not very different from that of Saddam Hussein. Neither the deposed Iraqi dictator nor the US ever favored a government dominated by Shi'ites, nor a realization of Shi'ite religious goals. But what if the majority of the Iraqi people did not desire an American form of democracy but something closer to Iranian Islamic theocracy? The US could refuse to recognize this desire in various ways. It could do everything in its power to impose something it calls "democracy," even against the will of the people. But democracy imposed by force or other means, is not democracy as normally understood, since it is not a system in which power belongs to the people. Hence, the very idea of imposing democracy from without, or from above, is self-contradictory.

This analysis provides a response to the third factor, namely, the assumption that Iraq was, is now, or is even potentially fertile ground for democracy in general, the style of democracy currently practiced in the US, or one of its other main forms. An important reason counting against the view that democracy as it is understood in the West is a likely or even a plausible outcome of the war in Iraq is the very strong influence of a conservative form of Islam in that part of the world. Another is that democracy, other than in name, is never the result of a simple transplant from one country to another. It is always the result of an indigenous movement in which the political process brings forth democracy as a stage in its development. Iraq, like other countries in the region, has a long cultural and political tradition, but nothing resembling a democratic government. The closest it seems to have come to democracy, however understood, is the period of constitutional monarchy instituted by the British in 1921, which ended with the assassination of the king in 1958. This led to the installation of what quickly became a Baathist Republic under General Kassem, who was rapidly overthrown. Yet no one would confuse the Baathist dictatorship, led by Saddam Hussein, with democracy.

Neither WMD nor the effort to bring about, or even to move toward, democracy appears to be a significant reason for the war in Iraq. In retrospect, the former reason is a mere excuse concocted by the administration of George W. Bush to promote public political support for military action by the US and its allies, and the latter reason is a weak talking point later introduced to justify an ongoing foreign occupation.

The more plausible "causes" lie elsewhere, beginning, for the allies of George W. Bush, with the neoconservative American political agenda.

The fourth and last factor presupposed by any effort to transform Iraq into a democracy is that the country must be viable as a more than nominally unified entity for a significant period of time. The history of the Middle East, which includes Southwest Asia and Egypt, dates back thousands of years, and throughout all this time has played an important role in world affairs. A unified kingdom of Egypt was already founded around 3150 BCE by King Menes. In comparison, the Republic of Iraq is still a very young country. After the First World War, Iraq was formed in August 1921 as a result of the League of Nations granting the area to the United Kingdom as a mandate. In simplest terms, two former Ottoman regions (*vilayets*), Baghdad and Basra, were joined together into a single country. This was supplemented five years later by the addition of the northern region of Mosul to create the boundaries of the modern Iraq.

There is an obvious analogy between Iraq and the former Yugoslavia. The Kingdom of Yugoslavia was a monarchy also formed after the First World War, a country of Serbs, Croats, and Slovenes, three peoples divided by language, religion, and tradition. It was renamed during the Second World War as the Socialist Federal Republic of Yugoslavia before eventually disintegrating in conflicts at the close of the twentieth century.

Contemporary Iraq similarly includes three very different populations, divided by history and interest: the Kurds (who number up to 35 million people in the region, and are arguably the largest "nation" in the world without a country), the Shia, and the Sunni. The Kurds, who comprise some 17–18 per cent of the population of Iraq, are said to be the fourth largest ethnic group in the region, after the Arabs, Persians (or Iranians) and Turks. The Kurds and Shia were brutally suppressed by Saddam Hussein. The Kurds have good reason not to trust the US government, which abandoned them to their fate after having encouraged an uprising against Saddam Hussein, one which was violently put down, at the time of the first Gulf War. The traditional religious enmity between the Shia and the Sunni was enormously exacerbated by the brutal treatment of the Shia by Saddam, a Sunni, while the US stood by. The deep differences between the Shia and the Sunni were not somehow magically overcome through the fall of Saddam. After he was toppled during the war in Iraq, the Sunni leaders of the country were determined to stop what they perceived as a march toward a majority Shia dictatorship.[24]

The deep antagonism between the various communities in Iraq had two effects. It made it extremely difficult for reasons of history, doctrine, and politics for the two Muslim communities as well as the Kurds to cooperate, for instance in holding together Iraq after the US led invasion. And it also made it difficult for any of the parties to trust the US, which at various times either supported Saddam Hussein against the Iranians, or betrayed the Kurds when they required support against Saddam, and in situation after situation showed it was simply not a dependable ally.

Effective dismemberment of Iraq, which had been held together by a brutal dictatorship, is foreseeable and in fact has arguably already occurred. The US and its military allies will not stay in Iraq forever, or even more than a short period of time when measured against the very long history of the region. The Kurds have in effect already withdrawn from a country in which they detect little common interest with other segments of the population. The Shia and Sunnis, locked in political struggle during the foreign occupation, are simultaneously engaged in a civil war: conflict between competing Muslim groups divided by everything except their relationship to Islam.

Qualified observers are skeptical about the prospects for the survival of Iraq as a unified country when the occupying forces finally leave. Peter Galbraith thinks the three main components of the Iraqi population have no common interest while much divides them, so that they cannot be brought together in a functioning democracy, however understood, and probably cannot even be held together.[25] This point is not new. It was already made at the time the country was coming into being. King Faisal, installed as monarch by the British when they formed the country of Iraq, had already complained in 1918 that Iraq lacked a unity of thought and ideals, or a sense of community. He pointed to the fact that the new state was run by the Sunni, who continued the historical oppression of the Shia merely because they were Shia.[26]

Other Possible Causes of the Iraq War

This book is focused on 9/11, but not on the Iraq war. Hence, mention of the war's other possible overt and/or covert causes (oil, Israel, stabilizing the situation in the Middle East, redrawing the map of the Middle East, removing a potential source of further trouble, warning other potential foes, and bringing about regime change) can be handled more rapidly.[27]

What is widely known as political realism simply brackets all moral questions in foreign policy. From this perspective, it is a good idea for the US to expand its access to, even its control over, the available but diminishing supply of fossil fuel, including oil and, if possible, natural gas. Concern with access to oil has dominated Western approaches to this region since the beginning of the twentieth century. In related ways, this theme has long governed Western actions with respect to Iran, Iraq, Saudi Arabia, and other countries in the region, and to peoples such as the Kurds, and so on.[28]

The presence of oil in the region, known from antiquity, attracted the attention of various nations, including Great Britain, as the Ottoman Empire was being dismembered. Iraq, which had never been a country, became one in the course of the British acquiring rights to its oil. The League of Nations granted the UK a mandate in Mesopotamia, which became known as Iraq, a term used by classical Arab geographers and the ordinary Arabic term to designate the region. Britain first acquired then expanded its control of oil in southern Iraq, which it had originally occupied in 1914, at the start of the First World War. This control was later expanded through the 1916 Sykes-Picot Agreement defining the spheres of British and French influence, which awarded Britain direct and exclusive control. This control was later extended to the north around Mosul. When the peace treaties were being negotiated in 1919 at the end of the war, the French premier, Clemenceau, apparently simply ceded French oil rights in the northern Mesopotamian region to Britain.[29] In exchange, France was granted similar control in Syria, and so on.

As for other modern industrial countries, concern with access to fossil fuels has been a concern of successive US governments over many years. It was especially emphasized around the time of the Second World War. Toward the end of the conflict, James Forrestal, the secretary of the navy, drew attention to the US need to encourage the development of oil resources in the Persian Gulf.[30] A report of the Special Ad Hoc Group of the State, War and Navy Departments' coordinating committee dated April 21, 1947 spelled out the importance of maintaining access to metals, oil, and other natural resources deemed strategically important.[31]

The importance of access to cheap oil increases as the available supply oil diminishes and there is increasing competition from other countries for the remainder. In the present context, to increase American access to oil would have two main advantages: it would decrease US dependence on other nations, and it might also decrease the cost of one or more necessary commodities. Advanced industrial capitalism requires fossil fuel in enormous and constantly increasing quantities. The US, which has the world's largest economy, is crucially dependent on other countries to supply it with oil.

Oil is becoming more expensive for a variety of reasons, including the rapid emergence of China as a major economic power with enormous and steadily growing energy requirements. It is not irrelevant that China recently has begun to consume even more energy than the US. In 2009, Saudi Arabia, the country that exports more oil than any other in the world, delivered more oil to China than to the US. It is not difficult to imagine that the rapid rise of China as a consumer of energy, including fossil fuels, and its importance as a partner for oil producing countries such as Saudi Arabia, could result in changes in historic alliances of oil producing countries with the West.

Naturally countries that have oil want to sell it for as much money as they can. Just as naturally, buyers want to pay as little as they can. Even better than buying is the idea of simply "taking" what one needs (or wants) without paying for it. It is true that war is costly. But it would ultimately have proven relatively less costly if the US government had been able to sell Iraqi oil to fund the costs of its occupation of that country. In practice, this was not the case. Yet, if followed out, this line of reasoning leads to the idea of waging war in order to secure possession of Iraqi oil fields.[32] Though this was certainly not the only reason pushing the US toward war in Iraq, it was a factor, which, even if it cannot be "quantified," is obviously significant. The same logic points to the possibility of other such "resource wars" in the Middle East and elsewhere. As concerns the Middle East, candidates might include Saudi Arabia, in order to expand and consolidate the US hold on oil in the region, or Iran to get hold of its natural gas reserves. This suggests that an unacknowledged desire for access to Iranian gas is one of the possible factors in the response to the Iranian nuclear program.

The US was not alone in wishing to gain control of Iraqi oil. Other countries interested in the same resources include those with companies that hold contracts for the delivery of this oil, which may or may not be honored once the Iraq war winds down. Much of the proven Iraqi oil reserves lie in Kurdish territory in northern Iraq. This is an obvious reason why a series of countries, including Great Britain, Turkey, and the US are not now and never have been favorable to the idea of an independent Kurdish country. It is an anomaly of the present situation that the US led coalition of the willing, which preaches democracy, is not very happy about extending it to everyone, for instance to the Kurds.

US support of Israel has been steady and unwavering since it was founded. Since the Carter administration, the US has been engaged in a difficult diplomatic exercise as it tries to achieve a settlement between the Israelis and the Palestinians despite its steady, and according to some observers excessive, engagement in favor of Israel. What is widely perceived as US tolerance of Israeli excesses is an obvious factor in the Muslim reaction to 9/11. Yet the role of this tolerance as a causal factor is harder to judge. During his period as president, George W. Bush was allied with Christian fundamentalists and was also clearly concerned with pleasing Jewish voters friendly to Israel. The concern to please Jewish voters carried over when Obama became president, though he never had nor sought ties to Christian fundamentalists.

An instance of uncritical American support lies in the Israeli invasion of Lebanon in July 2006. This invasion can be understood as the immediate reaction to a specific event: the kidnapping of two Israeli soldiers, which the Israeli government notoriously interpreted as a threat to Israel's survival. This kidnapping seemed vastly less important than the stated reaction, certainly not threatening enough to provoke a war, to most foreign observers. This invasion, which could probably never have taken place without US encouragement or at least tacit agreement, also included direct US military help.[33] The invasion points to the virtually unlimited depth of American support for Israeli policies, which has remained steady over many years. Though real and significant, this is clearly a secondary aspect, a factor that influences US policy in the region, all things being equal, but implausible in normal circumstances as a significant cause of the American decision to go to war.

When George W. Bush left office, a number of ideas that were prominent while he was president, such as stabilizing the Middle East or redrawing the map of the region, simply disappeared from the debate. As concerns the Iraq war, these ideas can be discussed together. At the time the war began, the region had been essentially stable since the end of the Gulf War in 1991. It is, hence, difficult to believe, unless the regime of George W. Bush was persuaded by its own baseless claims (in particular those concerning nonexistent Iraqi WMD), that a desire for stability in the Middle East functioned as an important factor in launching the conflict.

The meaning of the phrase "redrawing the map of the Middle East" was never defined. It is, hence, difficult to determine its precise role in the decision to go war. Obviously the result of that conflict has not been to stabilize, but rather to destabilize, the region, which was essentially stable under the Iraqi dictatorship, the fall of which quickly led to veritable chaos in Iraq. Since, even years later, suicide bombing and related incidents continued to occur, albeit with decreasing infrequency, the situation in Iraq, though substantially improved, was never fully mastered by the occupying forces. Arguably, the situation in Iran took a turn distinctly unfriendly to US interests through the replacement of a reformist president (Khatami) by a religious hard-liner (Ahmadinejad), the violent repression of reformist forces after the "reelection" of Ahmadinejad, the ratcheting up of international tensions through the Iranian decision to pursue the enrichment of uranium for supposedly peaceful purposes, and so on. One can speculate that the original intention on the part of those who planned the US invasion of Iraq was, after a rapid victory, to continue on into Syria, at least in principle a relatively easy foe, and perhaps into Iran, according to all observers a more difficult task. If that was the case, then the enormous scale of the apparently unexpected Iraqi insurgency—there is an unconfirmed rumor the US government expected the invading American soldiers to be welcomed with flowers[34]—not only created a difficult task for the US. It also scaled down whatever other ambitions it may have had in the region while George W. Bush was in office.

The question of whether the US went to war in part to remove a potential source of trouble partially depends on the "sincerity," which is difficult to measure, with which the WMD theme was initially embarked upon. If those responsible for launching the war thought at the time there really were WMD in Iraq and only later came to the opposite conclusion, then they were victims of their own misinformation, in this case shoddy intelligence. On this crucial point, there is a difference of opinion. One view is that the vastly mistaken CIA estimate of Iraqi WMD was due to political pressure. The argument runs as follows: the CIA, which advises the president, tells him what he wants to hear. Another argument is that the intelligence community in general, particularly the CIA, was simply inept.[35]

It has already been noted that the best information was that Iraq did not possess WMD when the US attacked. One can claim the Iraqi dictator was an unscrupulous character, someone who at some time in the future could possibly acquire such weapons, hence, believe that one day he was likely to represent a significant threat to American security, including its strategic interests, and so on. Yet, that line of reasoning, a form of political paranoia, is arguably as dangerous as the weapons themselves, for it leads to the conclusion that the US needs to be afraid of, as well as ready and willing to attack, virtually all countries.

Throughout this period, in line with NSS 2002, there was brave talk about fighting more than one war at the same time. As the war in Iraq continued, however, two things became clear: first, the US was clearly unable to put out the fires it had started; it did prove capable, after some very difficult times, of stemming the increasing slide into chaos through the military surge. Yet, other than merely declaring victory and leaving, it was still not clear, almost a decade after the war began, how it could be brought to an end. Second, the simultaneous prosecution of wars in Iraq and Afghanistan, together with a major recession, provided a strain on US resources. It became obvious that, despite claims to the contrary, America was simply not capable of fighting two such wars simultaneously. It was unclear whether it was even up to fighting (and winning) a single such war against a determined insurgency.

One should be realistic in evaluating the results of these military endeavors. Certainly the US did not win in Iraq and there is no reason to think it is winning, about to win, or will ever win in Afghanistan. Perhaps for that reason, when Obama became president the US scaled-down the inflammatory rhetoric with respect to Iran, which continues to flare up from time. Though it did not negotiate directly with Iran, the US was noticeably more careful, and not a little more skillful, in its handling of North Korea, with which it reached a negotiated agreement to stop the nuclear program. Though NSS 2002 permitted preemptive war, it is easier to believe that key players in the administration of George W. Bush were more concerned with justifying a rapid invasion of Iraq that had, in principle, already been decided on—perhaps even decided on prior to the beginning of his first term—than in meeting, or even in anticipating, a possible future problem.

The idea that the US went to war in Iraq to put other nations on notice about the constant possibility of American military intervention is a factor that can be an ingredient in any conflict in which the US is engaged. The US, which has been an expansionist nation almost from the beginning of the republic, has never been hesitant about interfering in the affairs of other countries.[36] A straight line leads from arrival of the Mayflower Pilgrims in the new world, then the massacre of the American Indians as they expanded their original foothold resulting in the push to evict the British, then the French and the Spanish from North America, including the forced annexations of Mexican territory, the Spanish-American War to expand American hegemony throughout the hemisphere and into the Pacific, and increasingly far-flung twentieth-century military operations in the Caribbean and Indochina.

This expansionist tendency was not created by George W. Bush, but was strengthened through the view associated with his presidency that America's role lies in bringing democracy to all nations. If that is the case, then the results must be sobering. The difficulties the US encountered in Iraq have not so far cowed, but rather apparently emboldened, other countries, particularly Iran, perhaps also Israel. About a decade after 9/11 there seemed to be considerable awareness that the US was tied down for the foreseeable future in the wars in Iraq and Afghanistan, unable to continue to risk other major military adventures. It is true that, with the help of the European Union, the US successfully pressured Syria to withdraw from Lebanon. Yet, it later met increasing resistance on matters concerning the spread of nuclear capabilities from Iran, a potential foe, even as it took steps to spread nuclear power to India, a historically friendly nation.

An Esoteric Cause of an Overt War?

The political justification of the war in Iraq goes back to the Gulf War, which was in fact the first US war against Iraq. The refusal of then-president George H. W. Bush (Bush the Elder) to authorize Norman Schwarzkopf, commander in chief of the US and Coalition forces, to push on to Baghdad left Saddam Hussein in place, creating a later opportunity for Bush the Younger. The apparent reasoning for this decision was to maintain an element of stability in Iraq, and more generally in the region, at the close of the conflict. The intention was to avoid the very complicated difficulties that later arose in the second conflict involving Iraq. This in fact resulted in the regime change Bush the Younger clearly desired, producing massive instability that neither the Iraqis nor the US and its allies wanted or were capable of fully mastering.

At the time of the Gulf War, the decision not to go after Saddam Hussein, hence not to bring about regime change, annoyed many neoconservative thinkers. A number of them believed it was a profound mistake not to have unseated the Iraqi dictator. They devoted considerably less attention to his massacre of the Kurds after the end of the war in retaliation for the Sha'aban Intifada in March 1991.[37]

George W. Bush's idea of bringing about regime change in Iraq by military means, which played well according to the neoconservative ideology he favored as he came into office, more in his first term than in the second, did not establish a precedent since it was depressingly familiar. It was fully consistent with established US practice over roughly the past half century, when the US directly or indirectly acted to overthrow undesirable rulers in countries from Panama to Grenada and Afghanistan, and from Haiti to Somalia. The list, which is depressingly long, includes Hawaii, Cuba, the Philippines, Puerto Rico, Vietnam, Guatemala, Nicaragua, Honduras, Panama, Chile, Iran, Grenada, Afghanistan, and . . . Iraq. The same US that "officially" favors democracy, did not hesitate to overthrow a series of democratically elected governments it considered unfavorable to American interests, including those of Allende in Chile, Arbenz in Guatemala, Mossadegh in Iran, and the Sandinista regime in Nicaragua.[38]

The neoconservative policies of the PNAC, mentioned above, provide an important link that ties together the three wars George W. Bush started after 9/11, and other less important actions, such as the Israeli invasion of Lebanon in July 2006, which the US clearly supported and even enabled. This is perhaps less the case for the war in Afghanistan, which can be regarded from two perspectives that probably fuse into one. These include the need to react strongly and immediately on political and psychological grounds, as noted, as well as the idea, an ingredient in the PNAC, that after the end of the cold war the world the world had not become a more peaceful but a more dangerous place. In the immediate aftermath of 9/11, this simplistic line of reasoning—simplistic since it was not based on analysis of the prevailing situation at the time—led to the inference that the only acceptable course of action was for the US to strive to attain world hegemony. The self-described mission of the PNAC was certainly important in deciding to go to war in Iraq, including the specific shape of that war as well as throughout the so-called global war on terror.

The war in Iraq seems to have served a different political function. In part, it is the tangible manifestation of a theoretical dispute, with dire practical consequences, between conservatives and neoconservatives, which played out on the world stage in the series of deadly conflicts that took place at the beginning of the new century. The theoretical conflict is in fact a conflict of two generations. It sets in opposition two parties, each of which regarded itself as legitimated by a special relationship to Ronald Reagan. His political view was interpreted for these purposes as supporting both the conservatism favored by the older and wiser generation, who were more comparatively cautious and more aware of their surroundings, and the neoconservatism favored by their younger offspring, who were comparatively less cautious, even incautious, and less aware of their surroundings. Conservatism is a traditional political approach that is wary of foreign engagements, and fiscally tightfisted. Neoconservatism reflects the opposite concern to engage whenever possible in working out a hegemonic relationship to the entire world with a willingness to devote apparently endless sums to foreign engagements.

This conflict took the form of an opposition between a father and his son, an opposition which in other times and places would have been a Greek tragedy. One party was composed of the conservatives around George H. W. Bush, an astute man who went to war when Saddam Hussein invaded Kuwait and threatened stability in the Middle East and American access to oil. Yet George H. W. Bush counseled caution toward the end of the Gulf War by leaving Saddam Hussein in place. He was concerned to avoid the many difficulties that were easy to anticipate, and which arose when this constraint was not observed. The other party featured the neoconservatives clustered around his less astute son, George W. Bush, an intellectually limited man, who did not foresee the consequences of his actions with any clarity, and who allowed himself to be drawn into situations which neither he nor his advisors understood, and for which there was apparently never even any clear plan in place.

The decision to declare war represented a resounding victory of the younger, more adventurous, less cautious neocons over their older, less adventurous conservative predecessors. For a brief shining moment in the history of the United States it looked as if one could disregard with impunity anything previously learned about the risks of an aggressive foreign policy, specifically including reluctance to plunge into military engagements that could not be won, such as in Vietnam. In concrete terms, there was really no difference between the call to action and the action that followed, between the neocon ideology George W. Bush and his followers not only recited but also seemed to believe, and actions based more on ideology than on a careful study of the situation. In practice, in the heady times after 9/11, before reality set in, there was a time when George W. Bush may have actually believed he had been chosen by God to lead the free world in spreading democracy far and near. Whether that is true or a fable recounted for exoteric consumption, he and those around him clearly thought they were justified—taking abstract, ideological claims for sacred foreign policy writ that would "work" because it was formulated by thinkers with impeccable neoconservative credentials—in plunging into the military fray.

The situation as concerns the global war on terror is somewhat different. Unlike the wars in Afghanistan and Iraq, this was never presented as a regional war in a single country, but in quasi-Miltonic terms as all-out war between the forces of good and evil at the level of the entire globe. If the PNAC can be believed, then the central aim here was less to strike a blow against a particular enemy, or to react against a specific possible future threat, or even to defeat terrorism in the world. It was rather to show through decisive action the kind of global leadership in world affairs called for by neoconservative ideology. The aim in view was to bring about a world favorable to American conceptions of politics and economics, the two main cornerstones of the supposed Pax Americana outlined in the founding documents of the PNAC. Left unclear is whether this is a justified reaction to a dire situation presenting a threat to the entire Western world in mortal peril or, as is more likely, an enormous overreaction based on a fatal misreading of the situation.

There are two main possibilities. This very strong reaction was appropriate on the supposition that the US is never safe, since there might be terrorists, visible and invisible, lurking literally everywhere. Yet, it was not justified, and simply likely to bring about the situation to which it claims to react as a kind of self-fulfilling prophecy if the global war on terror was the result of a conscious or possibly even unconscious overreaction that simply exaggerates the magnitude of the present problem.

Politicians are often politically astute but not necessarily intellectually capable. American presidents run the intellectual gamut from Woodrow Wilson, a university president of a very high intellectual order, to Dwight D. Eisenhower, who was last in his class at West Point but also became a university president. George W. Bush, intellectually very limited, was in this way closer to Eisenhower than Wilson. The decision to treat 9/11 as an act of war enabled someone whose presidency was widely regarded as illegitimate, and which was already starting to founder in the early days of September 2001, to assume "heroic" stature as a wartime president. In effect he "saved" his presidency at the same time as he plunged the country into war. We will never know what might have happened if, instead of treating the problem, not as an act of war but as a crime, George W. Bush had not embarked on a series of wars that were not to be won. If, instead of applying a predetermined course of action mandating regime change in Iraq, he had opted for a potentially more fruitful policy of containment, it is likely the world would have been a different place today.[39]

The Iraq War and the Iraq Study Group Report

The *Iraq Study Group Report*, the contents of which were abundantly leaked and then publicly presented at the end of 2006, represents another installment in the conflict of generations between the older and wiser conservatives and the younger and brasher neoconservatives.

In George W. Bush's initial presidential campaign, his self-description as a compassionate conservative, effectively concealed the neoconservative agenda for foreign politics that was applied after 9/11. Subsequent elections in 2002, 2004, and 2006 functioned in effect as public referenda on his administration's policies in response to these events. The "(re)election" of George W. Bush in 2004 indicated that at that time the American public narrowly approved, or at least preferred, his response to these events. This included his decision to cast the war in Iraq as a crucial element in his response to terror. From 2004 until 2006, faced with mounting American losses in Iraq, increasing chaos, particularly in Baghdad, revelations about mistreatment of prisoners in Abu Ghraib and elsewhere, continuing stories about Guantanamo and secret prisons around the world, the American public slowly changed its mind. Sweeping Republican losses in the November 2006 midterm elections indicated that a large majority of voters was no longer willing to back George W. Bush's foreign policies, especially the war in Iraq, which increasingly attracted unfavorable attention.

This electoral defeat was significant in a series of related ways. In shifting control of Congress from the Republican to the Democratic camp, it for the first time created the real possibility of congressional oversight with respect to George W. Bush's policies, including a public airing of unrealistic claims about the war in Iraq. Bush personally emerged from this election cycle as severely weakened, as able under certain conditions to resist changes in his policies but now increasingly unable to dictate policy by, in effect, circumventing the more normal series of checks and balances among the legislature, executive, and judiciary. After the election, it was clear the public at large was now blaming the Republic Party for the debacle in Iraq. Though the Democrats proved unable to end the war by bringing the troops home, the continued focus on Iraq convinced many people that there was in fact no military solution in sight. If, for no other reason, on merely political grounds, there was a widespread conviction that sweeping changes needed to be made before the next electoral cycle.

The two administrations of George W. Bush featured an unusually tight link between politics, foreign policy, and military engagement. His military engagement in Iraq was from the start driven by neoconservative political ideology. After the 2006 midterm elections, he might well have separated politics from his military engagement in Iraq in acknowledging what the report never directly says, but clearly implies, to wit: the war already was, or was rapidly becoming, a military defeat on the ground. Instead, he cut his losses in acknowledging his political defeat through a series of moves while refusing to concede military defeat in Iraq, hence refusing to concede the effective defeat of his foreign policy.

To "acknowledge" his electoral defeat, but not the military situation in Iraq, where the US and its allies were steadily losing the capacity to influence events, Bush initially made a series of three related moves intended to "save" his foreign policy in Iraq. In effect, he was offering something to his critics through a public mea culpa, pointing to, but certainly not publicly confessing, an admission of error, while attempting once again to make the policy his critics rejected work despite its increasingly visible flaws.

The first two moves were simple, but the third was more complex. First, Bush simply allowed the term of John R. Bolton, ambassador to the UN, to expire. Bolton, an extremely vocal, radical form of neoconservative, was when appointed, a well-known opponent of the UN. A controversial figure even among neoconservatives, he was only appointed when Congress was in recess and later needed, in the ordinary scheme of things, to be reappointed to remain in his job. Allowing his appointment to expire was at best symbolic in removing a highly visible neoconservative firebrand, someone who alienated nearly everyone, friend and foe. Second, Bush replaced Secretary of Defense Donald Rumsfeld—a highly visible and controversial symbol of the ostensibly failed policy in the war in Iraq—with Robert Gates, who had earlier been head of the CIA. This second move perhaps appeared to be more substantive than it in fact was. It removed someone Bush clearly depended to formulate military policy while publicly taking on the press and other critics. It was also perhaps a type of political slight of hand, since it signaled a deeper change of strategy than Bush, who was committed to continuity, was willing to make.

Both moves were mainly symbolic, since they did not signal a change of policy. Bolton's role had been twofold. It was to show the neoconservative wing of the Republic Party that Bush was listening to it. It was further to carry out the neoconservative policies of the Bush Administration, which Rumsfeld also had a hand in determining, but for which responsibility was largely shared. The limits of Bush's effort to cut his losses by giving up some visible symbols while remaining on roughly the same neoconservative course appeared in the third move.

The third move, potentially more significant, began earlier. It included the report of an important panel, which at least potentially prepared the way for a significant change of course in Iraq, through Bush's reaction to that report. Under considerable pressure well before the election, when electoral failure, looming on the horizon, was already seen as a real possibility, Bush formed the bipartisan Iraq Study Group, announced on March 15, 2006. Its co-chairs were James A. Baker, a conservative former secretary of state in the administration of George H. W. Bush and a close personal friend of the Bush family, hence someone unlikely to cause political waves, and Lee H. Hamilton, a conservative Democrat and former Congressman from Indiana. One can suppose that in appointing a study group headed by two well-known conservatives, Bush was preparing political cover in case he should later desire to revise his foreign policy, even to change course in Iraq. Yet, Bush was probably not prepared for what followed. The perhaps unanticipated result was a clear refutation of the policy it was intended to evaluate by those who could normally be expected to support it, as well as a suggested course change unlike anything previously publicly contemplated.

The subtitle of the report, "The Way Forward—A New Approach," clearly signals that by the time it was written its authors had come to the conclusion that the policy applied in the US invasion and occupation of Iraq had irremediably failed.[40] The report suggests the policy failed because it was based on a series of false premises. The original premise of the presence of significant quantities of WMD failed because there simply were none. This was replaced by related claims, including the reputed desire to bring democracy to the Middle East, a desire that, significantly, appeals to none of the countries in the region; and the proclaimed intention to defeat al Qaeda. Significantly, unlike the government rhetoric that preceded it, the report did not feature emphasize the creation of democracy in the region.

The report's treatment of al Qaeda, which over time increasingly became the "official" excuse for the continued US occupation of Iraq, is interesting. Over the years, George W. Bush continued to link the war in Iraq to the wider global war on terror. The report casts doubt on the importance of this supposed link. Though al Qaeda was present in Iraq, at the time the report was written the Iraqi branch of al Qaeda was largely composed of indigenous Sunni Arabs who financed its operations locally.

The report underlines the importance of Iraq to the US but castigates the strategy to secure it. It clearly states that Iraq is important for regional and global stability, its strategic location between Sunni and Shia Muslims, Kurdish and Arab populations, and, above all, as was now spelled out in black and white, because it has "the world's second-largest known oil reserves."[41]

According to the report, the policy applied by the Bush administration, which was based on the military defeat of al Qaeda in Iraq, failed for four main reasons. To begin with, as noted, the main current problem in Iraq was not due to al Qaeda but rather to religious strife between the Sunni and Shia, whose origins went back almost to the founding of Islam. Then, there was no consensus, either in the US or in Iraq, about support for the US effort. Further, the situation on the ground was worsening from day to day. And, finally, the US could not realistically expect to alter the slide into chaos, in which the American ability to influence events in Iraq was steadily decreasing despite a significant increase in American troop levels.

The conclusions drawn by the authors of the report and by George W. Bush were nearly unrelated, clearly incompatible. As concerns the report and the situation on the ground in Iraq to which it points, everything happened as if the neoconservative George W. Bush and his conservative critics inhabited different worlds. The report urged a break with policies it regarded as flawed. As if he were unable to see the same reality, or to see it as reality, Bush reacted by reaffirming a version of the very policies the report rejected.

The answer, according to the report, included at least the following: a broad consensus among Americans in support of the US policy, hence American support for US government policy in Iraq; a broad consensus among Iraqis in support of this policy, hence Iraqi support of US government policy; a political but not a military solution to the war in Iraq, combined with negotiation with all the countries, whether friendly or not to the US, with a stake in the stability of the region; and a negotiated solution to the Arab-Israeli conflict.

These separate points can be boiled down to a single essential insight, which is never clearly formulated but which underlies the spirit of the report. In essence what it said is that for a political, military, or other policy in the region to be successful it needed to be freely accepted as representing the shared view by Americans who were involved in the region as well as Iraqis and all other parties to the conflict. But it could not merely be forced down the throats of any parties, and certainly not enacted *manu militari* as Bush desired, since that precluded success. If this is the real criterion for Bush's policies to work, then it was no wonder he found it difficult to accept.

Each point raised in the report merits discussion. After the midterm elections it was clear that no consensus existed among Americans, and that American policy in Iraq was unpopular. Americans were widely, and nearly evenly, divided about the war in Iraq and continued to remain so years later. There was also no consensus among Iraqis, who were sharply divided along sectarian lines between the Sunnis and Shi'ites. This division was the result of a number of causes, obviously including the historical split between the Sunnis and the Shi'ites about the very nature of Islam. A further, proximate cause was the equally obvious bias of the Iraqi prime minister, Nouri al-Maliki; The US officially supported Maliki to achieve unity in Iraq, but he clearly favored the Shi'ites, to whom he belongs, over the Sunnis. Rather than bringing about a national reconciliation, which the American government desired, Maliki appeared prejudiced toward the Shia, who had historically been dominated by the Sunni. Instead of preparing a future in which all Muslims and even non-Muslims would have their say in a democratic country, which the US desired to put in place, he seemed to be concerned with making up for past injustices. The result was an obvious contradiction, with highly detrimental practical consequences tending to undermine American policy.

The authors of the report were conservatives, not neoconservatives. In essence, their report asked Bush to abandon neoconservatism for conservatism. An intellectually more astute, more agile person might have responded by conceding that the policies in place were not working and changes were necessary. Such a person could have utilized the report to make various changes in ongoing strategy. This was not in the cards for Bush, who was not prone to introspection and apparently incapable of analyzing his mistakes. He replaced the opportunity to adjust his policies with sheer stubbornness about maintaining them. Hence, it was not surprising, but rather in character, that Bush responded to the report not by tempering but rather by reaffirming his neoconservatism.

The key element in his response was the decision in favor of a "surge" in troop levels, sending to Iraq 21,500 more soldiers, about all that were then available. The effect was to disregard one of the main tenets of Rumsfeld's military approach. The latter was the architect of a leaner, supposedly more effective American fighting machine. His idea was to get the job done while keeping the number of American troops and their losses to a minimum to avoid the public protests that increasingly marked the later years of the Vietnam War. In ratcheting up the number of soldiers on the ground, Bush signaled that Rumsfeld's concept had simply failed. But otherwise he again insisted on a neoconservative approach that had given no sign of working—if the idea is to transform Iraq into a functioning democracy—no matter how much money, troops, and materiel were thrown into the fray. For Bush simply disregarded the report's claim that the increasingly visible slide into chaos could be slowed or stalemated, but not altered, by increasing troop levels. And in once again looking for a military solution, he appeared to disregard the (perhaps more important) observation that the solution in Iraq could not be military but only political.

The troop surge had two other results, one of which was certainly unexpected. The surge decreased violence in the Baghdad area. Yet, as Thomas Ricks points out, it did not succeed in other ways, strategically or politically.[42] It further failed to strengthen the support of the war in the US, where the public remained sharply divided. Congressional testimony in September 2007 by General David Petraeus, commander of the multi-national force in Iraq, asserting the surge was working, enabled the Bush administration to resist Democratic calls to shorten the war by bringing the troops home. This pointed to the effect of a worsening imbalance among the branches of government as the executive increasingly freed itself from legislative oversight. In practice, this meant Congress was unable halt White House efforts to pursue the war. Yet after Petraeus testified, everyone suddenly seemed to understand that a slight, or even a major, improvement in the military situation was no substitution for political progress.

The other point concerns the final disposition of the war. As soon as the US invaded Iraq, there was speculation about a possible exit strategy. The Bush administration did not have one, since it at first thought it did not need one. Later, it was simply unable to devise a plausible exit scenario. Its view of the end game emerged almost as a byproduct of the effort, through showcasing General Petraeus as the featured spokesman for what it said was going right about the intervention, in order to stave off any change in its prosecution of the war. For perhaps the first time after a period of years, Bush began to transform expectations of final victory, hence the idea of finally leaving Iraq (as happened in Vietnam), into the very different prospect that (as in Korea) US troops would remain on a permanent basis. Whether to adopt a Vietnam or a Korean approach to the wars in Iraq and Afghanistan confronted the Obama administration as it strove to pick up the pieces in taking office, as George W. Bush, arguably the author of the most important American foreign policy mistake ever, retreated from the national and international scene.

The War in Afghanistan

The war in Iraq was the centerpiece of American foreign policy when George W. Bush was president, but after Barack Obama became president, attention quickly shifted to Afghanistan. The differences in Iraq and Afghanistan are significant. The US entered into the war in Afghanistan very rapidly, without adequate reflection, but invaded Iraq after reflection (conducted very badly). In sum, the war in Iraq was a deliberate but bad choice, whereas the war in Afghanistan was the apparently the result of no thought at all.

Years later, as both wars were approaching a decade of involvement, the one in Afghanistan increasingly seemed even more difficult than the one in Iraq. In Iraq, the US and its allies did not win. But they also did not lose, achieving a perilous kind of stalemate, the stability of which must still be demonstrated. It remained to be seen as events continue to unfold if the reversal of Sunni domination over the Shia, resulting from the invasion of Iraq, will affect the maintaining of unity, for instance in holding on to the Kurdish minority, while achieving a functioning political entity

A brief remark on the history of Afghanistan will be useful for grasping the background of the war. Afghanistan, which was conquered (330–327 BCE) by Alexander the Great, has been frequently at war ever since. In recent years, the Afghan political situation has been unstable, at times chaotic, as the country was continually ravaged by a series of conflicts. Following a coup d'état in 1973, Muhammad Daoud Khan came to power and Afghanistan distanced itself from the Soviet Union. A civil war started as an insurgency against the People's Democratic Party of Afghanistan, which took power in what is known as the Saur Revolution on April 27, 1978. Saur is the Dari word for the second month of the Persian calendar, when the uprising occurred. This single event led indirectly to three important events, whose consequences continue to define the present situation: the Soviet military intervention in Afghanistan, the rise of the Taliban, and the intervention of the US and its allies.

The Soviet military intervention lasted from 1979 to 1989. This war also belongs to the cold war, because it involved the main protagonists, the Americans and Soviets. In late 1978, to avoid losing influence in the region, the Soviet Union militarily intervened in Afghanistan to support a regime favorable to Moscow. In 1979, further developments pushed the Soviets to intervene further, with additional forces. The justifications were to support the regime in power and to maintain calm in Central Asia.

The Soviet involvement ended with a full withdrawal of troops as a result of the Geneva Accords (1988) between Afghanistan and Pakistan. Soviet president Mikhail Gorbachev withdrew his forces from Afghanistan in 1989. The Soviets, who were opposed by Afghan mujahideen—Arabic for someone who struggles for freedom; "mujahid" means soldier of holy war—suffered heavy losses. Because of their anti-Communist stance, the Afghan mujahideen were assisted in the war by the CIA, Pakistan, and Saudi Arabia.

Osama bin Laden participated as a Soviet opponent through his Maktab al-Khidamat, which trained a small number of mujahideen and provided limited assistance. In 1988, he broke away from MAK to form al Qaeda, broadening his anti-Communist stance into an international Islamic movement. After the Soviet army withdrew, the Soviets continued to aid the Afghan government of Mohammed

Najibullah, and the CIA and Saudi Arabia continued to aid the mujahideen in armed opposition.

The Najibullah government was finally overthrown in 1992. This led to a civil was in Afghanistan that lasted from 1992–96. A confused situation ensued as various factions jockeyed for power, a situation that continued until September 1996, when the Taliban militia took power in Kabul. The Taliban (from Pashto: "Taliban," meaning "students"; a "Talib" is a student or seeker of knowledge) is a Sunni Islamist political movement that governed Afghanistan from 1996 until overthrown by the US invasion in late 2001. Since then it has been fighting a guerilla war against the governments of Afghanistan, Pakistan, and the International Security Assistance Force (ISAF) led by NATO.

The Taliban was led by its founder, Mullah Mohammed Omar, about whom little is known. Its members are mainly drawn from Pashtun tribes as well as volunteers from nearby Islamic countries. Omar is thought to be an ethnic Pashtun from the Hotak tribe. According to Goodson, Omar's original commanders were "a mixture of former small-unit military commanders and madrassa teachers."[43] Its rank and file members are said to be drawn from among Afghan refugees who studied at religious schools in Pakistan. Omar fought as a guerilla with the Harakat-i Ingilab-i branch of the anti-Soviet mujahideen from 1989 to 1992. After the Soviet military left Afghanistan, Omar went to Singesar, where he founded a madrassa.[44] He is said to have founded the Taliban in 1994 inspired by a dream. His movement quickly gathered recruits. It captured the whole of Kandahar Province and then captured Herat in September 1995.[45] In 1996, when the Taliban took power in Afghanistan, Omar's followers made him head of the government and awarded him the title of Commander of the Faithful. When the US-led "Operation Enduring Freedom" began in early October 2001, Omar went into hiding.

The Pashtuns are an Eastern Iranian ethno-linguistic group mainly in Afghanistan and the Northwest Frontier Province, now called Pakhtunkhwa, federally administered tribal areas, and the Balochistan (or Baluchistan) province of Western Pakistan. The Pashtuns speak Pashto and follow Pashtunwali, usually described as a traditional set of rules guiding individual and community conduct. Pashto, an Indo-European language, belongs to the Eastern Iranian branch of the Indo-Iranian language family. Pashtunwali (or Pathanwali), which means the "way of the Pashtuns," is an unwritten code of ethics that antedates Islam but does not contravene basic Islamic principles. Pashtunwali emphasizes courage (*tora*), revenge (*badal*), hospitality (*melmestia*), and so on. It favors self-respect, independence, hospitality, love, forgiveness, and tolerance toward all. Yet, when the Taliban came to power, they in fact promoted an extremely strict form of shari'a intermixed with influences of Saudi Wahabism as well as the pan-Islamic jihadism of Osama bin Laden.[46] They were especially strict with women, who were made to wear the burqa in public, were forbidden education after the age of eight, and forbidden to work.

The more recent war in Afghanistan was waged by a coalition cobbled together by George W. Bush in reprisal for the terrorist acts perpetrated in September 2001.

This war began in the immediate aftermath of 9/11 as part of what was initially called "Operation Infinite Justice" and was later called "Operation Enduring Freedom." According to Bush, what he had in mind was nothing less than a crusade. He said: "This crusade, this war on terrorism, is going to take a while."[47] The announced goals of this war in Afghanistan included capturing Osama bin Laden, destroying al Qaeda, which possessed bases in the country, and in pushing the Taliban from power.

The result of the initial attack was to replace the Taliban with Hamid Karzai. Karzai is from a politically prominent Pashtun family that strongly supported the former Afghan king, Zahir Shah. During the Soviet war, he was active in raising funds for the mujahideen and further cooperated with the CIA.[48] Karzai was not selected to be president by the Afghan people but was chosen a group of political leaders in a meeting in Germany in December 2001. Karzai was initially selected by Afghan political figures at the International Conference on Afghanistan on December 5, 2001 for a six-month term. He was then appointed as interim president by the Loya Jirga on 3 June 2002 for a two-year term in 2002. Karzai was elected president in October 2004, but he was accorded very little legitimacy and was unable to extend his control beyond Kabul. His reelection in 2009, after his only opponent withdrew in a fiasco widely considered to have been rigged by Karzai, further weakened him and his government in various ways.

When Bush was in office, the war in Afghanistan was considered an integral part of the war on terror. But after he left office, this was rarely mentioned, meaning the US was bogged down in a costly and unpopular military endeavor, which was never as popular as the war in Iraq, and which, in being detached from the war on terror as the latter faded from view, lost any vestige of its original flimsy justification.

When he took office, Barack Obama inherited the war in Afghanistan. Obama has sent mixed signals about his understanding of the situation. In December 2009, he announced he would deploy an additional 30,000 soldiers over six months (in effect a form of military surge comparable to the Bush surge in Iraq), but would also begin troop withdrawals to be completed (it was hoped) 18 months later. This amounted to stepping up the military engagement as a prelude to disengaging.

Meanwhile, from the American perspective the results of the war in Afghanistan can only be regarded as unsatisfactory. In part, the difficulty centers on the Taliban, about which there is altogether too much nonsense. Too many observers want to write the Taliban off as belonging now only to history, though they stubbornly refuse to fold up their tents and vanish.[49] In August 2008, there were some 70,000 foreign soldiers in the country. In 2009, this number, which did not include foreign mercenaries, or coalition "contractors," rose to 113,000. Yet in January 2009, the International Council on Security and Development estimated that the Taliban was active in some 72 per cent of the territory. It is no clearer now, after all these years of war, that a military defeat of the Taliban is a real possibility. A six-year archive of classified military documents made available by WikiLeaks and published by the *New York Times* offers what in a headline is described as "an unvarnished and grim picture of the Afghan war," considerably less positive than the view depicted by the administrations of George W. Bush and Barack Obama. The main point seems to be that since 2001 the Taliban has never been stronger.[50]

As for Iraq, one can ask the obvious questions: what is the US policy and what is its likely outcome? It is a pleonasm to say that the US goals in Afghanistan have never been clear. For this reason, it is difficult to say whether they can be accomplished. If they include overturning a Taliban regime, then this was already accomplished in 2002. If they include getting rid of al Qaeda, then in 2010 all observers agreed it was gone. Indeed, at that point it was years since al Qaeda had an important presence in Afghanistan. It makes no sense to fight a war based on the incorrect premise there is a significant al Qaeda presence in Afghanistan if that is seriously incorrect. Yet, there seems to be another goal, one which is less easily achieved, and which makes the war in Afghanistan, a very different country than Iraq, suddenly look exceedingly like the latter: a war with no obvious end in sight. For in Afghanistan as in Iraq, the US seems to be taken with the old idea of nation building. This idea worked in Germany and in Japan after the Second World War, but it requires time, money, and the right kind of country for it to succeed. It is not clear that either Iraq or Afghanistan offers the right kind of country in which to work the American will in building an Afghan nation according to Western democratic specifications. It is further clear that the recent fascination with nation building, central to the foreign policy of George W. Bush, does not interest Barack Obama to the same degree. What, then, are the choices for the US?

One choice is to reach out to the Taliban in acknowledging what should by now be obvious: the Taliban has not been and probably cannot be defeated by military means. Karzai, who seems aware of this fact, has always been a nervous, unstable ally. Since he was rightly not confident that the US has the necessary will to prevail, or that it will even stay engaged, he began to reach out to the Taliban for a political settlement while the US was still playing the military card. On January 26, 2010, at the International Conference on Afghanistan in London, he announced a peace initiative with the Taliban. This created a bizarre situation in which General Petraeus, as the newly-anointed commander of the American-led forces, was striving to kill as many Taliban as he could before the foreign forces begin to withdraw according to plan in July 2011, while Karzai was seeking to include the same people in a coalition government. In fact, there is a further irony in that foreign military forces and the US government did not even appear to be on the same page. Petraeus, who took over as commander from McChrystal, was focusing on containing the Taliban. But Joe Biden, the US vice-president, was mainly concerned to prevent the return of al Qaeda.[51] It is up to Obama, who has not done nearly enough to distance himself from Bush, to seize the occasion to establish a coherent policy, one that will finally be his own. As this book went into production, the US and coalition forces seemed to be following a two-track approach in applying as much military pressure as possible on the Taliban while simultaneously supporting talks between the Karzai government and selected Taliban elements, excluding Mullah Omar, aimed at ending the war.

Barack Obama and 9/11

Many of the difficulties encountered in the Western response to 9/11 depend on the personality of George W. Bush. It is not difficult to imagine that if someone else had been president of the US at the time, what was in fact a very serious crime would not have been treated as a *casus belli*, hence would not have led the country into a series of costly, perhaps unnecessary, wars from which the US and its Western allies have found it difficult to extricate themselves.

It is arguable that the US is on the decline. Yet, at least in the near future, American political fortunes and, in virtue of his key role in what is still the world's strongest country by any measure, even after the electoral reverses of 2010 Western political fortunes, are firmly in the hand of Barack Obama, elected in 2008 to succeed Bush as the American president. This raises two questions central to any effort to understand what is in store for the US and the world: Who is Barack Obama? And what does that have to do with 9/11?

In trying to answer these questions, one must resist the temptation to write the future history of Obama's presidency, which will only be known over time. The differences between George W. Bush and Barack Obama run wide and deep, so much so that one can wonder if, as the title of David Remnick's recent book suggests, with Obama we have not finally crossed a bridge.[52] Remnick has in mind a specific incident and a specific bridge: the Edmund Pettis Bridge in Selma, Alabama, where on March 7, 1965, Governor George Wallace's state troopers attacked a group of peaceful civil rights marchers. Remnick, who is thinking of the race story in America, believes that through the election of Obama a historical bridge had been crossed and change had come to the country.[53] Yet, he hedges his bets in noting the obvious: the day of postracial America has not yet come,[54] and since nothing has ended, numerous problems still lie ahead.[55] Obama, who detects progress, is equally cautious. In referring to minority groups in the American context, he notes that "We didn't quite get there, but that journey continues."[56] He further states in retrospect:[57]

> Nobody should have been under the illusion—certainly I wasn't, and I was very explicit about this when I campaigned—that by virtue of my election, suddenly race problems would be solved or conversely that the American people would want to spend all their time talking about race. I think it signifies progress, but the progress preceded the election. The progress facilitated the election. The progress has to do with the day-to-day interaction of people. . . .

The election of Obama clearly is, as Remnick thinks, an amazing story, which should be celebrated. It says something hopeful about the US that less than a century and a half after the Civil War, whose effects continue to be felt throughout life in America, a black could be elected president. Lest one forget, it was still scarcely more than a half century after the monumental decision in *Brown v. Board of Education of*

Topeka (1954) that struck down *Plessy v. Ferguson* (1896), a decision which, even after the Civil War permitted segregation.

Obama's success in becoming president might, but need not, lead to progress concerning the many problems that confronted the US as he took office. Certainly the establishment of health reform, which had been on the table for many years, was a genuine turning point. But it was not significant, other than that it committed government money, which could not be diverted for other purposes, as concerns the vast array of issues linked to 9/11.

Obama, who came into office in underlining his differences with George W. Bush, might still alter his views. Yet, several years after he reached the White House he was still committed to winning the war on terror. This goal, which was never clear during the Bush years, is no clearer during the Obama years. It is still unclear what this means and where the desire to win, or at least continue a war or wars, runs up against the reality of the situation, which so far has proven refractory, both in Iraq and in Afghanistan, despite the best efforts of two American presidents, and of those thousands of soldiers willingly or often unwillingly thrown into the balance to work the will of successive administrations devoted to waging war on terror to win the peace.

As concerns the war on terror, the policy differences between Obama and his immediate predecessor that have so far surfaced have been less substantial than meets the eye. The number and difficulty of the problems is daunting. Nonetheless, a pattern has emerged in which a commitment is made to do something, such as a phased withdrawal from Iraq or Afghanistan, or closing Guantanamo, a commitment that is then followed by postponement, in effect a retreat. For instance, in "Executive Order 13492—Review and Disposition of Individuals Detained at the Guantánamo Bay Naval Base and Closure of Detention Facilities" (January 22, 2009), President Obama stated that the Guantanamo facility would be closed as soon as possible, and no more than a year from that date, which deadline continues to recede into the past.

Further, Obama's principled stand against the war in Iraq is diluted by the fact that as president he has surrounded himself by those who supported it. These include Hillary Rodham Clinton, his main adversary in the fight for the nomination of the Democratic Party, and someone with known hawkish views, who after his election became secretary of state. Obama campaigned against Clinton on the fact that he voted against, but she voted for, authorizing the war in Iraq. His administration further includes Robert Gates, secretary of defense under Bush. Gates is now in the same role under Obama, and is still in charge of the Pentagon. *Plus ça change*.

It is clearly easier to discuss what has happened than to speculate about what might later occur. Since presidents inherit the ongoing situation, Obama's hands are certainly far from free. Though he is president, hence immensely powerful during the time span of his mandate, he cannot simply do what he wants. Whatever he is inclined to do is subject to many obvious constraints: the character of the ongoing political debate, which has never been more partisan; the present situation in the country, which has struggled with the deepest financial crisis in the US and in the world since 1929; and so on, including the kind of person he is.

The politics one favors are never independent of who one is as a person. In comparison to his predecessor, Obama is clearly intellectually gifted, and triply able: to think through problems, to learn from experience and, if necessary, to revise his views. In this and other ways he differs from his predecessor, who offered no more than sheer stubbornness in place of insight. Remnick's comment that Obama uses the language of reconciliation rather than the language of insistence[58] corresponds to the latter's intellectual agility, which replaces Bush's simple doggedness.

In a more perfect world, these character traits ought in principle to enable Obama to distance himself from the policies of his predecessor. Yet, there is a distinction in the real world between what one would like and what in the end one is able to do. For whatever reason, the differences with respect to the conduct of foreign policy as concerns 9/11 are not always apparent, certainly not apparent to the extent one might have wished. Reasons include the desire not to appear too radical, the very difficult political and economic situation, as well as the conciliatory way in which Obama proceeds. The result is that there is unfortunately more continuity than change in Obama's policy.

Consider the following themes: for much of a decade the US government was in thrall to neoconservative rhetoric about the central threat of international terrorism to the American way of life. A very dark Christian understanding of the world heavily influenced Bush's response to 9/11 and foreign policy in general. Not surprisingly, since he is a born again Christian, everything in his mind seems to correspond to a broadly Abrahamic view of the devil as real and human beings everywhere as besieged by sheer wickedness immortally described in Milton's famous lines[59]:

> Rocks, caves, lakes, fens, bogs, dens, and shades of death,
> A universe of death which God by curse
> Created evil, for evil only good. . . .

When George W. Bush was president, this dark view of a world in which evil lurks in every nook and cranny justified cutting back on civil liberties, warrantless wiretapping, illegal use of torture, indefinite detention, and other abuses. Yet, surprisingly and certainly sadly Obama has not broken, or not broken sufficiently, with these disastrous precedents. Instances include the proposals to loosen the Miranda rules in questioning terror suspects, whose presentation before a judge can be delayed, and the maintenance of possible future "renditions," the trials of suspected terrorists in military tribunals, while expanding the war in Afghanistan, and so on.

Bush was fond of issuing grand doctrinal statements. If an Obama doctrine is emerging, it is one more oriented toward *Realpolitik* than his predecessor's, more focused on relations with traditional powers, especially Russia and particularly China, while relegating issues like human rights and democracy to the international backburner. The shape of Obama's take on foreign policy is contained in a speech entitled "On the way forward in Afghanistan and Pakistan," which he gave at West Point in December 2009 to address the topic of Afghanistan, and in his first formal statement of National Security Strategy, a 52-page document released in May 2010.

NSS 2010 correctly argues that preserving American leadership in the world hinges on learning to accept and manage the rise of many competitors. It helpfully dismisses as far too narrow the Bush era doctrine that fighting terrorism should be the nation's overarching objective. It merges idealism with realism, and the defense of perceived American interests with recognition that the US must now move from a defensive strategy based on counterterrorism to a broader agenda in shifting from confrontation to more traditional diplomacy, hence increasing international cooperation as opposed to disregarding it. NSS 2010 acknowledges, as George W. Bush did not, that the US simply cannot continue to prosecute extended wars in Iraq and Afghanistan and still meet its other responsibilities. And it is of more than anecdotal interest that the expression "global war on terror," central to American foreign policy when George W. Bush was in office and still a recurrent expression at the end of his term, does not even appear in NSS 2010. This can only be the result of a policy decision to break with the recent past and its inflammatory rhetoric

The treatments of Iraq and Afghanistan are dissimilar but revealing. With respect to Iraq, the document proclaims: "Going forward, we have a responsibility, for our own security and the security of the region, to successfully end the war through a full transition to Iraqi responsibility."[60] The end game in Iraq is increasingly clear. The central idea, a variation on the Vietnam solution, is to hand over the reins to whatever government is in power when the date for phased withdrawal arrives, hoping all the while that things hold together while the US and Coalition forces depart. The difference in Iraq with respect to Vietnam is that there—especially in the wake of the Tet offensive at the beginning of 1968 resulting ultimately in the fall of Saigon in April 1975—it became apparent to all observers that the US and its South Vietnamese allies had in fact lost the war. As a direct result, US forces, diplomats, and assorted dependents needed to get out of town in a hurry. In Iraq the US and allied forces have presumably selected a date or series of possible dates, subject to conditions on the ground, to disengage at leisure. But the effect is the same: in both cases, despite a massive commitment of forces and finances, the US simply failed to enforce its will on a sovereign nation.

The situation is more muddled as concerns the war in Afghanistan. The wars in Iraq and in Afghanistan were not thrust on George W. Bush. They were wars of his choosing. The war in Iraq will be forever identified with his presidency. It is the single defining act and the measure of his achievement. If the war is a failure, then so is his presidency. In winding down the war in Iraq, Obama is putting a limit to a major, self-inflicted problem, a problem which will not just go away and which has important domestic and international consequenes.

Afghanistan is a different story. The war is not of Obama's choosing, but one he inherited and arguably even embraced. Yet, in deciding to focus on this war,

Obama is making two points. First, he is responding to the evolution of the situation in the region since the US attacked Afghanistan in the immediate aftermath of 9/11. What at the time appeared as a simple operation has over time become increasingly complicated. As Obama took office it was already beginning to look not only as if the US and its allies might not win in Afghanistan, but that in a worst case scenario similar to Vietnam they might even lose the war. Second, Obama can be understood to be suggesting that for the US the deeper priority was never Iraq, but Afghanistan.

The NSS 2010 document contains a number of statements about Afghanistan (and Pakistan) in linking Al Qaeda and the Taliban. It indicates that "our focus [is] on defeating al-Qa'ida and its affiliates in Afghanistan, Pakistan, and around the globe."[61] This statement singles out al Qaeda in stressing the relationship between Afghanistan, Pakistan, and other countries, and perhaps soon Yemen. The document continues in affirming the US commitment to defeating al Qaeda as well as the Taliban:

> We will disrupt, dismantle, and defeat al-Qa'ida and its affiliates through a comprehensive strategy that denies them safe haven, strengthens front-line partners, secures our homeland, pursues justice through durable legal approaches, and counters a bankrupt agenda of extremism and murder with an agenda of hope and opportunity. The frontline of this fight is Afghanistan and Pakistan, where we are applying relentless pressure on al-Qa'ida, breaking the Taliban's momentum, and strengthening the security and capacity of our partners. In this effort, our troops are again demonstrating their extraordinary service, making great sacrifices in a time of danger, and they have our full support.

And it further sums up the US position in linking al Qaeda, the Taliban, Afghanistan, and Pakistan:

> This is the epicenter of the violent extremism practiced by al Qa'ida. The danger from this region will only grow if its security slides backward, the Taliban controls large swaths of Afghanistan, and al-Qa'ida is allowed to operate with impunity. To prevent future attacks on the United States, our allies, and partners, we must work with others to keep the pressure on al-Qa'ida and increase the security and capacity of our partners in this region. In Afghanistan, we must deny al-Qa'ida a safe haven, deny the Taliban the ability to overthrow the government, and strengthen the capacity of Afghanistan's security forces and government so that they can take lead responsibility for Afghanistan's future. Within Pakistan, we are working with the government to address the local, regional, and global threat from violent extremists.

This document restates a series of themes in remarkably similar language, themes Obama sounded in his speech on Afghanistan. In this speech, Obama points out that he opposed the war in Iraq, saying: "I opposed the war in Iraq precisely because

I believe that we must exercise restraint in the use of military force, and always consider the long-term consequences of our actions." This statement does not go far enough. It blames Obama's predecessor to failing to see the limits of what could reasonably be done but fails to take a position on whether it was reasonable even to consider a military move in Iraq. It would be more interesting to know if, like George W. Bush, he thinks substantial American interests were at stake in Iraq. He clearly thinks like Bush that, to employ the same phrase, substantial American interests were and still are at stake in Afghanistan, interests which justify stepping up the fight in order later to gradually disengage. "So, no, I do not make this decision lightly. I make this decision because I am convinced that our security is at stake in Afghanistan and Pakistan. This is the epicenter of violent extremism practiced by al Qaeda. It is from here that we were attacked on 9/11, and it is from here that new attacks are being plotted as I speak." What is the aim, what is it Obama thinks one ought to accomplish in Afghanistan? He answers: "I set a goal that was narrowly defined as disrupting, dismantling, and defeating al Qaeda and its extremist allies, and pledged to better coordinate our military and civilian efforts."

Both the speech on Afghanistan and NS 2010 are problematic, longer on rhetoric than substance, different from, but unfortunately still too similar to views crafted when George W. Bush was president to be more than marginally helpful. Both the speech and NSS 2010 continue to identify al Qaeda and the Taliban as extremist allies, as working together. Yet since that relationship apparently already ended in 2008, perhaps, depending on the source even as early as 2002, it seems that, like the Iraq war intended to address non-existent WMD, the Afghan war, which is directed against al Qaeda's supposed continued presence in Afghanistan, is also based on a mistake. Since it is unclear that al Qaeda is still present in a significant way in Afghanistan, it is unclear that it can be driven out of the country. Observers indicate this is not the case. Finally, it is unclear that the Taliban, which is in fact an indigenous religious movement and not one imported from outside or imposed on the Afghan people, can in fact be destroyed, hence unclear that this objective can even in principle be met.

In the speech, Obama acknowledges the comparison between the war in Afghanistan and the war in Vietnam. He attempts to deflect the comparison in two ways: through a reference to what Bush called the "coalition of the willing," and which Obama describes as a broad coalition; and through the statement that, "Unlike Vietnam, we are not facing a broad-based popular insurgency." Since it is known that the US partners in the coalition were often coerced, this is not a significant claim. The deeper problem is whether, as Obama suggests, the Taliban is a more tractable foe than the Viet Cong, since it not a popular insurgency. It has already been noted that the Taliban is a Sunni Pashtun movement. Both Karzai and Omar are Pashtuns, the strongest group in the multi-ethnic Afghan state. This suggests, on the contrary, that the Taliban is not going away soon, but will still be there when foreign troops leave, since it incarnates in part the will of the Afghan people.

As concerns Afghanistan, one issue that has moved to the center of the debate is the increasing use of drones to assassinate individuals in Afghanistan and Pakistan. This falls into the category of the assassination of leaders, already a priority when George W. Bush was president. According to Jenna Jordan, who has studied what is called leadership decapitation in counterterrorism activity, this technique is actually ineffective, as other leaders step into the breach, tending to perpetuate terrorist groups that otherwise would have simply disbanded.[62]

What are the consequences of not winning in Afghanistan? What if, after prosecuting the war to the bitter end, or even if at some earlier point in time the US and its allies finally come to the conclusion that it is not in their best interest to continue the conflict? Many observers think it is not really possible to withdraw from Afghanistan, since some version of the following catastrophe would ensue: The Taliban would take over, provide bases for al Qaeda, and suddenly there would once again be the kind of situation that led to 9/11. At this point in the tale, Afghanistan begins to resemble Vietnam. Before the Tet offensive, it was widely thought that the consequences of withdrawing from Vietnam were worse than remaining. Yet the US withdrew, South Vietnam fell to North Vietnam, and very little else occurred to threaten American interests. A withdrawal from Afghanistan might well be messy. It would further threaten stability in the land, which has probably never been stable, and even threaten stability in the region. But it might also interrupt an ongoing series of wars that has lasted many years. In fact, there seems to be a choice between two main scenarios, with many possible variations: either the US and its allies continue to fight in Afghanistan in opposing the Taliban, hence the Afghan people, in a war that apparently cannot be won, or at some point they decide it is not worth continuing the war and withdraw.

On the Global War on Terror

If all things have an end, then one day the wars in Iraq and in Afghanistan will finally come to an end. It is less clear that the global war on terror will come to an end soon, or in the distant future—one hesitates to say ever. The fact that NSS 2010 does not employ this term, global war on terror, hence no longer refers explicitly to it in the way that George W. Bush used to do, does not mean that, in virtue of a change in linguistic practice, the problem to which the term referred had in the meantime somehow vanished.

Though they differ, at least initially the wars in Afghanistan and Iraq featured a traditional opposition between one or more countries in armed conflict. The global war on terror, on the contrary, like the international war on drugs, concerns both nation-states as well as other groups with shifting alliances, which are not identified with any country, and which operate freely across national borders.

Many aspects of the global war on terror remain obscure, starting with what the term is supposed to mean. A comparison might be helpful. Presumably, the American war on drugs is directed at impeding the cultivation, production, and entry of illegal drugs, which can be identified in the form of a list. Yet, since there are no defining characteristics, no way to pin down the semantic reference, it is unclear how to understand a global war on terrorism.

One difficulty concerns the familiar term "war" in the locution "global war." In the wake of the Treaty of Westphalia (1648) that eventually led to the emergence of the modern nation-state, conflicts arose between states over the intervening centuries. It is possible, even likely, that the age of the nation-state, or at least that age as it earlier existed, is now drawing to a close. We appear increasingly to be entering into a period in which the nation-state as we have known it is being weakened, and/or replaced, by a variety of supranational entities such as the United Nations, the World Court, the World Bank, the European Union, and so on. It is clear what it means to go to war against one or more nation-states, which occupy a definable geographical location. It is unclear what it means to go to war against an enemy such as al Qaeda that is neither a nation-state nor in some way identified, even loosely, with one or more such national entities, and which is not geographically situated.

A further difficulty concerns the word "terrorism." It is, for instance, as difficult to distinguish between terrorism and physical violence as it is to differentiate between freedom fighters, insurgents and other actors on the contemporary stage. Since these terms are only meaningful relative to a conceptual framework, their usage depends on a point of view. The members of Hamas are regarded by many Palestinians as freedom fighters, but are condemned by the US as terrorists and whenever possible killed by the Israelis. Muslims who participated in 9/11 were described in the immediate aftermath by the US government as extremists, mere fringe elements supposedly out of touch with their religion. Yet, for many in the Arab countries they were and still are regarded as martyrs and held up as examples of young people seeking to defend the Islamic world against the encroachments, economic or otherwise, of industrially advanced Western countries.

The global war on terror is the means the US chose to defend the country against what years later still looks like a continuing and unforeseeable terrorist threat. It seems obvious that the US is entitled to defend itself against terrorism. It is unclear that to do so required, requires, and will continue to require a war, no less a global war in which virtually the entire US armed forces as well as an appreciable chunk of available finances are mobilized for an indefinite period and for an equally indefinite goal in a struggle against an enemy who has never been clearly described.

The global war on terror has attracted criticism: as exaggerated in scope in view of the terrorist threats, as giving rise to human rights abuses, and as decreasing the very personal freedom it is intended to defend. Not everyone is convinced this war is justified. Rashid Khalidi, for instance, argues that George W. Bush's interventionist posture toward the Middle East was no mere post-9/11 aberration, but rather a bellicose expression of a longstanding campaign. Yesterday's enemy was Communism and today's is terrorism. And just as the threat of Communism was wildly exaggerated a half century ago, so today "the global war on terror is in practice an American war in the Middle East against a largely imaginary set of enemies."[63]

Though clearly psychologically unsettling, and though morally reprehensible, in real terms the terrorist threat, which is far from benign, is still relatively small. No more than 3,000 people died on 9/11 as compared to more than 40,000 in a given year in the US from automobile accidents, and between 20 and 40 million worldwide in the 1918 flu pandemic. The relatively small size of the terrorist threat creates, in turn, the impression that when George W. Bush was president, though not afterwards, it was often "hyped" for partisan political effect. This was especially the case as elections approached. It is at least possible that in launching a total war against what could easily have been taken as a crime, the Bush administration was trying to garner political support by focusing attention on a very terrible but invisible adversary. The repeated alerts after 9/11 were arguably often unjustified, based on faulty and incomplete information, about as reliable as the US government expectation that in invading Iraq American soldiers would be welcomed as heroes. The US responded to its perception of the threat by embarking on what for all the world looked like a permanent state of emergency in which the government at all levels, but also the public, was continuously mobilized against a grievous threat that was never reliably identified. Obviously the terrorist threat was real. Yet if one thinks it is not as widespread or as profound as depicted, then such emergency measures as the Patriot Act, which restricted civil liberties in the name of freedom, seem unwarranted.

While George W. Bush was in office, representatives of the US government always insisted the US would settle for nothing less than a full and total defeat of the enemy. What does that mean? How can the enemy be defeated? Who is the enemy? These apparently simple questions are very difficult to answer.

If we remove partisan politics as a factor—the Republicans consistently claim that the Democrats are "soft" on terrorism, by implication less than fully patriotic—we can focus on the problem of "protecting" the US against its enemies. It is not only not clear who that enemy is; it is not even clear what it would mean to "win" the war on terror. Does this mean that the US intends to kill every last terrorist in the world? If that is the aim, it seems very unlikely to succeed, so improbable as to be scarcely worth undertaking. It is likely that the Afghanistan war, in all probability the Iraq war and more probably the global war on terror, cannot simply be won through military action, and it is not clear what it would mean to "win" in any of these cases. This difficulty, which, after Obama took office, is still a major impediment to understanding the aim and evaluating the policies of the US in all three wars, is especially significant with respect to the global war on terror.

Would it suffice for terrorism to decrease in frequency? As concerns the number of people or the rate at which they die? All indications are that resistance to the US and its allies has not decreased, but steadily increased as a result of military action. In Afghanistan, years of war have had the result that recruits were being attracted to the ranks of the mujahideen at least as fast as and probably faster than they were killed on the battlefield. The increased use of drones, which led to the multiplication of unintended civilian deaths, has only hardened public opinion against the Americans and their allies in both Afghanistan and Pakistan. The advent of "local" terrorism in which would be terrorists who have lived most, or even all, their lives in such countries as England, the US, Norway, and so on represents a further deterioration of the situation. Since national borders are porous at best, it is very hard to protect against those who come from abroad. It is harder still to anticipate homegrown terrorists, such as Major Nidal M. Hasan, a US army psychiatrist, the suspect in the Fort Hood shootings in November 2009, who was born and grew up in the US. It should be of concern that Hasan, accused of 13 counts of premeditated murder and 32 counts of attempted murder, was not linked to any terrorist group.

These and other developments suggest two points about the global war on terror. First, it apparently cannot be won, however "won" is interpreted, through military action alone—the basic approach taken throughout the administrations of George W. Bush. Perhaps the most generous thing to say about the military approach is that it utterly failed. Time will tell. But there is no reason to think that approximately a decade of military action brought the war on terror closer to a resolution, or even improved the situation in any durable way. Terrorism, which is a real problem, was not eradicated or even significantly diminished by the Bush administration. After Obama took office, it remained at least as important after abundant military action than before.

Second, it would be hasty to proclaim victory over al Qaeda, which has not been defeated. Indeed, there is reason to think that the problem of terrorism in the Middle East region is on the verge of spreading to yet another country: Yemen. There are now a number of signs indicating that the situation in that country, the poorest in the Arab world, deeply conservative but with a weak and corrupt government, is a likely candidate for expansion by al Qaeda.[64]

Third, if the global war on terror can be won or even stalemated in any meaningful way, this is likely to be through a combination of military action, diplomacy, and economic moves rather than through military action alone, on which up to the end of George W. Bush's time in office, the US and allied forces relied. This implies a return to the normal ways in which nations deal interact, including diplomacy, attention to the consequences of economic and social themes, and so on, which Bush largely ignored.

On Politics, Economics, and War

In the aftermath of 9/11, three wars broke out. In Afghanistan, the US and its allies attacked and largely destroyed a poor country unable to defend itself against First World military powers, a country in which the Taliban had given safe haven to al Qaeda, which was presumably responsible for 9/11. The Taliban and al Qaeda are different. The former is an indigenous Islamic movement that arose to defend Afghanistan against foreign encroachment, whereas al Qaeda is a pan-Islamic movement that arose as an offshoot of the struggle against the Soviet invasion, but which is not directly related to Afghanistan. The war in Vietnam was an indication of how difficult it is finally to defeat a people committed to defending themselves. If final defeat of an enemy was the main objective, then the US led war in Afghanistan did not succeed. The invasion of Iraq by the US and its allies was successful in forcing Saddam Hussein from power, hence in bringing about regime change. But merely replacing the Iraqi dictator did not lead to improving, but rather to worsening, the security of the Western world. Western powers apparently did not anticipate, and were unable to defeat, the ensuing insurgency, which gradually slipped from the control of the US and into increasing chaos until the time of the military "surge," which restored a semblance of order inside Iraq but not outside it.

These wars are superficially dissimilar. But on a deeper level they are in fact similar and closely related through their relationship to neoconservative politics that led the US to target real, as well as suspected, Muslim terrorists. All three wars were begun and later waged by the administration of George W. Bush after 9/11 in the name of fighting terrorism even when, as in the case of the war in Iraq, there was apparently no terrorism or even a credible threat of terrorism against American or allied interests. All three further exemplify the influence of domestic politics on war.

It is at least arguable that war should only be entered into as a last resort, when diplomacy or other means appear to be ineffective to defend the country against its real enemies. By this criterion, these wars exemplify not only the decision of the US to defend itself against threats, real or more likely imagined, but also to seize on an occasion to further an esoteric political agenda largely hidden from public view and often very different from the public, exoteric justifications offered up to justify its actions.

It is as important to defend the US through appropriate action in cases of clear and present danger, that is, if the danger is real and not imaginary, as it is to avoid war when at all possible through diplomacy and other means. Mere political considerations should not be considered to be sufficient reasons to go to war.

We can bring out this point through a brief comparison between the wars in Vietnam and in Iraq. The public justification of the Vietnamese War depended on two factors: the supposed attacks on US naval forces in the Gulf of Tonkin, and the infamous domino theory. In August 1964, President Lyndon B. Johnson in part correctly, but in part mendaciously, claimed North Vietnamese forces had in the space of three days twice attacked American destroyers in the Gulf of Tonkin. According to a report published in 2005 by the National Security Agency, there was a first attack, provoked in response to South Vietnamese commando raids on the North Vietnamese coast. But historians now believe the second attack never occurred. Yet, Johnson used the alleged incidents to secure the passage in Congress of the Southeast Asia Resolution, better known as the Gulf of Tonkin Resolution, which granted him the power to assist any Southeast Asian country in resisting "Communist aggression." The best information currently available indicates that at the time of his assassination President Kennedy had been almost certain to withdraw US troops then in South Vietnam rather than expand the war.[65] Less than a year later, Johnson seized on the resolution to greatly expand the Vietnam conflict.

The war in Vietnam was "sold" to the public and Congress through the manipulation of faulty intelligence to justify an attack by the US on North Vietnam as a "means" of entering into military conflict. The war in Iraq is apparently the product of neoconservative ideology unconstrained by the reality of the situation insofar as it could be ascertained either at the time or while the conflict was proceeding. It is now common knowledge that in the events leading up to this war, available intelligence information was manipulated to "justify" a military engagement through the conjunction of two criteria: an unsupported, unverifiable, and erroneous claim for WMD, and the newly revised national security doctrine authorizing preemptive war.

The claim for the existence of WMD was evaluated both before, and in greater detail after, the US and its allies had occupied Iraq. There was not the slightest reputable report that WMD were present in the country at the time war was waged on Iraq to counter that very threat. After the report by David Kay, no reputable party still insisted that such weapons did exist.[66] If a factual allegation can be empirically disproved, then that result was in fact accomplished in this case.[67]

The infamous domino theory, which played an analogous role in the war in Vietnam, presents a more difficult problem. This term refers to an idea advanced by President Dwight Eisenhower in a 1954 press conference. The domino theory arose during the cold war as a way of justifying American intervention around the globe. Churchill's famous "Iron Curtain" speech at Westminster College in Fulton, Missouri, in 1946, led to an effort to contain international Communism. In the speech, Churchill said:

> From Stettin in the Baltic to Trieste in the Adriatic an "iron curtain" has descended across the continent. Behind that line lie all the capitals of the ancient states of Central and Eastern Europe. Warsaw, Prague, Belgrade, Bucharest and Sofia: all these famous cities and the populations around them lie in what I must call the Soviet sphere, and all are subject, in one form or another, not only to Soviet influence but a very high and in some cases increasing measure of control from Moscow.

Containment, which, as noted, was recommended around the same time by Kennan, was regarded as threatened by the tendency of Communism, much like an infectious disease, to propagate itself. The basic insight was that Communism was like an infectious disease, which, once it broke out in one area, was liable to spread throughout the region yielding increasing Soviet control. In his news conference on April 7, 1954, Eisenhower said:

> Finally, you have broader considerations that might follow what you would call the "falling domino" principle. You have a row of dominoes set up, you knock

> over the first one, and what will happen to the last one is the certainty that it will go over very quickly. So you could have a beginning of a disintegration that would have the most profound influences.

Eisenhower's statement about the falling domino principle quickly gave rise to the domino theory, which was a staple of American foreign policy debate from the 1950s to the 1980s. President John F. Kennedy applied this theory in Southeast Asia. He authorized the military intervention in Vietnam in the 1960s, which led to the war in Vietnam, since he feared the spread of Communism to South Vietnam and Laos. A version of the domino theory was still a factor in the war in Iraq. The US decision to go to war in that country was sometimes justified on the grounds that otherwise Iran, which, like Iraq, has a Shi'ite majority, would take control in the region.

The domino theory, which has never been demonstrated, remains controversial. In retrospect the United States was forced to withdraw from Vietnam without attaining either its military, political, or other objectives. South Vietnam fell to North Vietnam and after reunification the North Vietnamese Communists and their Viet Cong allies took power in that country. And the Soviet bloc and even the Soviet Union eventually disintegrated. At the time the Vietnam War was in progress, it was widely asserted and commonly believed that if the US did not stop Communist expansion in Southeast Asia, the Communists would, so to speak, shortly be landing in San Francisco. The US was unable to stop the Communists in Vietnam, and the Pathet Lao came to power in Laos in 1975. But nothing further happened with respect to US interests, and the US gradually resumed trade with Communist countries in the region, including a united Vietnam and, above all, with China, the major ally of the Vietnamese Communists.

The US economically depends, and is likely to depend increasingly, on China, a Communist country, in a complex interrelationship of benefit to both countries. If the domino theory asserts that the spread of Communism is basically inimical to American interests, then the opposite inference seems closer to the mark. If it is possible to refute the domino theory by experience, we can conclude that it has been abundantly refuted by events since it was formulated. Yet that may not be possible. Mere experience is often inadequate to evaluate political claims, which are based on underlying political commitments, which are often immune to evaluation. The latter are very much like religious beliefs, which are normally unaffected by experience. Organized religion frequently invokes enemies, who are not less frightening merely because they are imaginary. It is not difficult to imagine a future US administration later claiming that a specific enemy—fill in the blank with "Communists," "Muslim radicals," and so on—must be stopped through war to save the free world.

In hindsight, we can conclude that the process of intelligence evaluation that was supposed to inform us about the "real" situation on the ground as the US went down the road to the post-9/11 wars broke down in two ways: the intelligence was faulty, and the use made of it was even more faulty. In fact, the decision-making process seems to have been based on a generally neoconservative political commitment entered into before, hence apart from, 9/11. Everything points to the fact that the decision to go to war in fact depended on esoteric reasons never presented to the public, and that the exoteric public process was, and was intended to be, no more than a propaganda campaign undertaken to sway public opinion. In fact, throughout the period of George W. Bush's presidency the same propaganda machine continued to function after 9/11 in ways designed to present a biased, tendentious view, one which invariably supported the Bush administration's view without presenting available counterevidence, and while impeding other views from being presented. Two of the more blatant strategies employed including "embedding" journalists with soldiers in the field, and paying journalists both in Iraq and the US to provide favorable coverage of the administration's point of view.

Politics and military action are often entwined. The wars in Vietnam and in Iraq exemplify the intrusion of politics into the decision-making process, leading to arguably unjustified military conflicts. As concerns Iraq, the result was an unnecessary but enormous financial sacrifice by an administration in principle committed to fiscal conservatism, and an unnecessary loss of life engendered by moral conservatives otherwise committed to the protection of life at all costs. There is an outright contradiction between George W. Bush's public opposition to stem cell research on grounds of compassion for the unborn and his lack of compassion for thousands of American soldiers (and an untold but much greater number of Iraqis) apparently sacrificed for objectives that were never justified or even clarified.

George W. Bush was interested in nation building in order to spread democracy. He willingly went to war on the basis of his deeply held neoconservative principles. Waging war for ideological reasons is hardly a novel occurrence. Yet, it must be resisted whenever and wherever it is encountered if a meaningful form of democracy is to survive. The problem emphatically does not lie in finding out how to bring democracy to the Islamic world. It rather lies in preserving democracy worthy of the name, in which war is not merely entered into because it corresponds to preselected political goals, or because some politicians are committed to a version of the ancient view that might makes right.

Rousseau's Problem, Democracy, and the Road Ahead?

The modern world can be characterized in many different ways: as arising out of the Copernican revolution in astronomy, as deriving from the emancipation of reason from religious faith, as the locus of the emergence and incessant growth of capitalism, and so on. A thesis of this book is that the ceaseless expansion of capitalism, reaching a new and perhaps final peak in economic globalization, engenders, in overcoming all differences through further forms of itself, deep resistance. This resistance, which is not a mere accident, is rooted in the nature of capitalism. From Adam Smith's invisible hand to Ronald Reagan's trickle down economics, there is persistent faith that mere economic development will solve any and all the practical problems we face in daily life. But what if the ceaseless expansion of modern capitalism were itself problematic in generating, not only increased wealth, but also problems it cannot itself solve through still further economic development?

The idea that there are intrinsic limits to economic development is about as old as modern capitalism. Rousseau suggested in the middle of the eighteenth century that modern social life has miscarried, since what he describes as natural liberty in the so-called state of nature has only been transformed into a kind of self-induced slavery. Rousseau's problem concerns the question of real human freedom in respect to the social context. There seem to be three main responses to Rousseau's problem, which can be indicated in simple form. One, due to Rousseau, is the suggestion to return behind the modern world to an earlier, mythical state of nature to recover "natural" freedom or freedom in nature. The difficulty of this suggestion is that since the idea of freedom in nature is mythical, one cannot return to it. A second response, identified with Hegel, is to achieve social freedom within the modern state, hence within the modern world, in the identification of the individual with the state. Marx, who rejects the idea that there can be meaningful freedom within the framework of modern capitalism, later interprets Rousseau's problem as resulting from self-induced submission to an increasingly embracing economic framework. The difficulty is not a loss of tradition, or a lack of religious spirituality, but rather the very conviction, in itself a basic article of modern faith, that merely growing the economy is in and of itself sufficient to address the questions, or at least the main questions, we currently face. The third response, devised by Marx, consists in finding in the modern world (defined in economic terms through private ownership of the means of production, or capitalism) the conditions of transcending it through the transition from capitalism to Communism.

Hegel was skeptical about the alleged promise of capitalism. Those who are committed to capitalism as the main instrument of meaningful social freedom think that, if not already, then later at least, it will overcome problems that have so far arisen. Yet continued economic expansion generates difficulties and concerns not always foreseen, and on occasion difficult to resolve. One, increasingly in the news, is global warming, leading to extreme weather phenomena. Instances include more frequent and more dangerous hurricanes, the increasingly rapid breakup of the polar icecaps, and the rising level of the world's oceans, which threatens eventually to flood the major cities of the world. We do not know if this problem can later be resolved in a satisfactory way. Another is increasing restriction of the traditional Western view of respect for others as human beings, famously formulated in Kant's view of human beings as always ends and never simply as means. This view has been replaced in practice, as Marx notes, by a very different approach to human beings as reduced to their quantifiable economic importance for others, for instance, their employer, through the replacement of quality by quantity. There is an obvious tension between increasingly secular capitalist societies, which are based on the "commodification" of human beings, and such alternatives as traditional Islamic society, where there is no distinction between religion and politics, and fewer concessions to the economic imperatives of capitalism.

Western and Islamic views of the "good" for human beings are incompatible. The Western view of the good life is linked to modern industrial society, which features ceaseless economic expansion requiring constant change. The Islamic view of the good life requires simple reproduction of the type of human existence as specified in the Qur'an.

This difference can be described in terms of a widely known anthropological model between basically different kinds of society. The French cultural anthropologist Claude Lévi-Strauss concentrates on kinship systems, which he analyzes in terms of social function.[68] Roughly speaking, he argues that social circumstances exist because they are functional for the social order, not because they are functional for the person. On this basis, he suggests that tribal societies feature a basic structure that is reproduced over time. This leads to a contrast between self-reproducing societies, which resist change of any kind—such as the traditional Islamic society that Muslim fundamentalists favor, and which, in the sense that they are self-reproducing without change, are not historical—and those societies, in practice those associated with modern capitalism, in which change at any cost in order to maximize financial gain through economic expansion is a paramount value.

The ceaseless economic expansion characteristic of modern life in the West is not innocent. There is a twofold price to pay. On one hand, there is the zero-sum game in which, at least schematically, wealth is accumulated in ways that enable some to profit through their economic relation to others. Western economic expansion has not, so far, solved the difficulties of the very poor. Close to a billion people are chronically hungry. The United Nations Food Agency claims that some 920 million people currently subsist on less than 1900 calories a day. According to Jean Ziegler, United Nations special rapporteur on the right to food in the period 2000–08, one in twelve people is malnourished, and 58 per cent of all deaths during a given year are due to malnutrition. He calculates that in 2006 some 36 million people died of hunger or associated diseases.[69] On the other hand, the need to continually expand the economic base of modern industrial society runs up against social differences that must be "overcome," as it were, in the process of striving for Western economic goals.

The result is a form of alienation located outside capitalism but within the modern world in which it is a central component. Marx, who was concerned with the effect of the normal functioning of a modern form of free market economy on people who work within it, insightfully describes ways in which such individuals are alienated by the very system that is in principle intended to realize the good life. He famously analyzes types of alienation arising within capitalism.[70] What we are confronted with now is a form of alienation arising not within, but outside of, hence in reaction against capitalism itself, which to many individuals situated both within and outside capitalism, seems inimical to their understanding of the good life.

There is an obvious social "contradiction" between two prominent views of the good life, which are now locked in a deadly confrontation. On the one hand, there is the Western view that the human good lies in ceaseless economic expansion. On the other, there is the fundamentalist Islamic conviction that the human good lies in the ceaseless maintenance of traditional life focused on the religious repetition of the same.

This "contradiction" suggests the West faces a deep problem that cannot be corrected through a global war on terror. This difficulty clearly cannot merely be assimilated to the "mistaken" actions of a few dissident, rogue elements within Islam. Many in the Islamic world reject Islamic fundamentalism, but many more also reject as mistaken the pursuit of a Western way of life, including Western democracy, however that term is understood, as well as the ubiquitous economic incentives of modern industrial capitalism. Al Qaeda, the "official" enemy of the US and its allies, is only the currently most visible form of the fundamentalist view of Islam, and in that sense similar to the fundamentalist Protestant movement in Christianity—which is engaged in a struggle for the heart and soul of Islam.

It is hard to be sanguine about the road ahead. Those exerting political, economic, and military power in the West seem to know astonishingly little, and to be mainly uninterested in learning more, about the Islamic world. The difficulty is not, as some experts about the region think, that the Americans now dominating events in the Middle East know less than their British counterparts did several generations ago, hence choose policies inappropriate for this region.[71] One suspects that, even if they had intimate knowledge of the region, it would not substantially alter the thrust of their engagement with it, which thrust is not due to ignorance but, in the final analysis, to their allegiance to the expansive nature of modern capitalism itself.

The problem is not that capitalism is intrinsically self-realizing in simply sweeping away any and all obstacles. To accept that view is to deny that human beings are capable of meaningful forms of freedom, of doing otherwise than they in fact do in their daily lives. Individuals who have nothing or next to nothing, for instance those who live in the very poorest countries of the world, have very little economic choice. They are in effect literally modern slaves to the economic round. But it is illusory to believe that the captains of contemporary Western capitalism, those who through word and deed determine the political and economic policies of the industrialized countries of the world, are obliged to do what they do through powers beyond their control. They seek to extend capitalism literally everywhere, not because capitalism somehow forces them to do so, but rather because they identify with it and even find their version of the good life in this way.

The wars in Iraq and Afghanistan have not improved, but rather substantially worsened, the problem in several ways. It is mistaken to believe that, say, with a still greater effort, with more soldiers and material, the US and its allies could have successfully prosecuted the wars they began after 9/11. An important lesson of Vietnam, which seems now to be being ignored in the Middle East, is that it is very difficult, in practice perhaps not possible, for a foreign power to impose itself against the will of a "united" people. Indeed, that seems impossible if a meaningful form of democracy is a necessary condition of doing so. Another difficulty lies in the widespread view that the war on terrorism can be won by militarily defeating the possibility of terrorism. A third is the erroneous idea that the solution lies in beginning yet another war, for instance through the Israeli invasion of Lebanon or Iran.

If the intention of these conflicts was to overcome terrorism wherever it might be, then results of this approach are far from satisfying. Despite his best efforts, George W. Bush was unsuccessful in Iraq, Afghanistan, and in the global war on terrorism. His main "success" lies in toppling Saddam Hussein, but at the significant cost of creating what appears to be a highly instable situation in the Middle East and at an enormous and rapidly growing cost in money, lives, and good will. Bush's other "success" lies in uniting a whole series of disparate observers who would normally be opposed, like Noam Chomsky on the left and Brent Scowcroft and former secretary of state James Baker, on the right, observers who agree that Bush failed to solve or even dent the problem of terrorism, but significantly reduced America's standing in the world, while alienating friends and creating new enemies.

The truth of the matter is that economic globalization begets not a stable but rather an unstable world, a world in which ever bigger economies compete in a delocalized way for markets and natural resources, leading to conflict between starkly different types of society. This conflict, which is not a mere accident, is lodged at the epicenter of the modern world. It is a crisis of capitalism of a new kind, which, contrary to the prevalent interpretation of Marx, is not due to a failure to find new markets, resulting in oversupply. It is rather a crisis in which capitalism generates its own opposition as a result of its success, which in turn sets intrinsic limits to its continued expansion. Though there are differences in religion and civilization between the Islamic world and that West, the present conflict is not caused by, hence cannot fairly be ascribed to, such differences. It is rather the vanguard of the fundamentalist Muslim reaction to the modern world—especially to the global extension of capitalism in every corner of the world, which is regarded as threatening a fundamentalist Islamic view of the good life. For that reason, an ordinary style conflict centered on nation-states is probably unavailing in the short run, and perhaps even in the long run. For the adversary does not consist in a few unrepentant elements, but rather in all those who adhere to a traditional view of Islam, that is, a religion which, in this sense, is basically opposed to the incessant global expansion of capitalism.

Notes

1. See Pervez Musharraf, *In the Line of Fire: A Memoir*, New York: Free Press, 2006.
2. See *The IRAQ Study Group Report: The Way Forward—A New Approach*, New York: Vintage, 2006.

3. Murphy explores basic analogies between the US and Rome, including such factors as power and basic social health, such as what he calls the hollowing out of government, the mismatch of ambitions and resources, the growing inequality, the lack of manpower, and the increasing reliance on military force. See Cullen Murphy, *Are We Rome? The Fall of an Empire and the Fate of America*, New York: Houghton Mifflin Company, 2007.
4. See Paul Kennedy, *The Rise and Fall of the Great Powers, Economic Change and Military Conflict from 1500 to 2000*, New York: Random House, 1987, pp. 54–540.
5. See Ferguson, *Colossus*, and Immanuel Wallerstein, "The Eagle has crashed," in *Foreign Policy*, August/September 2002.
6. See Bob Brecher, *Torture and the Ticking Bomb*, Oxford: Blackwell, 2007.
7. On the selective torture of 14 suspected central terrorism suspects, who were held and each interrogated separately by the CIA at so-called black sites, who were interviewed separately by representatives of the International Committee of the Red Cross when they arrived at Guantanamo after having been held captive elsewhere, see Mark Danner, "US Torture: Voices from the Black Sites," *New York Review of Books*, vol. 56, number 6, April 9, 2009.
8. For an account of CIA torture of prisoners, see Jane Mayer, "The Black Sites: A rare look Inside the C.I.A.'s secret interrogation program," in *The New Yorker*, August 13, 2007. Other prisoners are tortured on behalf of the US government by such countries as Egypt, Jordan, and Syria.
9. There is reason to think that what happened at Abu Ghraib was known to, tolerated by, and perhaps orchestrated with the help of Donald Rumsfeld, then secretary of defense, and the Pentagon. See Seymour M. Hersh, "The General's Report: How Antonio Taguba, who investigated who investigated the Abu Ghraib scandal, became one of its casualties, in *The New Yorker*, June 19, 2007.
10. According to the *New York Times*, even after publicly denying it was engaged in torture the US continued to practice various forms of torture surreptitiously. See Scott Shane, David Johnston and James Risen, "Secret U. S. Endorsement Of Severe Interrogations. Justice Dept. Said to Back Harshest Tactics After Declaring Torture 'Abhorrent,'" *New York Times*, Thursday, October 4, 2007, p. 1.
11. "The Military-industrial Complex," in *Public Presidential Papers, Dwight D. Eisenhower*, 1960, pp. 1035–40.
12. See Paul Collier, *The Bottom Billion: Why the Poorest Countries Are Failing and What Can Be Done About It*, Oxford: Oxford University Press, 2007, pp. 18–26.
13. For discussion of pre-emption as a substitute for so-called hot pursuit, see "A Clean Break: A New Strategy for Securing the Realm." This is a report prepared by The Institute for Advanced Strategic and Political Studies' "Study Group on a New Israeli Strategy Toward 2000." The lead author of the report was Richard Perle, a close associate of Defense Secretary Donald Rumsfeld. Perle was forced, because of a conflict of interest, to resign from his position as chair of the Pentagon's Defense Policy Board in March 2003.

14. See "The Memo, the Press, and the War: An Exchange," in *The New York Review of Books*, August 11, 2005, pp. 60–63.
15. Before the war, the United Nations Monitoring, Verification and Inspection Commission (UNMOVIC) was created through the adoption of Security Council resolution 1284 on December 17, 1999. UNMOVIC was to replace the former United Nations Special Commission (UNSCOM) in continuing the latter's mandate to disarm Iraq of its WMD as well as to conduct ongoing monitoring and verification to check Iraq's compliance with its obligations not to reacquire the same weapons prohibited to it by the Security Council. This team was headed by Hans Blix, a former Swedish diplomat, Blix eventually came to the conclusion that there were no WMD as described by the US and that the US and British governments had dramatized the situation in order to legitimate the war in Iraq.
16. See Wolfowitz Interview with *Vanity Fair*'s Sam Tannenhaus, May 30, 2003, 2:17 Press Release: US Department of DefenceWeb Version: http://dod.mil/transcripts/2003/tr20030509-depsecdef0223.html
17. See Bob Woodward, *Plan of Attack*, New York: Simon and Schuster, 2004, p. 249.
18. See George Tenet, *At the Center of the Storm*, New York: Harper Collins, 2007.
19. See "Amartya Sen, "Democracy as a Universal Value," in *American Educator*, Summer 2000, p. 20.
20. The single exception is Marcus Aurelius (121–80), Roman emperor from 161 until his death.
21. United States Department of State (2006–01–18).
22. See Julius K. Nyere, *Freedom and Unity/ Uhuru Na Ujamaa*, Oxford: Oxford University Press, 1967, p. 104: "It was possible for the ancient Greeks to boast of 'democracy' when more than half the population had no say at all in the conduct of affairs of the State. It was possible for the framers of the Declaration of Independence to talk about 'the inalienable right of Man' although they believed in exceptions; it was possible for Abraham Lincoln to bequeath to us a perfect definition of democracy although he spoke in a slave-owning society; it was possible for my friends the British to brag about 'democracy' and still build a great Empire for the glory of the Britons."
23. See Plato, *Republic*, (338c), in *Plato: Complete Works*, p. 983.
24. See Ali. A. Allawi, *The Occupation of Iraq: Winning the War, Losing the Peace*, New Haven: Yale University Press, 2006, p. 386.
25. See Peter W. Galbraith, *The End of Iraq: How American Incompetence Created A War Without End*, New York: Simon and Schuster, 2006.
26. "Iraq is one of those countries that lack a key requirement of a social polity., namely a unity of thought and ideals, and a sense of community." King Faisal, cited in Allawi, *The Occupation of Iraq: Winning the War, Losing the Peace*, p. 22.
27. This list is not exhaustive. Different observers cite different possible causes. Khalidi gives such other reasons as the demonstration that the US did not need

to follow international law or operate within friendly alliances, and the desire to establish permanent military bases in the Middle East. See Rashid Khalidi, *Resurrecting Empire: Western Footprints and America's Perilous Path in the Middle East*, Boston: Beacon Books, 2004, pp. x–xi.

28. See chapter 3: "The Middle East: Geostrategy and oil," in Khalidi, *Resurrecting Empire*, pp. 74–117.
29. See Khalidi, *Resurrecting Empire*, p. 94.
30. "It is distinctly in the interest of the United States to encourage industry to promote the orderly development of petroleum resources in . . . areas such as the Persian Gulf . . . The buying power of the United States . . . will depend in some degree on the retention by the United States of such oil resources. . . . Indeed the actual expansion of such holdings is very much to be desired." James Forrestal, United States Secretary of the Navy, 1944, cited in Khalidi, *Resurrecting Empire*, p. 74.
31. "It is important to maintain in friendly hands areas which contain or protect sources of metals, oil, and other natural resources, which contain strategic objectives or areas strategically located, which contain substantial industrial potential, which possess manpower and organized military forces in substantial quantities, or which for political or psychological reasons enable the US to exert a greater influence for world stability, security and peace." Cited in Tony Judt, *Postwar: A History of Europe Since 1945*, London: Penguin, 2005, p. 95.
32. This view is supported by Phillips. See Kevin Phillips, *American Theocracy: The Peril and Politics of Radical Religion, Oil, and Borrowed Money in the 21st Century*, New York: Viking, 2006.
33. It is known that during the invasion the Israelis made use of a new American experimental weapons system known as DIME (Dense Inert Metal Explosive) in much the same way as the Germans experimented with aerial bombing in 1937 in the Spanish Civil War.
34. This is apparently not the first time the intelligence services of the US have succumbed to this kind of rosy view of their activities. According to Johnson, in 1961 Richard Bissell, then head of the Directorate of Operations, claimed that Cubans would shower insurgents sponsored by the US to invade Cuba with rose petals. See Chalmers Johnson, *Nemesis*, p. 96.
35. See, on this point, the exchange between Robert Jervis and Thomas Powers in *The New York Review of Books*, July 15–August 15, 2010, vol. LVII, 12., pp. 56–57. See Galbraith, *The End of Iraq: How American Incompetence Created A War Without End*. See further Robert Jervis, *Why Intelligence Fails: Lessons from the Iranian Revolution and the Iraq War*, Ithaca, NY: Cornell University Press, 2010.
36. For recent discussion, see Kagan's discussion of the history of US foreign policy in Robert Kagan, *Dangerous Nation: America's Place in the World From its Earliest Days to the Dawn of the Twentieth Century*, New York: Knopf, 2006.
37. See Allawi, *The Occupation of Iraq: Winning the War, Losing the Peace*, pp. 45–50.
38. See Stephen Kinzer, *Overthrow: America's Century of Regime Change from Hawaii to Iraq*, New York: Times Books, 2006.

39. On the distinction, in respect to 9/11, between a crime and a *casus belli*, see Samantha Power, "Our War on Terror," in *New York Times Book Review*, 29 July 2007, p. 1.
40. See *The IRAQ Study Group Report: The Way Forward—A New Approach*, New York: Vintage, 2006.
41. *The IRAQ Study Group Report: The Way Forward—A New Approach*, p. 2.
42. See Thomas E. Ricks, *The Gamble: General David Petraeus and the American Military Adventure*, New York: Penguin, 2009.
43. Larry Goodson, *Afghanistan's Endless War: State Failure, Regional Politics, and the Rise of the Taliban*, Seattle: University of Washington Press, 2001, p. 114.
44. See Dexter Filkins, *The Forever War*, New York: Vintage Books/Random House, 2009, p. 30.
45. See Larry P. Goodson, *Afghanistan's Endless War: State failure, Regional politics and the rise of the Taliban*, University of Washington Press, 2001, p. 107.
46. See Ahmed Rashid, *Taliban: Militant Islam, Oil and Fundamentalism*, New Haven: Yale University Press, 2001.
47. President: Today We Mourned, Tomorrow We Work, Georgewbush-whitehouse.archives.gov. 2001–09-17
48. Nick Mills, Karzai: *The Failing American Intervention and the Struggle for Afghanistan*, John Wiley and sons, 2007, p. 240.
49. See e.g., Neamatollah Nojumi, chapter 2: "The Rise and Fall of the Taliban," pp. 90–117, and Lutz Rzehak, chapter 5: "Remembering the Taliban," pp. 182–211, in Robert D. Crews and Amin Tarzi, editors, *The Taliban and the Crisis of Afghanistan*, Cambridge: Harvard University Press, 2008.
50. See *The New York Times*, Monday, July 26, 2010, p. 1.
51. See Alain Frachon, "Pourquoi sommes-nous en Afghanstan?," in *Le Monde*, Vendredi 2 juillet 2010, p. 17.
52. See David Remnick, *The Bridge: The Life and Rise of Barack Obama*, New York: Knopf, 2010.
53. See Joseph Lelyveld, "Who Is Barack Obama?," in *The New York Review of Books*, May 13–26, 2010, vol. LXII, number 8, p. 4.
54. See Remnick, *The Bridge: The Life and Rise of Barack Obama*, p. 578.
55. See Remnick, *The Bridge: The Life and Rise of Barack Obama*, p. 587.
56. Remnick, *The Bridge: The Life and Rise of Barack Obama*, p. 586.
57. Remnick, *The Bridge: The Life and Rise of Barack Obama*, p. 584
58. See Remnick, *The Bridge: The Life and Rise of Barack Obama*, p. 3.
59. See Milton, *Paradise Lost*, II, lines 621–23.
60. National Security Strategy 2010, p. 25
61. National Security Strategy 2010, p. 1.
62. See Jenna Jordan, "When Heads Roll: Assessing the Effectiveness of Leadership Decapitation," in *Security Studies*, 18:719–755, 2009.
63. Rashid Khalidi, *Sowing Crisis: The Cold War and American Dominance in the Middle East*, New York: Beacon Press, 2010, p. 245.

64. See Robert F. Wirth, "Is Yemen the next Afghanistan?" *The New York Times Magazine*, July 11, 2010.
65. See Gordon W. Goldstein, *Lessons in Disaster: McGeorge Bundy and the Path to War in Vietnam*, New York: Holt, 2010. Goldstein reports Kennedy's view that eventually the outside forces leave but the insurgents stay. Pfaff regards the evidence presented as conclusive that, if he had not been assassinated, Kennedy would have withdrawn the still limited number of American troops in Vietnam. See William Pfaff, "Mac Bundy Said He Was 'All Wrong,'" in *The New York Review of Books*, June 10–23, 2010, vol. LVII, no. 10, pp. 59–64.
66. David Kay was head of the Iraq Survey Group, which was charged with searching for WMD. It issued an Interim Report in October 2003 saying that Iraq did not have such weapons. Kay resigned on January 23, 2004.
67. It is interesting to note that at least some neoconservatives consider the failure to find WMD as irrelevant in arguing that the Iraq War is otherwise fully justified. See Robert Kagan and William Kristol, "The Right War for the Right Reasons," in *The Weekly Standard*, February 23, 2004, reprinted as an Appendix in "Iraq: Setting the Record Straight," A Report of the Project for the New American Century, April 2005, pp. 78–93.
68. See Claude Lévi-Strauss, *Structural Anthropology*, Garden City: Anchor Books, 1967.
69. See Jean Ziegler, *L'Empire de la honte*, Paris: Fayard, 2007, p. 130.
70. There is an important literature on this topic. See, e.g. Bertell Ollman, *Alienation: Marx's Conception of Man in a Capitalist Society*, New York: Cambridge University Press, 1977; and Richard Schacht, *Alienation*, Garden City: Doubleday, 1970.
71. For this argument, see chapter 5: "Raising the ghosts of empire," in Khalidi, *Resurrecting Empire*, pp. 152–77.

Index